# R

# MEDICINE

## Library of Congress Classification

1999 EDITION

Prepared by the
Cataloging Policy
and Support Office,
Library Services

Library of Congress, Cataloging Distribution Service, Washington, D.C.

The additions and changes in Class R adopted while this work was in press will be cumulated and printed in List 277 of *LC Classification — Additions and Changes*

**Library of Congress Cataloging-in-Publication Data**

Library of Congress.
Library of Congress classification. R. Medicine / prepared by the Cataloging Policy and Support Office, Collections Services. — 1999 ed.
p. cm.
Includes index.
1. Classification, Library of Congress. 2. Classification—Books—Medicine. I. Title: Medicine. II. Library of Congress. Cataloging Policy and Support Office. III. Title.
Z696.U5R 2000
025.4'661—dc21 99-086967
CIP

ISBN 0-8444-1004-7



For sale by the Library of Congress,
Cataloging Distribution Service,
Washington, DC 20541-5017

# PREFACE

The first edition of Class R, Medicine, was published in 1904, the second in 1921, the third in 1952, and the fourth in 1980. An edition cumulating additions and changes made during the period 1980-1995 was published in 1995. This 1999 edition cumulates additions and changes that have been made since 1995.

New or revised numbers and captions are added to the L.C. Classification schedules as a result of development proposals made by the cataloging staff of the Library of Congress and cooperating institutions. Upon approval of these proposals by the weekly editorial meeting of the Cataloging Policy and Support Office, new classification records are created in the master database or existing records revised. The Classification Editorial Team, consisting of Lawrence Buzard, editor, and Barry Bellinger, Kent Griffiths, Nancy Jones, and Dorothy Thomas, assistant editors, is responsible for creating new classification records, maintaining the master database, and creating index terms for the captions.

Thompson A.Yee, Acting Chief
Cataloging Policy and Support Office

December 1999

OUTLINE

| | | |
|---|---|---|
| R | 5-920 | Medicine (General) |
| | 5-130.5 | General works |
| | 131-687 | History of medicine. Medical expeditions |
| | 690-697 | Medicine as a profession. Physicians |
| | 702-703 | Medicine and the humanities. Medicine and disease in relation to history, literature, etc. |
| | 711-713.97 | Directories |
| | 722-722.32 | Missionary medicine. Medical missionaries |
| | 723-726 | Medical philosophy. Medical ethics |
| | 726.5-726.8 | Medicine and disease in relation to psychology. Terminal care. Dying |
| | 727-727.5 | Medical personnel and the public. Physician and the public |
| | 728-733 | Practice of medicine. Medical practice economics |
| | 735-854 | Medical education. Medical schools. Research |
| | 855-855.5 | Medical technology |
| | 856-857 | Biomedical engineering. Electronics. Instrumentation |
| | 858-859.7 | Computer applications to medicine. Medical informatics |
| | 864 | Medical records |
| | 895-920 | Medical physics. Medical radiology. Nuclear medicine |
| RA | 1-1270 | Public aspects of medicine |
| | 1-418.5 | Medicine and the state |
| | 396 | Regulation of medical education. Licensure |
| | 398 | Registration of physicians, pharmacists, etc. |
| | 399 | Regulation of medical practice. Evaluation and quality control of medical care. Medical audit |
| | 405 | Death certification |
| | 407-409.5 | Health status indicators. Medical statistics and surveys |
| | 410-410.9 | Medical economics. Economics of medical care. Employment |
| | 411-415 | Provisions for personal medical care. Medical care plans |
| | 418-418.5 | Medicine and society. Social medicine. Medical sociology |
| | 421-790.95 | Public health. Hygiene. Preventive medicine |
| | 428-428.5 | Public health laboratories, institutes, etc. |
| | 440-440.87 | Study and teaching. Research |

OUTLINE

| Class | Numbers | Subject |
|---|---|---|
| RA | | Public aspects of medicine |
| | | Public health. Hygiene. Preventive medicine - Continued |
| | 565-600 | Environmental health |
| | | Including sewage disposal, air pollution, nuisances, water supply |
| | 601-602 | Food and food supply in relation to public health |
| | 604-618 | Parks, public baths, public carriers, buildings, etc. |
| | 619-637 | Disposal of the dead. Undertaking. Burial. Cremation. Cemeteries |
| | 638 | Immunity and immunization in relation to public health |
| | 639-642 | Transmission of disease |
| | 643-645 | Disease (Communicable and noninfectious) and public health |
| | 645.3-645.37 | Home health care services |
| | 645.5-645.9 | Emergency medical services |
| | 646-648.3 | War and public health |
| | 648.5-767 | Epidemics. Epidemiology. Quarantine. Disinfection |
| | 771-771.7 | Rural health and hygiene. Rural health services |
| | 773-788 | Personal health and hygiene |
| | | Including clothing, bathing, exercise, travel, nutrition, sleep, sex hygiene |
| | 790-790.95 | Mental health. Mental illness prevention |
| | 791-954 | Medical geography. Climatology. Meteorology |
| | 960-1000.5 | Medical centers. Hospitals. Dispensaries. Clinics |
| | | Including ambulance service, nursing homes, hospices |
| | 1001-1171 | Forensic medicine. Medical jurisprudence. Legal medicine |
| | 1190-1270 | Toxicology. Poisons |
| RB | 1-214 | Pathology |
| | 1-17 | General works |
| | 24-33 | Pathological anatomy and histology |
| | 37-56.5 | Clinical pathology. Laboratory technique |
| | 57 | Post-mortem examination. Autopsies |
| | 127-150 | Manifestations of disease |
| | 151-214 | Theories of disease. Etiology. Pathogenesis |
| RC | 31-1245 | Internal medicine |
| | 49-52 | Psychosomatic medicine |

OUTLINE

OUTLINE

OUTLINE

| | | |
|---|---|---|
| RE | | Ophthalmology - Continued |
| | 91-912 | Particular diseases of the eye |
| | 918-921 | Color vision tests, charts, etc. |
| | 925-939 | Refraction and errors of refraction and accommodation |
| | 939.2-981 | Optometry. Opticians. Eyeglasses |
| | 986-988 | Artificial eyes and other prostheses |
| | 991-992 | Ocular therapeutics |
| RF | 1-547 | Otorhinolaryngology |
| | 110-320 | Otology. Diseases of the ear |
| | 341-437 | Rhinology. Diseases of the nose, accessory sinuses, and nasopharynx |
| | 460-547 | Laryngology. Diseases of the throat |
| RG | 1-991 | Gynecology and obstetrics |
| | 104-104.7 | Operative gynecology |
| | 133-137.6 | Conception. Artificial insemination. Contraception |
| | 138 | Sterilization of women |
| | 159-208 | Functional and systemic disorders. Endocrine gynecology |
| | 211-483 | Abnormalities and diseases of the female genital organs |
| | 484-485 | Urogynecology and obstetric urology. Urogynecologic surgery |
| | 491-499 | Diseases of the breast |
| | 500-991 | Obstetrics |
| | 551-591 | Pregnancy |
| | 600-650 | The embryo and fetus |
| | 648 | Spontaneous abortion. Miscarriage |
| | 651-721 | Labor. Parturition |
| | 725-791 | Obstetric operations. Operative obstetrics |
| | 801-871 | Puerperal state |
| | 940-991 | Maternal care. Prenatal care services |
| RJ | 1-570 | Pediatrics |
| | 47.3-47.4 | Genetic aspects |
| | 50-51 | Examination. Diagnosis |
| | 52-53 | Therapeutics |
| | 59-60 | Infant and neonatal morbidity and mortality |
| | 91 | Supposed prenatal influence. Prenatal culture. Stirpiculture |
| | 101-103 | Child health. Child health services |
| | 125-145 | Physiology of children and adolescents |
| | 206-235 | Nutrition and feeding of children and adolescents |

OUTLINE

| | | |
|---|---|---|
| RJ | | Pediatrics - Continued |
| | 240 | Immunization of children (General) |
| | 242-243 | Hospital care |
| | 245-247 | Nursing of children. Pediatric nursing |
| | 250-250.3 | Premature infants |
| | 251-325 | Newborn infants |
| | | Including physiology, care, treatment, diseases |
| | 370-550 | Diseases of children and adolescents |
| | 499-507 | Mental disorders. Child psychiatry |
| RK | 1-715 | Dentistry |
| | 58-59.3 | Practice of dentistry. Dental economics |
| | 60.7-60.8 | Preventive dentistry |
| | 280 | Oral and dental anatomy and physiology |
| | 301-493 | Oral and dental medicine. Pathology. Diseases |
| | 501-519 | Operative dentistry. Restorative dentistry |
| | 520-528 | Orthodontics |
| | 529-535 | Oral surgery |
| | 641-667 | Prosthetic dentistry. Prosthodontics |
| RL | 1-803 | Dermatology |
| | 87-94 | Care and hygiene |
| | 95 | Pathological anatomy |
| | 110-120 | Therapeutics |
| | 130-169 | Diseases of the glands, hair, nails |
| | 201-331 | Hyperemias, inflammations, and infections of the skin |
| | 391-489 | Atrophies. Hypertrophies |
| | 675 | Chronic ulcer of the skin. Bedsores |
| | 701-751 | Diseases due to psychosomatic and nerve disorders. Dermatoneuroses |
| | 760-785 | Diseases due to parasites |
| | 790 | Pigmentations. Albinism |
| | 793 | Congenital disorders of the skin. Nevi. Moles |
| RM | 1-950 | Therapeutics. Pharmacology |
| | 138 | Drug prescribing |
| | 139 | Prescription writing |
| | 146-146.7 | Misuse of therapeutic drugs. Medication errors |
| | 147-180 | Administration of drugs and other therapeutic agents |
| | 182-190 | Other therapeutic procedures |
| | | Including acupuncture, pneumatic aspiration, spinal puncture, pericardial puncture |
| | 214-258 | Diet therapy. Dietary cookbooks |

OUTLINE

| | | |
|---|---|---|
| RM | | Therapeutics. Pharmacology - Continued |
| | 259 | Vitamin therapy |
| | 260-263 | Chemotherapy |
| | 265-267 | Antibiotic therapy. Antibiotics |
| | 270-282 | Immunotherapy. Serotherapy |
| | 283-298 | Endocrinotherapy. Organotherapy |
| | 300-666 | Drugs and their actions |
| | 671-671.5 | Nonprescription drugs. Patent medicines |
| | 695-893 | Physical medicine. Physical therapy<br>Including massage, exercise, occupational therapy, hydrotherapy, phototherapy, radiotherapy, thermotherapy, electrotherapy |
| | 930-931 | Rehabilitation therapy |
| | 950 | Rehabilitation technology |
| RS | 1-441 | Pharmacy and materia medica |
| | 125-131.9 | Formularies. Collected prescriptions |
| | 139-141.9 | Pharmacopoeias |
| | 151.2-151.9 | Dispensatories |
| | 153-441 | Materia medica |
| | 160-167 | Pharmacognosy. Pharmaceutical substances (Plant, animal, and inorganic) |
| | 189-190 | Assay methods. Standardization. Analysis |
| | 192-199 | Pharmaceutical technology |
| | 200-201 | Pharmaceutical dosage forms |
| | 250-252 | Commercial preparations. Patent medicines |
| | 355-356 | Pharmaceutical supplies |
| | 400-431 | Pharmaceutical chemistry |
| | 441 | Microscopical examination of drugs |
| RT | 1-120 | Nursing |
| | 89-120 | Specialties in nursing |
| RV | 1-431 | Botanic, Thomsonian, and eclectic medicine |
| RX | 1-681 | Homeopathy |
| | 211-581 | Diseases, treatment, etc. |
| | 601-675 | Materia medica and therapeutics |
| RZ | 201-999 | Other systems of medicine |
| | 201-275 | Chiropractic |
| | 301-397.5 | Osteopathy |
| | 399 | Osteo-magnetics, neuropathy, etc., A-Z |
| | 400-408 | Mental healing |
| | 409.7-999 | Miscellaneous systems and treatments<br>Including magnetotherapy, mesmerism, naturopathy, organomic medicine, phrenology, radiesthesia |

Medicine (General)
Periodicals. Societies. Serials
5 International periodicals and serials
10 Medical societies
Including aims, scope, utility, etc.
International societies
10.5.A3 General works
10.5.A5-Z Individual societies
America
English
United States. Canada
11 Periodicals. Serials
15 Societies
British West Indies. Belize. Guyana
18 Periodicals. Serials
20 Societies
Spanish and Portuguese
Latin America
21 Periodicals. Serials
25 Societies
27.A-Z Other, A-Z
27.F7 French
Europe
English
31 Periodicals. Serials
35 Societies
Dutch
37 Periodicals. Serials
39 Societies
French
41 Periodicals. Serials
45 Societies
German
51 Periodicals. Serials
55 Societies
Italian
61 Periodicals. Serials
65 Societies
Spanish and Portuguese
71 Periodicals. Serials
75 Societies
Scandinavian
81 Periodicals. Serials
85 Societies
Slavic
91 Periodicals. Serials
95 Societies
96.A-Z Other European languages, A-Z
96.H8 Hungarian
Asia
97 English
97.5.A-Z Other European languages, A-Z
97.7.A-Z Other languages, A-Z

| | |
|---|---|
| | Periodicals. Societies. Serials -- Continued |
| | Africa |
| 98 | English |
| 98.5.A-Z | Other European languages, A-Z |
| 98.7.A-Z | Other languages, A-Z |
| | Australasia and Pacific islands |
| 99 | English |
| 99.5.A-Z | Other European languages, A-Z |
| 99.7.A-Z | Other languages, A-Z |
| | Indexes, see Z6658+ |
| 101 | Yearbooks |
| 104 | Calendars. Almanacs |
| | Cf. AY81.M4, American popular medical almanacs |
| 106 | Congresses |
| 108 | Medical laboratories, institutes, etc. |
| | Class here papers and proceedings |
| | For works about these organizations, see R860+ |
| | Collected works (nonserial) |
| | Cf. R126+, Ancient Greek and Latin works |
| 111 | Several authors |
| 114 | Individual authors |
| | Communication in medicine |
| | Cf. PN4192.M43, Public speaking |
| 118 | General works |
| | Information centers |
| 118.2 | General works |
| 118.4.A-Z | By region or country, A-Z |
| 118.6 | Medical literature |
| 119 | Medical writing. Abstracting and indexing |
| | Including practical manuals and stylebooks |
| | Cf. PE1475, Preparation of scientific papers in English |
| | Cf. PN4784.M4, Medical journalism |
| | Cf. R853.P75, Proposal writing |
| | Medical illustration, see R836.A1+ |
| 119.8 | Medical archives |
| | Medical telecommunication. Television in medicine |
| 119.9 | General works |
| 119.95 | Medical telematics |
| 120 | Atlases. Pictorial works |
| 121 | Dictionaries |
| 123 | Nomenclature. Terminology. Abbreviations |
| | Cf. RB115, Pathology |
| 125 | Encyclopedias |
| | General works |
| | Through 1800 |
| 126.A-Z | Ancient Greek |
| 126.A1A-Z | Collected works |
| 126.A1C6 | Corpus medicorum graecorum |
| 126.A2-Z | Individual works |
| | Dioscorides |
| 126.D5-D6 | Works |

General works
Through 1800
Ancient Greek
Individual works
Dioscorides -- Continued
126.D7 Biography and criticism
For philological and textual criticism, see PA3968.D6
Galen
126.G2-G7 Works
126.G8 Biography and criticism
For philological and textual criticism, see PA3997
Hippocrates
Collected and selected works
By date
126.H4 Greek
126.H5 Greek and Latin
126.H51 Latin
126.H54 English
126.H55 French
126.H56 German
126.H57 Other
126.H59 Selections. By editor or compiler
126.H6.A-Z Individual works, A-Z
126.H6A3-H6A5 De aere, aquis et locis
126.H6A6-H6A9 Aphorismi
126.H6C3 De capitis vulneribus
126.H6E6 Epidemiorum libri (I and III)
126.H6F7 De fracturis
126.H6H2 De haemorrhoidibus
Jusjurandum, see R724.5
126.H6L6 Lex
126.H6M6 Mochlicus
126.H6M8 De morbo sacro
De prisca medicina, see R126.H7P6
126.H6P8 Prognostica
126.H6U8 De ulceribus
126.H6V6 De victus ratione in morbis acutis
126.H7A-Z Spurious and doubtful works, A-Z
126.H7A1 Collected works
126.H7A4 De alimento
126.H7A7 De articulis
126.H7C5 Coacae praenotiones
126.H7C7 De corde
126.H7D3 De decenti habitu
126.H7E2 Epidemiorum libri (II)
126.H7E4 Epidemiorum libri (IV)
126.H7E5 Epidemiorum libri (V)
126.H7E6 Epidemiorum libri (VI)
126.H7E7 Epidemiorum libri (VII)
126.H7F6 De flatibus
126.H7G3 De genitura

General works
Through 1800
Ancient Greek
Individual works
Hippocrates
Spurious and doubtful works, A-Z -- Continued

126.H7H8 De humoribus
126.H7I5 De insomniis
126.H7I7 De internis affectionibus
126.H7L8 De locis in homine
126.H7M3 De medicamentis purgatoriis
126.H7M5 De medicorum astrologia
126.H7M7 De morbis
126.H7M9 De mulierum morbis
126.H7N3 De natura humana
126.H7P6 De prisca medicina
126.H7S5 De septimanus
126.H8 Works about Hippocrates
For philological and textual criticism, see PA4016
126.M52 Michigan Medical Codex
126.P37 Paul of Niceae
126.P7 Praxagoras
Ancient Latin
127.A1A-Z Collected works
127.A1C6 Corpus medicorum latinorum
127.A2-Z Individual works
127.C2-C6 Celsus
127.C2-C5 Works
127.C6 Biography and criticism
For philological and textual criticism, see PA6277.C2+
127.1 Ancient Chinese works
127.2 Ancient Indic works
127.3 Ancient Egyptian works
127.5 Other ancient works
Medieval works
Class here works chiefly in medieval Latin
128 General works
128.3 Arabic
Early modern works
128.6 15th-16th centuries
128.6.P2-P33 Paracelsus
Cf. R147.P2, Biography
128.7 17th-18th centuries
1801-
129 Comprehensive systematic works
130 Theories. Principles
Cf. R733, Special schools and theories of medicine
130.3 Outlines, syllabi, etc.
130.5 Juvenile works

General works
1801- -- Continued
Addresses, essays, lectures, see R708
History
Cf. GN477+, Primitive medicine
Cf. GR880, Folk medicine
131.A1 Periodicals. Societies. Serials
131.A2 Congresses
131.A3-Z General works
133 General special
133.5 Juvenile works
133.6 Addresses, essays, lectures
Biography
For medical missionaries, see R722.3+
For biography of specialists in particular fields, see the field, e.g., Ophthalmology RE31+
Collective
134 General
134.5 Collections of portraits
Individual and national biography, see R153+
By period
134.8 Paleopathology
Ancient
Biography, see R126.A+
135 General works
135.3 Assyro-Babylonian medicine
135.5 Biblical and Talmudic medicine
135.6 Buddhist medicine
135.8 Shinto medicine
137 Egyptian medicine
137.3 Minoan medicine
137.5 Scythian medicine
137.8 Persian medicine
138 Greek medicine
138.5 Roman medicine
Medieval
141 General works
143 Arabic
Biography
144.A1 Collective
144.A2-Z Individual, A-Z
144.A7 Arnaldus de Villanova
Modern
145 General works
15th-16th centuries
146 General works
Biography
147.A1 Collective
147.A2-Z Individual, A-Z
147.P2 Paracelsus
Cf. BF1598.P2, Hermetic philosophy
Cf. R128.6.P2+, Medical works
17th-18th centuries

History
By period
Modern
17th-18th centuries -- Continued
148 General works
Biography, see R134+, R153+
19th-20th centuries
149 General works
Biography, see R134+, R153+
By region or country
150 America
United States
151 General works
152 General special
Biography
Collective
153 General
153.5 Collections of portraits
154.A-Z Individual, A-Z
154.5.A-Z By region, A-Z
For biography, see R153+
For local, see R155+
By state
155-157 Alabama (Table R2)
159-161 Alaska (Table R2)
163-165 Arizona (Table R2)
167-169 Arkansas (Table R2)
171-173 California (Table R2)
175-177 Colorado (Table R2)
184-186 Connecticut (Table R2)
188-190 Delaware (Table R2)
193-195 District of Columbia (Table R2)
197-199 Florida (Table R2)
201-203 Georgia (Table R2)
204-204.3 Hawaii (Table R2)
205-207 Idaho (Table R2)
209-211 Illinois (Table R2)
217-219 Indiana (Table R2)
221-223 Iowa (Table R2)
225-227 Kansas (Table R2)
229-231 Kentucky (Table R2)
233-235 Louisiana (Table R2)
237-239 Maine (Table R2)
241-243 Maryland (Table R2)
245-247 Massachusetts (Table R2)
249-251 Michigan (Table R2)
254-256 Minnesota (Table R2)
258-260 Mississippi (Table R2)
263-265 Missouri (Table R2)
267-269 Montana (Table R2)
271-273 Nebraska (Table R2)
275-277 Nevada (Table R2)
279-281 New Hampshire (Table R2)

History
By region or country
United States
By state -- Continued
283-285 New Jersey (Table R2)
287-289 New Mexico (Table R2)
291-293 New York (Table R2)
294-296 North Carolina (Table R2)
297-299 North Dakota (Table R2)
301-303 Ohio (Table R2)
305-307 Oklahoma (Table R2)
309-311 Oregon (Table R2)
313-315 Pennsylvania (Table R2)
317-319 Rhode Island (Table R2)
321-323 South Carolina (Table R2)
325-327 South Dakota (Table R2)
329-331 Tennessee (Table R2)
333-335 Texas (Table R2)
337-339 Utah (Table R2)
341-343 Vermont (Table R2)
345-347 Virginia (Table R2)
349-351 Washington (Table R2)
353-355 West Virginia (Table R2)
357-359 Wisconsin (Table R2)
361-363 Wyoming (Table R2)
Other regions or countries
461-464 Canada (Table R3)
464.2 Greenland
Latin America
464.5 General works
465-468 Mexico (Table R3)
469 Central America
General works
471.A-Z By country, A-Z
Biography
472.A1 Collective
472.A2-Z Individual, A-Z
473 West Indies
General works
475.A-Z By country, A-Z
Biography
476.A1 Collective
476.A2-Z Individual, A-Z
South America
480 General works
482.A-Z By country, A-Z
Biography
483.A1 Collective
483.A2-Z Individual, A-Z
Europe
484 General works
486-489 Great Britain. England (Table R3)

History
By region or country
Other regions or countries
Europe
Great Britain. England -- Continued
491-493 Northern Ireland (Table R3)
For biography, see R489
495-497 Scotland (Table R3)
For biography, see R489
498.2-4 Wales (Table R3)
For biography, see R489
498.6-9 Ireland (Table R3)
499-502 Austria (Table R3)
504-507 France (Table R3)
Biography
507.A1 Collective
507.A2-Z Individual, A-Z
Schweitzer, Albert, see R722.32.S35
509-512 Germany (Table R3)
Including West Germany
512.2-5 East Germany (Table R3)
513-516 Greece (Table R3)
517-520 Italy (Table R3)
Benelux countries. Low countries
521-524 Belgium (Table R3)
526-529 Netherlands (Table R3)
531-534 Russia. Soviet Union (Table R3)
535-538 Poland (Table R3)
Scandinavia
538.5 General works
539-542 Denmark (Table R3)
543-546 Iceland (Table R3)
547-550 Norway (Table R3)
551-554 Sweden (Table R3)
555-558 Spain (Table R3)
559-562 Portugal (Table R3)
563-566 Switzerland (Table R3)
575.A-Z Other European regions or countries, A-Z
*Under each country:*
*.x* *General works*
*.x2* *General special*
*.x3* *Local, A-Z*
*.x4* *Biography*
*.x4A1-.x4A29* *Collective*
*.x4A3-.x4Z* *Individual, A-Z*
Asia
581 General works
591-594 Saudi Arabia (Table R3)
601-604 China (Table R3)
604.2-5 Pakistan (Table R3)
605-608 India (Table R3)
608.2-5 Sri Lanka (Table R3)
608.6-9 Burma (Table R3)

History
By region or country
Other regions or countries
Asia -- Continued
Southeast Asia. Indochina
Including Cambodia, Laos, Malaysia, Thailand, Vietnam
609 General works
611.A-Z By country, A-Z
Biography
612.A1 Collective
612.A2-Z Individual, A-Z
614-617 Indonesia (Table R3)
618-621 Philippines (Table R3)
623-626 Japan (Table R3)
627-630 Korea (Table R3)
631-634 Iran (Table R3)
635-638 Former Soviet Union in Asia (Table R3)
For Transcaucasia, see R531+
640-643 Turkey (Table R3)
644.A-Z Other Asian regions or countries, A-Z
Apply table at R575.A-Z
Israel, see R644.P3
644.P3 Palestine. Israel
Africa
651 General works
653.A-Z By region or country, A-Z
Biography
654.A1 Collective
654.A2-Z Individual, A-Z
Atlantic Ocean islands
654.5 General works
655.A-Z Individual islands or groups of islands, A-Z
*Under each:*
*.x General works*
*.x2 General special*
*.x3 Local, A-Z*
*.x4 Biography*
*.x4A1-.x4A29 Collective*
*.x4A3-.x4Z Individual, A-Z*
671-674 Australia (Table R3)
675-678 New Zealand (Table R3)
681-684 Pacific islands
*Under each country:*
*1 General works*
*2 General special*
*3 Local, A-Z*
*4.A-Z Biography*
*4.A1A-Z Collective*
*4.A2-Z Individual, A-Z*
687 Medical expeditions. Medical voyages and travels
Medicine as a profession. Physicians
690 General works

Medicine as a profession. Physicians -- Continued
692 Women in medicine. Women physicians
Minorities in medicine
693 General works
694 Jews in medicine. Jewish physicians
695 Blacks in medicine. Black physicians
Including Afro-Americans
696 Indians in medicine. Indian physicians
696.5 Hispanics in medicine. Hispanic physicians
697.A-Z Other personnel, A-Z
697.A4 Allied health personnel
Assistant medical officers, see R697.P45
697.F6 Foreign medical personnel
697.P45 Physicians' assistants
699 Awards, prizes, etc.
Medicine and the humanities. Medicine and disease in relation to history, literature, etc.
Cf. R723+, Medical philosophy
For the relation of special medical topics and diseases to history, literature, etc., see the topic or the disease
702 General works
702.5 Medicine and the arts. Arts medicine
Clinical studies of famous persons
703 Collective
Individual
see the biography of the individual in classes B-Z
Physicians to famous persons
see the biography of the person in classes B-Z
705 Anecdotes, humor, etc.
Cf. NC1763.M4, Pictorial humor
Cf. PN6231.M4, Medical wit and humor
Cf. PN6268.M4, Medical anecdotes
706 Curiosities of medicine
Personal life of physicians
Cf. R134+, Biography
Cf. R727+, Professional relations
Cf. RC451.4.P5, Mental health
707 General works
707.2 Family and marital life
707.3 Artistic interests. Physicians as artists, writers, musicians, etc.
Cf. PN492, Physicians as authors
Cf. PQ150.P4, French physicians as authors
Cf. PR120.P6, English physicians as authors
Cf. PT170.A+, German physicians as authors
Physicians as portrayed in art, literature, etc.
see N8223, PN56.5.P56, etc.
Portraits of physicians
see R134.5, R153.5, R154, etc.
707.4 Recreation. Hobbies
708 Addresses, essays, lectures

Directories
Cf. R101, Yearbooks of the progress of medicine
711 General
By region or country
711.3 America
North America
711.5 General works
United States
712.A1 General
712.A2A-Z By region or state, A-Z
712.A3-Z By city, A-Z
713.01 Canada
713.03 Mexico
713.04 Central America
713.05 West Indies
South America
713.06 General works
713.07 Argentina
713.09 Bolivia
713.11 Brazil
713.13 Chile
713.15 Colombia
713.17 Ecuador
713.19 Guianas
713.21 Paraguay
713.23 Peru
713.25 Uruguay
713.27 Venezuela
Europe
713.28 General works
Great Britain
713.29 General works
713.31 England
713.32 Wales
713.33 Scotland
713.35 Northern Ireland
713.36 Ireland
713.37 Austria
713.39 Belgium
713.41 Denmark
713.43 France
713.45 Germany
Including West Germany
713.46 East Germany
713.47 Greece
713.49 Netherlands
713.51 Italy
713.53 Norway
713.55 Portugal
713.57 Russia
713.59 Spain
713.61 Sweden
713.63 Switzerland

Directories
By region or country
Other regions or countries
Europe -- Continued
713.67.A-Z Other European regions or countries, A-Z
713.67.F5 Finland
Asia
713.68 General works
713.69 China
713.7 Taiwan
713.71 India
713.73 Japan
713.75 Iran
713.79 Former Soviet Union in Asia
713.8 Turkey
713.81.A-Z Other Asian regions or countries, A-Z
Israel, see R713.81.P3
713.81.P3 Palestine. Israel
713.81.P6 Philippines
713.82 Arab countries (General)
Africa
713.83 General works
713.85 Egypt
713.87.A-Z Other African regions or countries, A-Z
713.89 Australia
713.93 New Zealand
713.97 Pacific islands
Missionary medicine. Medical missionaries
Cf. RA390.A2+, Medical missions for promoting medical knowledge and service
722 General works
Biography
722.3 Collective
722.32.A-Z Individual, A-Z
722.32.S35 Schweitzer, Albert
Cf. B2430.S37, Schweitzer as philosopher
Cf. BX4827.S35, Schweitzer as theologian
Cf. CT1018.S45, Schweitzer (General biography)
Cf. ML416.S33, Schweitzer as musician
Medical philosophy. Medical logic
Cf. BC161.P5, Logic for physicians
723 General works
723.5 Decision making
Cf. R859.7.D42, Data processing
Medical ethics. Medical etiquette
For ethical aspects of medical specialties, see the specialty, e.g., Critical care ethics, RC86.95
724 General works
724.5 Hippocratic oath
725 Codes of ethics
725.3 Medical ethics committees
725.5 Special aspects

Medical ethics. Medical etiquette -- Continued
Religious aspects
Cf. BL65.M45, Medicine and religion
725.55 General works
725.56 Christian ethics
725.57 Jewish ethics
725.59 Islamic ethics
726 Prolongation or termination of life-sustaining care. Euthanasia. Assisted suicide
726.2 Advance directives
Medicine and disease in relation to psychology
Cf. RA776.9+, Health behavior and habits
Cf. RC49+, Psychosomatic medicine
Cf. RC435+, Psychiatry
Cf. RJ499+, Mental disorders of children and adolescents
Cf. RT86, Psychology of nursing
726.5 General works
726.7 Clinical health psychology
726.8 Terminal care. Dying
Cf. BF789.D4, Psychology
Cf. RA1000+, Terminal care facilities
Cf. RC451.4.T47, Psychiatry
Cf. RJ249, Pediatrics
Cf. RT87.T45, Nursing
For ethical and moral aspects, see R726
Medical personnel and the public. Physician and the public
Including community relations, advice to physicians
Cf. RT86.4, Nurse and physician
727 General works
727.2 Assaults against medical personnel
Medical personnel and patient. Physician and patient
727.3 General works
Advance directives, see R726.2
727.35 Involuntary treatment
727.4 Patient education and health counseling
Cf. RA975.5.P38, Patient education programs in hospitals
Cf. RT90+, Nursing
727.42 Patient participation
727.43 Patient compliance
727.45 Patient advocacy
Cf. RA965.6, Patient representative services in hospitals
727.47 Medical personnel and patient's family. Medical personnel-caregiver relationships
727.5 Medical personnel and other professions
727.8 Physician and other physicians or health professionals
Including medical referral and consultation
Cf. RA971.9, Hospital physician relations
Cf. RT86.4, Nurse and physician
For organized practice relationships, see R729+

Practice of medicine. Medical practice economics
Including business methods
Cf. HG8054, Physicians' insurance
Cf. RA410+, Economics of medical care
728 General works
Medical corporations. Corporate practice
728.2 General works
728.25 Physician management companies
728.3 Trade unions for physicians
Medical fees. Income of physicians
728.5 General works
728.6 Capitation fees
Including global capitation
728.8 Medical secretaries, office assistants, etc.
Types of medical practice
729 General works
729.5.A-Z Special types, A-Z
Family practice, see R729.5.G4
729.5.G4 General practice. Family practice
729.5.G57 Government practice
Cf. RA5, Health officers
729.5.G6 Group practice
729.5.H4 Health care teams
729.5.H43 Health maintenance organization practice
Including managed care practice
Managed care practice, see R729.5.H43
729.5.N87 Nurse-physician joint practice
729.5.P37 Partnership
729.5.R87 Rural practice
Cf. RA771+, Rural health services
729.5.S6 Specialty practice. Specialization
729.8 Medical errors
Cf. RA1056.5, Malpractice
Cf. RC90, Iatrogenic diseases
Cf. RC455.2.E76, Psychiatric errors
Cf. RD27.85, Surgical errors
729.9 Medical misconceptions
730 Quackery
Cf. GV1800+, Medicine shows
Cf. RA1056.5, Malpractice
733 Special theories and systems of medicine (General). Alternative medicine. Holistic medicine
Class here works describing the theories and philosophy of several therapeutic systems
For clinical aspects of physiological therapeutics, see RM695+
For particular systems, see the system, e.g. RV, Eclectic medicine; RX, Homeopathy; RZ, Chiropractic, Osteopathy, Mental healing, etc.
Medical education. Medical schools
Cf. RA975.T43, Teaching hospitals
Cf. RA975.U5, University hospitals
735.A1 Periodicals. Societies. Serials

Medical education. Medical schools -- Continued

735.A2 Congresses
735.A4 Directories
735.A5 History
735.A6-Z General works
737 General special
740 Addresses, essays, lectures
Teaching techniques and practices, see R834+
By region or country
741 America
North America
743 General works
United States
745 General works
746.A-Z By region or state, A-Z
747.A-Z Individual institutions. By name, A-Z
749 Canada (Table R1)
Latin America
750 General works
751 Mexico (Table R1)
753 Central America (Table R1)
755 West Indies (Table R1)
South America
757 General works
758 Argentina (Table R1)
759 Bolivia (Table R1)
761 Brazil (Table R1)
762 Chile (Table R1)
763 Colombia (Table R1)
764 Ecuador (Table R1)
765 Guianas (Table R1)
766 Paraguay (Table R1)
767 Peru (Table R1)
768 Uruguay (Table R1)
769 Venezuela (Table R1)
Europe
771 General works
Great Britain
772 General works
773 England (Table R1)
774 Wales (Table R1)
775 Scotland (Table R1)
777 Northern Ireland (Table R1)
778 Ireland (Table R1)
779 Austria (Table R1)
781 Belgium (Table R1)
783 Denmark (Table R1)
784 France (Table R1)
Germany
Including West Germany
785.A1-A3 General works
785.A5-Z By state, A-Z
786.A-Z Individual institutions. By name, A-Z

Medical education. Medical schools
By region or country
Europe -- Continued
786.6 East Germany (Table R1)
787 Greece (Table R1)
789 Netherlands (Table R1)
791 Italy (Table R1)
793 Norway (Table R1)
795 Portugal (Table R1)
796 Russia (Table R1)
797 Scandinavia
Cf. R783, Denmark
Cf. R793, Norway
Cf. R799, Sweden
798 Spain (Table R1)
799 Sweden (Table R1)
801 Switzerland (Table R1)
804.A-Z Other European regions or countries, A-Z
*Under each country:*
*.x General works*
*.x2 Local, A-Z*
*.x3 Individual institutions. By name, A-Z*
Asia
810 General works
812 China (Table R1)
814 India (Table R1)
816 Japan (Table R1)
817 Iran (Table R1)
819 Former Soviet Union in Asia (Table R1)
For Transcaucasia, see R796
820 Turkey (Table R1)
821.A-Z Other Asian regions or countries, A-Z
Apply table at R804.A-Z
Africa
822 General works
823 Egypt (Table R1)
824.A-Z Other African regions or countries, A-Z
Apply table at R804.A-Z
831 Australia (Table R1)
832.5 New Zealand (Table R1)
833 Administration and planning of medical schools
Including allocation of space and resources
833.5 Teacher training
Teaching techniques
Including curriculum planning
834 General works
834.5 Problems, exercises, examinations
Cf. R838.5, Entrance examination aids
Cf. RC58, Examinations in internal medicine
835 Audiovisual aids

Medical education. Medical schools
Teaching techniques -- Continued
Medical illustration
Cf. NC760, Art anatomy
Cf. NC765+, Art anatomy
Cf. QM25, Pictorial works (Human anatomy)
Cf. QM531+, Surgical anatomy
Cf. QM557, Pictorial works (Human histology)
Cf. RB33, Atlases (Pathological anatomy)
836.A1 Periodicals. Societies. Serials
836.A2-Z General works
Medical photography, see TR708
837.A-Z Other, A-Z
837.A2 Ability testing
837.C6 Computer assisted instruction
837.I53 Independent study
837.S55 Simulated patients
Premedical education
837.8 Periodicals. Societies. Serials
837.9 Congresses
838 General works
Admission to medical school. Entrance requirements
838.4 General works
838.5 Entrance examination aids
840 Graduate medical education
Including fellowships, internships, residencies
845 Postgraduate medical education. Continuing medical education
Including refresher courses
Paramedical education
847.A1 Periodicals. Societies. Serials
847.A2-Z General works
By region or country
United States
847.5 General works
847.6.A-Z By region or state, A-Z
847.7.A-Z Other regions or countries, A-Z
Research. Experimentation
850.A1 Periodicals. Societies. Serials
850.A2 Congresses
850.A3-Z General works
852 General special
853.A-Z Special topics, A-Z
853.A53 Animal experimentation
853.C55 Clinical trials
Cf. RM301.27, Clinical drug trials
853.C76 Crossover trials
853.D37 Data processing
Grants, Research, see R853.R46
853.G76 Group-randomized trials
853.H8 Human experimentation
853.I53 Interdisciplinary research
853.I57 International cooperation

Research. Experimentation
Special topics, A-Z -- Continued
853.M3 Mathematics
853.O87 Outcome assessment
853.P75 Proposal writing
853.R46 Research grants
853.S44 Self-experimentation
853.S64 Social aspects
853.S7 Statistical methods
853.S94 Systematic reviews
853.T58 Tissue culture
854.A-Z By region or country, A-Z
Medical technology
855 Periodicals. Societies. Serials
855.2 Congresses
855.3 General works
855.4 Juvenile works
855.5.A-Z By region or country, A-Z
Biomedical engineering. Electronics. Instrumentation
Cf. HD9994+, Medical instruments and apparatus industry
Cf. RM950, Rehabilitation technology
For special equipment, see RD, RE, etc.
856.A1 Periodicals. Societies. Serials
856.A2 Congresses
856.A3 Dictionaries and encyclopedias
856.A4 Directories
856.A5 History
856.A6-Z General works
856.15 Handbooks, manuals, etc.
856.2 Juvenile works
856.25 Biomedical engineering as a profession. Biomedical technicians
856.3 Study and teaching
856.4 Research. Experimentation
856.48 Catalogs
856.5 Maintenance and repair of equipment
For maintenance and repair of special equipment, see the equipment in RC, RD, etc.
856.6 Safety measures. Standards
857.A-Z Other special topics, A-Z
857.A4 Aluminum
857.B5 Biochips
857.B52 Biological transport
857.B54 Biosensors
857.C4 Ceramics
857.C6 Clean air systems
Cf. RA969.43, Hospitals
857.C63 Cobalt-chromium-nickel alloys
857.C66 Colloids
857.C9 Cybernetics
857.D47 Digital signal processing
857.D5 Disposables

Biomedical engineering.
Electronics. Instrumentation
Other special topics, A-Z -- Continued

857.E49 Electricity
857.E52 Electrochemical sensors
857.E54 Electromagnetic compatibility
Fiber optics, see R857.O59
857.F68 Fourier transformations
857.G55 Glass in medicine
857.H64 Holography
Imaging systems, see R857.O6
857.L37 Lasers
857.M28 Mass spectrometry
857.M3 Materials
Cf. RD132, Artificial implant materials
Cf. RK652.5+, Dental materials
857.M37 Metals
857.M4 Metric system
857.M64 Monitor alarms
857.N65 Nonwoven fabrics
857.O59 Optical fibers. Fiber optics
857.O6 Optical instruments
Including imaging systems
857.P33 Packaging of medical instruments and apparatus
857.P36 Patient monitoring system
857.P49 Photogrammetry
857.P52 Picture archiving and communication system
857.P53 Piezoelectric polymer biosensors
857.P55 Plastics
857.P6 Polymers
857.P64 Polyurethanes
857.S47 Signal processing
Signal processing, Digital, see R857.D47
857.S5 Silicones
857.S63 Sound equipment
857.S67 Space telemetry
857.S83 Starch
857.S85 Strain measurement
857.T32 Tactile sensors
857.T43 Thin films
857.T47 Three-dimensional imaging
857.T57 Titanium alloys
857.T7 Transducers
857.U48 Ultrasonics

Computer applications to medicine. Medical informatics
Including electronic data processing
Cf. R119.95, Medical telematics
Cf. R853.D37, Medical research
Cf. RA409.5, Medical statistics
Cf. RA427.6, Multiphasic screening
Cf. RA971.6, Hospital administration
Cf. RB38, Clinical pathology
Cf. RC78.7.D35, Diagnosis
Cf. RC683.5.D36, Cardiology
Cf. RD29.7, Surgery
Cf. RE79.E38, Ophthalmology
Cf. RG547, Obstetrics
Cf. RT50.5, Nursing

858.A1 Periodicals. Societies. Serials
858.A2 Congresses
858.A3-Z General works
Study and teaching
859 General works
859.2.A-Z By region or country, A-Z
859.7.A-Z Special topics, A-Z
859.7.A78 Artificial intelligence
859.7.B37 Bar coding
859.7.C65 Computer simulation
859.7.C67 Computer vision
859.7.D36 Database searching
859.7.D42 Decision making
859.7.E43 Electronic data interchange
859.7.F89 Fuzzy systems
859.7.T45 TEDIUM (Computer system)

Medical laboratories, institutes, etc.
Cf. R108, paper and proceedings
Cf. RD28.5.A+, Surgery
860 General works
862.A-Z Individual. By city, A-Z
864 Medical records
Including methods of record-keeping, e.g. Punched-card systems
Cf. RA976+, Medical record departments and administration
Cf. RC65, Case history taking and recording

Museums. Exhibitions
871 General works
881 Individual exhibits and exhibitions. By date
891.A-Z Individual museums. By city, A-Z
Including museums of medical education institutions

Medical physics. Medical radiology. Nuclear medicine
Cf. RA569, Public health
Cf. RA766.R2, Radiation sterilization (Public health)
Cf. RA1231.R2, Toxicology
Cf. RC78+, Radiography
Cf. RC78.7.R4, Radioisotope scanning
Cf. RC91+, Diseases
Cf. RD33.55+, Interventional radiology
Cf. RD96.5, Surgery
Cf. RM845+, Radiotherapy

| | |
|---|---|
| 895.A1 | Periodicals. Societies. Serials |
| 895.A2 | Congresses |
| 895.A3 | Dictionaries and encyclopedias |
| 895.A4 | Directories |
| 895.A5-Z | General works |
| | Collected works (nonserial) |
| 895.15 | Several authors |
| 895.16 | Individual authors |
| 895.2 | Laboratories, institutes, etc. |
| 895.3.A-Z | Individual. By city, A-Z |
| 895.5 | History |
| 895.6.A-Z | By region or country, A-Z |
| 896 | Problems, exercises, examinations |
| 896.5 | Outlines, syllabi, etc. |
| 896.7 | Handbooks, manuals, etc. |
| 898 | Medical physics, medical radiology, nuclear medicine as a profession |
| 899 | Study and teaching |
| 905 | Mathematics. Statistical methods |
| 906 | Radiation dosimetry |
| 907 | Computer applications. Data processing |
| 920 | Instruments, apparatus, and appliances |

Public aspects of medicine
Medicine and the state
1 Periodicals. Societies. Serials
Hospitals, clinics, etc , see RA960+
2 Congresses
5 Departments of public health. Boards of health
Class here general works on organization and administration, and health officers
For reports of special boards, see RA11+
For training of health officers, inspectors, etc., see RA440.8
Directories of sanitary authorities, boards of health, etc.
7 General
United States
7.5 General works
7.6.A-Z By region or state, A-Z
7.8.A-Z Other regions or countries, A-Z
World Health Organization
8.A1-A4 Official publications
8.A1-.A29 Serials
8.A2 Official records
8.A3A-Z Monographs. Official conference publications. By title
8.A4A-Z Committees, etc.
8.A4A8 World Health Assembly. Journal
8.A5-Z Other publications
Including official publications of the preliminary conferences and of the various regions or countries
Government health agencies (General)
Including reports of boards of health
Cf. RA407+, Medical statistics
By region or country
10 America
10.7 North America
United States
11 Federal health agencies
National Board of Health
11.B1-B13 Serial reports
11.B14 Other
Public Health Service
Originally "The Marine Hospital Service." Name changed in 1902 to "The Public Health and Marine Hospital Service," and in 1912, to "The Public Health Service"
11.B15 Reports
11.B16 Lists of officers
11.B17 Weekly abstract
Other
11.B18 Official. By date
11.B19 Nonofficial. By author
11.B2 Reports of annual public health conferences

Medicine and the state
Government health agencies (General)
By region or country
United States
Federal health agencies -- Continued
National Institutes of Health
Originally "The Hygienic Laboratory." Name changed in 1930 to "The National Institute of Health, and in 1948, to "The National Institutes of Health"
For the Heart Institute, Cancer Institute, etc., see RC

11.D1 Serials, etc.
11.D5 Separate reports. By date
11.D6A-Z Nonofficial publications
11.F1-F6 Veterans' Administration (Medical activities)
Cf. UH201+, Administrative aspects
11.F1-F4 Serials, etc.
11.F5 Separate reports. By date
11.F6A-Z Nonofficial publications
13 States or cities collectively
By state
15-16 Alabama (Table R4)
18-19 Alaska (Table R4)
21-22 Arizona (Table R4)
24-25 Arkansas (Table R4)
27-28 California (Table R4)
31-32 Colorado (Table R4)
34-35 Connecticut (Table R4)
37-38 Delaware (Table R4)
41 District of Columbia
44-45 Florida (Table R4)
47-48 Georgia (Table R4)
49-50 Hawaii (Table R4)
51-52 Idaho (Table R4)
54-55 Illinois (Table R4)
61-62 Indiana (Table R4)
64-65 Iowa (Table R4)
67-68 Kansas (Table R4)
71-72 Kentucky (Table R4)
74-75 Louisiana (Table R4)
77-78 Maine (Table R4)
81-82 Maryland (Table R4)
84-85 Massachusetts (Table R4)
87-88 Michigan (Table R4)
91-92 Minnesota (Table R4)
94-95 Mississippi (Table R4)
97-98 Missouri (Table R4)
101-102 Montana (Table R4)
104-105 Nebraska (Table R4)
107-108 Nevada (Table R4)
111-112 New Hampshire (Table R4)
114-115 New Jersey (Table R4)

| | |
|---|---|
| | Medicine and the state |
| | Government health agencies (General) |
| | By region or country |
| | United States |
| | By state -- Continued |
| 117-118 | New Mexico (Table R4) |
| 121-122 | New York (Table R4) |
| 124-125 | North Carolina (Table R4) |
| 127-128 | North Dakota (Table R4) |
| 131-132 | Ohio (Table R4) |
| 134-135 | Oklahoma (Table R4) |
| 137-138 | Oregon (Table R4) |
| 141-142 | Pennsylvania (Table R4) |
| 144-145 | Rhode Island (Table R4) |
| 147-148 | South Carolina (Table R4) |
| 151-152 | South Dakota (Table R4) |
| 154-155 | Tennessee (Table R4) |
| 157-158 | Texas (Table R4) |
| 161-162 | Utah (Table R4) |
| 164-165 | Vermont (Table R4) |
| 167-168 | Virginia (Table R4) |
| 171-172 | Washington (Table R4) |
| 174-175 | West Virginia (Table R4) |
| 177-178 | Wisconsin (Table R4) |
| 181-182 | Wyoming (Table R4) |
| | Other regions or countries, A-Z |
| | Canada |
| 184 | General works |
| 185.A-Z | Provinces, A-Z |
| 186.A-Z | Cities, A-Z |
| 186.5-6 | Greenland (Table R5) |
| 187-188 | Mexico (Table R5) |
| 191.A-Z | Central America. By country, A-Z |
| 192 | Panama Canal Zone |
| 194.A-Z | West Indies, A-Z |
| | South America |
| 198 | General works |
| 201-202 | Argentina (Table R5) |
| 204-205 | Bolivia (Table R5) |
| 207-208 | Brazil (Table R5) |
| 211-212 | Chile (Table R5) |
| 214-215 | Colombia (Table R5) |
| 217-218 | Ecuador (Table R5) |
| | Guianas |
| 221 | General works |
| 222.A-Z | Local |
| 222.B7 | Guyana. British Guiana |
| 222.D8 | Surinam. Dutch Guiana |
| 224-225 | Paraguay (Table R5) |
| 227-228 | Peru (Table R5) |
| 231-232 | Uruguay (Table R5) |
| 234-235 | Venezuela (Table R5) |
| 237.A-Z | South Atlantic islands, A-Z |

Medicine and the state
Government health agencies (General)
By region or country
Other regions or countries, A-Z
South Atlantic islands, A-Z -- Continued
237.F3 Falkland Islands
Europe
239 General works
241-242 Great Britain. England (Table R5)
For colonies collectively, use RA241.X2+
243-244 Scotland (Table R5)
246-247 Northern Ireland (Table R5)
248-249 Wales (Table R5)
251-252 Austria (Table R5)
254-254 Belgium (Table R5)
257-258 Denmark (Table R5)
261-262 France (Table R5)
264-265 Germany (Table R5)
Including West Germany
East Germany
266 General works
266.2.A-Z Local, A-Z
267-268 Greece (Table R5)
271-272 Netherlands (Table R5)
Ireland
273 General works
273.2.A-Z Local, A-Z
274-275 Italy (Table R5)
277-278 Norway (Table R5)
281-282 Portugal (Table R5)
284-285 Russia (Table R5)
287-288 Spain (Table R5)
291-292 Sweden (Table R5)
294-295 Switzerland (Table R5)
299.A-Z Other European regions or countries, A-Z
299.C95 Czechoslovakia
299.F5 Finland
299.M3 Malta
299.P7 Poland
299.Y8 Yugoslavia
Asia
303 General works
305-306 China (Table R5)
307-308 Taiwan (Table R5)
309 Hong Kong
309.5-6 Pakistan (Table R5)
311-312 India (Table R5)
312.2-3 Sri Lanka (Table R5)
312.5-6 Burma (Table R5)
Southeast Asia
313-314 Thailand (Table R5)
315-316 Vietnam (Table R5)
316.5-6 Malaysia (Table R5)

Medicine and the state
Government health agencies (General)
By region or country
Other regions or countries, A-Z
Asia
Southeast Asia -- Continued
317-318 Indonesia (Table R5)
319-320 Philippines (Table R5)
321-322 Japan (Table R5)
331-332 Former Soviet Union in Asia (Table R5)
340.A-Z Other Asian regions or countries, A-Z
340.I7 Iraq
340.M2 Macao
340.S55 Singapore
Africa
345 General works
352.A-Z By region or country, A-Z
Indian Ocean islands
361 General works
363.A-Z By island or group of islands, A-Z
371-372 Australia (Table R5)
373-374 New Zealand (Table R5)
Pacific islands. Oceania
376 General works
Hawaii, see RA49+
388.A-Z Other, A-Z
Medical missions. Medical assistance
Class here works on missions for the promotion of medical knowledge and service
For missionary medicine and medical missionaries, see R722+
390.A2 General works
390.A3-Z By region or country originating the mission, A-Z
393 General works
394 General special
394.6 Addresses, essays, lectures
394.8 Mathematical models
394.9 Health planning
By region or country
United States
395.A3 General works
395.A4A-Z By region or state, A-Z
395.A5-Z Other regions or countries, A-Z
Regulation of medical education. Licensure
Cf. R735+, Medical education
396.A1 General works
396.A3-A4 United States
396.A3 General works
396.A4A-Z By region or state, A-Z
396.A5A-Z Other regions or countries, A-Z
Expert testimony, etc , see RA1056

| | |
|---|---|
| | Medicine and the state -- Continued |
| 398.A-Z | Registration of physicians, pharmacists, etc. |
| | Cf. RK5+, Dentistry |
| | Cf. RS4+, Pharmacy |
| 398.A1 | General works |
| 398.A3-A4 | United States |
| 398.A3 | General works |
| 398.A4A-Z | By region or state, A-Z |
| 398.A5-Z | Other regions or countries, A-Z |
| | Regulation of medical practice. Evaluation and quality control of medical care. Medical audit |
| | Including professional standards review organizations and physician practice patterns |
| | Cf. RA1056.5, Malpractice |
| 399.A1 | General works |
| 399.A3-A4 | United States |
| 399.A3 | General works |
| 399.A4A-Z | By region or state, A-Z |
| 399.A5 | Other regions or countries, A-Z |
| 399.5 | Disease management |
| | Pharmaceutical policy |
| 401.A1 | General works |
| 401.A3-A4 | United States |
| 401.A3 | General works |
| 401.A4A-Z | By region or state, A-Z |
| 401.A5-Z | Other regions or countries, A-Z |
| 404.A-Z | Reporting cases of sickness |
| | Cf. RC267.5+, Cancer |
| 404.A1 | General works |
| 404.A3-A4 | United States |
| 404.A3 | General works |
| 404.A4A-Z | By region or state, A-Z |
| 404.A5-Z | Other regions or countries, A-Z |
| | Death certification |
| | Cf. RB115, Nomenclature, classification, and nosology of diseases |
| 405.A1 | General works |
| 405.A3-A4 | United States |
| 405.A3 | General works |
| 405.A4A-Z | By region or state, A-Z |
| 405.A5-Z | Other regions or countries, A-Z |
| | Health status indicators. Medical statistics and surveys |
| | Cf. HA38+, Registration of vital statistics |
| | Cf. HB848+, Vital statistics |
| 407.A1 | Periodicals. Societies. Serials |
| 407.A2 | Congresses |
| 407.A3-Z | General works |
| | By region or country |
| | United States |
| 407.3 | General works |
| 407.4.A-Z | By region or state, A-Z |
| 407.5.A-Z | Other regions or countries, A-Z |

Medicine and the state
  Health status
      indicators. Medical statistics
      and surveys -- Continued
407.6 Developing countries
  Special groups, A-Z
408.A3 Aged
408.B33 Baby boom generation
408.B5 Blind
408.F3 Farmers
408.I49 Indians
  Infants, see RJ59+
408.M4 Men
408.M5 Migrant
408.M54 Minority aged
  Mothers, see RG530+
408.P59 Political prisoners
408.P6 Poor
408.P75 Prisoners of war
408.W65 Women
408.5 Health survey methods
  Statistical methods
409 General works
409.5 Computer programs. Computer calculations
  Medical economics. Economics of medical care
    Cf. HG9371+, Health insurance
    Cf. HV687+, Medical charities
    Cf. R728+, Practice of medicine
410.A1 Periodicals. Societies. Serials
410.A2 Congresses
410.A3 Dictionaries and encyclopedias
410.A5-Z General works
410.5 General special
  By region or country
    United States
410.53 General works
410.54.A-Z By region or state, A-Z
410.55.A-Z Other regions or countries, A-Z
410.56 Marketing
410.58 Hospital-physician joint ventures. Medical practice acquisitions
  Employment surveys, manpower requirements, distribution and utilization of physicians and medical personnel
410.6 General works
  By region or country
    United States
410.7 General works
410.8.A-Z By region or state, A-Z
410.9.A-Z Other regions or countries, A-Z
  Provisions for personal medical care
    State and private medical care plans
411 General works

Medicine and the state
Provisions for personal medical care
State and private medical care plants -- Continued
By region or country, see RA395.A+
State medical care plans. Socialized medicine.
National health insurance. Compulsory health insurance
Cf. HX550.M4, Communism/socialism and medicine

| | |
|---|---|
| 412 | General works |
| | By region or country |
| | United States |
| 412.2 | General works |
| | Medicare |
| | Including pharmaceutical assistance for the aged |
| 412.3 | General works |
| 412.35.A-Z | By region or state, A-Z |
| | Medicaid. Public medical assistance |
| 412.4 | General works |
| 412.45.A-Z | By region or state, A-Z |
| 412.5.A-Z | Other regions or countries, A-Z |
| | Private medical care plans |
| | Class here plans that provide medical care, including managed care plans, health maintenance organizations, preferred provider organizations |
| | Cf. R729.5.H43, Health maintenance organization practice. Managed care practice |
| | Cf. RK59.3.D45, Dental health maintenance organizations |
| | For private health insurance, see HG9371+ |
| 413 | General works |
| (413.3) | For special plans<br>see RA413.5 |
| 413.5.A-Z | By region or country, A-Z<br>*Under each country:*<br>.x *General works*<br>.x2 *Local, A-Z* |
| 413.7.A-Z | Special groups, A-Z |
| 413.7.A4 | Aged |
| | Cf. HV1450+, Free medical advice for the aged |
| | Cf. RA412.3+, Medicare |
| | Cf. RA997+, Nursing homes |
| | Government employees<br>see JK794.H38; JN450.H4, etc. |
| 413.7.I7 | Iron and steel workers |
| 413.7.M55 | Miners |
| 413.7.M57 | Minorities |
| 413.7.R3 | Railroad workers |
| 413.7.S54 | Small business employees |
| | Steel workers, see RA413.7.I7 |

Medicine and the state
Provisions for personal medical care
Special groups, A-Z -- Continued
413.7.U53 Uninsured persons
(414-415) Special types of care
see the type of care, e. g. RA960+, Hospital care RK52+, Dental care, etc.
Medical savings accounts
416 General works
416.5.A-Z By region or country, A-Z
Apply table at RA413.5.A-Z
Medicine and society. Social medicine. Medical sociology
418 General works
418.3.A-Z By region or country, A-Z
418.5.A-Z Special aspects, A-Z
418.5.F3 Family
Cf. RA418.5.F36, Fatherless family
Cf. RA777.7, Personal health
For clinical aspects of family practice, see RC46
For non-clinical aspects of family practice, see R729.5.G4
418.5.F36 Fatherless family
Homelessness, see RA564.9.H63
418.5.M4 Medical innovations
418.5.P6 Poor. Poverty
Poverty, see RA418.5.P6
418.5.T73 Transcultural medical care
418.5.U53 Unemployed. Unemployment
Unemployment, see RA418.5.U53
Public health. Hygiene. Preventive medicine
Including community health services
Cf. RK52+, Public health dentistry
Cf. RT97, Public health nursing
421 Periodicals. Societies. Serials
422 Congresses
422.5 Collected works (nonserial)
422.9 Nomenclature. Terminology. Abbreviations
423 Dictionaries and encyclopedias
423.2 Communication in public health
423.5 Directories
Cf. RA7+, Directories of sanitary authorities
424 History
Biography
424.4 Collective
424.5.A-Z Individual, A-Z
General works
424.8 Through 1900
425 1901-
427 General special
427.2 Handbooks, manuals, etc.
427.25 Moral and ethical aspects

Public health. Hygiene.
Preventive medicine -- Continued

427.3 Health risk assessment
Cf. RA566.27, Environmental health

Medical screening

427.5 General works

427.6 Multiphasic screening

427.8 Health promotion
Cf. RA975.5.H4, Health promotion services in hospitals
Cf. RC969.H43, Industrial medicine
Cf. RT90.3, Nursing

427.9 Primary health care

Public health laboratories, institutes, etc.
Including laboratory technique

428 General works

428.3.A-Z Individual laboratories, A-Z

428.5 Instruments, apparatus, and appliances

430 Problems, exercises, examinations

430.5 Outlines, syllabi, etc.

431 Popular works
Cf. RA773+, Personal health

432 Juvenile works

436 Addresses, essays, lectures

Museums. Exhibitions

437 General works

438.A-Z By region or country, A-Z
*Under each country:*
.x *General works*
.x2 *Special. By city, A-Z*

Study and teaching
Cf. LB1140.5.H4, Preschool education
Cf. LB1587+, Elementary education
Cf. LC1621, Higher education (Women)
Cf. QP39+, Physiology and hygiene
Cf. RA975.5.P38, Patient education programs in hospitals
Cf. RG973, Childbirth education
Cf. RK60.8, Dental health education
Cf. RT90.3, Nursing

440.A1 Periodicals. Societies. Serials

440.A15 Congresses

440.A2-Z General works

440.3.A-Z By region or country, A-Z
Apply table at RA413.5.A-Z

440.4 Evaluation

440.5 Health education of the public
Including safety education, materials, and methods
Cf. HV675+, Accidents

440.55 Audiovisual aids
For catalogs of materials, see RA440.55.Z9A-Z

Higher education in public health and health services administration

Public health. Hygiene. Preventive medicine
Study and teaching
Higher education in public health and health services administration -- Continued
440.6 General works
440.7.A-Z By region or country, A-Z
Apply table at RA413.5.A-Z
440.8 Training of health officers, inspectors, etc.
Research. Experimentation
440.85 General works
440.87.A-Z By region or country, A-Z
440.9 Public health as a profession
441 World health. International cooperation
Cf. RA8.A+, World Health Organization
441.5 Developing countries
Cf. RA390.A2+, Medical missions. Medical assistance
Cf. RA427.9, Primary health care
Tropics, see RC960+
By region or country
Including public and community health services, health centers, etc.
Cf. RA791+, Medical geography
For medical centers, see RA966+
For medical centers, see RA980+
For reports of government health agencies, see RA10+
America
442 General works
North America
443 General works
United States
445 General works
446 States (Collectively). Counties
446.5.A-Z By region, A-Z
447.A-W By state, A-W
448.A-Z By city, A-Z
Ethnic groups, etc.
448.4 General works
448.5.A-Z Individual, A-Z
Afro-Americans, see RA448.5.N4
448.5.A83 Asian Americans
448.5.C45 Chinese Americans
448.5.H38 Hawaiians
448.5.H57 Hispanic Americans
448.5.I44 Immigrants
448.5.I5 Indians
Cf. E98.M4, American Indian medicine and medicine men
448.5.J5 Jews
448.5.K65 Korean Americans
448.5.M4 Mexican Americans
448.5.M5 Migrant laborers

Public health. Hygiene. Preventive medicine
By region or country
America
North America
United States
Ethnic groups, etc.
Individual, A-Z -- Continued
Minority women, see RA564.86

448.5.N4 Negroes. Afro-Americans
448.5.P33 Pacific Islander Americans
448.5.P83 Puerto Ricans
448.5.T48 Thais
449-450 Canada (Table R5)
Latin America
450.5 General works
451-452 Mexico (Table R5)
Central America
453 General works
454.A-Z By country, A-Z
West Indies
455 General works
456.A-Z By country, A-Z
South America
457 General works
459-460 Argentina (Table R5)
461-462 Bolivia (Table R5)
463-464 Brazil (Table R5)
465-466 Chile (Table R5)
467-468 Colombia (Table R5)
469-470 Ecuador (Table R5)
Guianas
471 General works
472.A-Z By country, A-Z
475-476 Paraguay (Table R5)
477-478 Peru (Table R5)
479-480 Uruguay (Table R5)
481-482 Venezuela (Table R5)
Europe
483 General works
Great Britain
485 General works
487-488 England (Table R5)
488.2-3 Wales (Table R5)
489-490 Scotland (Table R5)
491-492 Northern Ireland (Table R5)
492.2-3 Ireland (Table R5)
493-494 Austria (Table R5)
495-496 Belgium (Table R5)
497-498 Denmark (Table R5)
499-500 France (Table R5)
500.5 Overseas departments and territories (General)
501-502 Germany (Table R5)
Including West Germany

Public health. Hygiene. Preventive medicine
By region or country
Europe -- Continued

502.5-6 East Germany (Table R5)
503-504 Greece (Table R5)
505-506 Netherlands (Table R5)
507-508 Italy (Table R5)
509-510 Norway (Table R5)
511-512 Portugal (Table R5)
513-514 Russia (Table R5)
515-516 Spain (Table R5)
517-518 Sweden (Table R5)
519-520 Switzerland (Table R5)
523.A-Z Other European regions or countries, A-Z
Apply table at RA413.5.A-Z

Asia

525 General works
527-528 China (Table R5)
528.5-6 Taiwan (Table R5)
528.7-8 Pakistan (Table R5)
529-530 India (Table R5)
530.2-3 Sri Lanka (Table R5)
530.5-6 Burma (Table R5)
531-532 Japan (Table R5)
533-534 Iran (Table R5)
535-536 Former Soviet Union in Asia (Table R5)
For Transcaucasia, see RA513+
537-538 Turkey (Table R5)
541.A-Z Other Asian regions or countries, A-Z
541.P6-P7 Philippines

*Subarrangement:*

*1* *General works*
*2.A-Z* *Local, A-Z*

543 Islamic countries

Africa

545 General works
549-550 Egypt (Table R5)
552.A-Z Other African regions or countries, A-Z
Apply table at RA413.5.A-Z

Indian Ocean islands

552.5 General works
552.6.A-Z By island or group of islands, A-Z

*Under each island:*

*.x* *General works*
*.x2A-Z* *Local, A-Z*

Australia

553 General works
554.A-Z Local, A-Z

New Zealand
Cf. DU423.M38, Maori medicine

555 General works
556.A-Z Local, A-Z

Pacific islands

Public health. Hygiene. Preventive medicine
By region or country
Pacific islands -- Continued
557 General works
558.A-Z By island or group of islands, A-Z
Hawaii, see RA447.A+
558.S6 Solomon Islands
*Subarrangement:*
*.x* *General works*
*.x2A-Z* *Local, A-Z*
Developing countries, see RA441.5
By ethnic group, etc.
Cf. RA448.5.A+, Ethnic groups, etc., in the United States
561 Jews
562 Blacks
563.A-Z Other, A-Z
563.C54 Chinese
563.I58 Inuit
563.M56 Minorities
Minority women, see RA564.86
563.P35 Palestinian Arabs
By age group, class, etc.
Cf. RA408.A+, Medical statistics
Cf. RA773+, Personal health and hygiene
Cf. RC965.A+, Occupations
Children, see RJ101+
Infants, see RJ59+, RJ251+
Prison hygiene, see HV8833+
School hygiene, see LB3401+
564.5 Youth
Adults
564.7 General works
564.8 Aged
Including retirees
Cf. RC952+, Geriatrics
564.83 Men
Women
Cf. RC963.6.W65, Industrial medicine
Cf. RG1+, Gynecology and obstetrics
564.85 General works
564.86 Minority women
564.87 Lesbians
564.88 Physically handicapped women
564.9.A-Z Other, A-Z
564.9.H63 Homeless persons
564.9.H65 Homosexuals
Poor, see RA418.5.P6
564.9.P72 Princes
564.9.P74 Prisoners of war
564.9.R43 Refugees
564.9.T73 Transsexuals

Public health. Hygiene.
Preventive medicine -- Continued
Environmental health
Cf. RA1226, Environmental toxicology
Cf. RB152.5+, Environmentally induced diseases
Cf. TD1+, Environmental technology
565.A1 Periodicals. Societies. Serials
565.A2 Congresses
565.A3-Z General works
566 General special
566.22 Handbooks, manuals, etc.
566.23 Problems, exercises, examinations
566.235 Juvenile works
566.24 Environmental health as a profession
566.25 Study and teaching
566.26 Research. Experimentation
566.27 Health risk assessment
566.29 Planning
By region or country
United States
566.3 General works
566.4.A-Z By region or state, A-Z
566.5.A-Z Other regions or countries, A-Z
566.6 Indoor environments
Cf. RA577.5, Indoor air pollution
Cf. RA616+, Public buildings
Cf. RA770, Housing
Urban health. Urbanization in relation to public health
566.7 General works
By region or country, see RA566.3+
Rural health, see RA771+
Sanitation. Waste disposal. Sewage disposal
567 General works
567.5.A-Z By region or country, A-Z
567.7 Infectious wastes
568 Drainage in relation to health
Cf. TC970+, Drainage engineering
568.2.A-Z By region or country, A-Z
568.5 Energy development in relation to public health
569 Radioactive substances and ionizing radiation
Cf. RA648.3, Nuclear warfare
Cf. RA1231.R2, Toxicology
569.3 Noniodizing radiation in relation to public health
Including electromagnetic waves, radiofrequency radiation, and microwaves
569.5 Laser beams
569.8 Ozone layer depletion
Carcinogens, see RC268.6+
Soil
570 Soils and soil moistures in relation to public health

Public health. Hygiene. Preventive medicine
Environmental health
Soil -- Continued.
571 Soil pollution. Soil remediation
Cf. RA642.S6, Transmission of disease
Cf. TD878+, Environmental technology, sanitary engineering
Air
Cf. RA642.A5, Transmission of disease
Cf. RA791+, Medical climatology
575 General works
575.5 General special
Air pollution (General)
Including gases. odors, and smoke
Cf. QP82.2.A3, Physiological effect
Cf. TD881+, Sanitary engineering
For nuisances, see RA580+
For economic aspects, see HC, e.g. HC110, United States; HC120, Canada
576.A1 Periodicals. Societies. Serials
576.A2 Congresses
576.A3-Z General works
By region or country
United States
576.5 General works
576.6.A-Z By region or state, A-Z
576.7.A-Z Other regions or countries, A-Z
577.A-Z By substance, A-Z
577.A68 Aromatic compounds
577.A9 Automobile exhaust gas. Gasoline
577.C36 Carbon monoxide
577.C45 Chlorine
577.C63 Coal
577.D53 Diesel motor exhaust gas
577.D8 Dust
577.F55 Fluorine compounds
577.L4 Lead
Cf. RA1231.L4, Toxicology
577.M28 Manganese
577.M4 Mercury
577.M86 Mutagens
577.N52 Nickel
577.N56 Nitrogen
577.O97 Ozone
577.P56 Photochemical oxidants
577.P6 Pollen
577.S9 Sulphur compounds
577.V35 Vanadium
577.5 Indoor air pollution
578.A-Z By activity, industry, manufacturing process, etc., A-Z

Public health. Hygiene. Preventive medicine
Environmental health
Air
Air pollution (General)
By activity, industry, manufacturing process, etc., A-Z -- Continued
578.A6 Abattoirs. Slaughterhouses
Cf. HD9410+, Animal industry
Cf. TS1960+, Butchering, slaughterhouses
578.B8 Breweries and distilleries
578.C5 Chemical plants
Distilleries, see RA578.B8
578.F4 Fertilizer factories
578.G5 Glue factories
578.H38 Hazardous waste incineration
578.L43 Leaf burning
578.M4 Metal industries
578.N8 Nuclear reactors
578.R4 Rendering works
Slaughterhouses, see RA578.A6
578.S5 Smelting
578.S6 Soap making
578.S94 Synthetic fuels industry
578.T2 Tanning
578.W4 Welding
Industrial pollution (other than air)
579 General works
579.5.A-Z By activity, industry, manufacturing process, etc., A-Z
579.5.C63 Coal-fired power plants
Nuisances (other than industrial)
580 General works
581 Garbage and refuse, offal, dead animals, etc.
Animal culture
Including livestock
581.5 General works
582 Stables
583 Swine
Water supply in relation to public health. Water pollution
Cf. RA642.A+, Transmission of disease
For technical aspects (Examination and analysis), see TD380+
For technical aspects (Purification), see TD429.5+
For technical aspects (Qualities of water), see TD370+
For technical aspects (Water supply engineering), see TD201+
591 General works
591.5 General special
591.6 Hard water. Water softening
Cf. TP263, Chemical technology

Public health. Hygiene. Preventive medicine
Environmental health
Water supply in relation to public health -- Continued

591.7 Fluoridation
Cf. QP801.F5, Physiology
Cf. RK52+, Dental public health
Cf. RK331, Caries
Cf. RK341, Endemic fluorosis
Cf. TD467, Water supply engineering

By region or country

United States

592.A1 General works

592.A2-Z By region or state, A-Z

Other American regions or countries, A-Z

593.A1 General works

593.A2-Z By region or country, A-Z

Europe

594.A1 General works

594.A2-Z By region or country, A-Z

Asia

595.A1 General works

595.A2-Z By region or country, A-Z

Africa

596.A1 General works

596.A2-Z By region or country, A-Z

Australia

597.A1 General works

597.A2-Z By state or territory, A-Z

597.5 New Zealand

Pacific islands, A-Z

598.A1 General works

598.A2-Z By island or group of islands, A-Z

598.5 Developing countries

599 Ice and ice supply in relation to public health
Cf. QR105.5, Bacteriology

600 Seawater. Ocean
Cf. RA606, Bathing beaches
Cf. RC1000+, Submarine medicine

Food and food supply in relation to public health
Cf. QR115+, Microbial ecology
Cf. TX341+, Home economics

601 General works

601.5 Foodborne diseases

602.A-Z Special foods, A-Z

602.E5 Eggs

602.F5 Fish

602.M54 Milk
Cf. QP144.M54, Nutrition
Cf. RC596, Food allergies
Cf. SF254.A1+, Milk contamination
Cf. SF257, Milk hygiene
Cf. TX379, Food

Public health. Hygiene. Preventive medicine
Food and food supply in relation to public health
Special foods, A-Z -- Continued
602.O9 Oysters
602.S6 Shellfish (General)
602.V4 Veal
604 Parks, recreation areas, camp grounds, etc.
Cf. GV191.74, Sanitary measures in camping
Cf. GV198.S3, Sanitation of organized camps
Cf. TD931, Sanitary engineering
Public baths, comfort stations, etc.
Cf. NA7010, Architecture
605 General works
606 Bathing beaches. Baths and swimming pools
Cf. RA780, Personal hygiene
607 Comfort stations
Hygiene of special groups of the population, see RA561+
Industrial hygiene, prevention of disease in industry, see RC967
Military hygiene, see UH600+
Naval hygiene, see VG470+
Prison hygiene, see HV8833+
Public health aspects of transportation
Cf. RA655+, Quarantine
For traffic accidents, see RA772.T7
615 General works
615.1 Railroads. Streetcars and buses
Cf. TF445+, Railroad car sanitation
615.2 Airplanes
615.3 Ships, boats, etc.
615.5.A-Z Other, A-Z
Public buildings
616 General works
Government buildings, see JK1613+
617 Barber shops. Beauty shops
Cf. TT950+, Hairdressing, barbers' work, beauty culture, etc.
618 Hotels
Cf. HD7285+, Housing
Cf. HD7393, Restaurants, etc.
Cf. TX911.3.S3, Sanitary measures in hotels
Disposal of the dead
Cf. GT3150+, Manners and customs
Cf. RA405.A+, Death certification
Cf. UH570, Army treatment of the dead
619 General works
Morgues
620 General works

Public health. Hygiene. Preventive medicine
Disposal of the dead
Morgues -- Continued
621.A-Z By region or country, A-Z
*Under each country:*
*.x* *General works*
*.x2* *Capital city*
*.x3A-Z* *Other local, A-Z*
Undertaking and embalming
622.A1 Periodicals. Serials
622.A5 Societies
622.A7 Directories
622.A8-Z General works
622.5 Dictionaries and encyclopedias
Biography
622.7.A1 Collective
622.7.A2-Z Individual, A-Z
622.8 Study and teaching
Catalogs, see TS2301.U5
Boards of undertaking and embalming examination and registration
622.95 General works
By region or country
United States
623.A2 General works
623.A3A-Z By region or state, A-Z
623.A5A-Z Other regions or countries, A-Z
623.A6-Z Embalming
Cf. DT62.M7, Egyptian mummies and embalming
Cf. GT3340, Manners and customs
623.5 Mortuary cosmetology. Post-mortem plastic surgery
623.6.A-Z By region or country, A-Z
623.7 Importation and transportation of dead bodies
624 Cryonics. Long-term cold storage of dead bodies
Burial. Interment
Cf. GT3320+, Manners and customs
625 General works
Cemeteries
Including management, laying-out, etc.
For sepulchral monuments, see NA6120+
For sepulchral monuments, see NB1800+
626 Periodicals. Societies. Serials
626.3 Directories
627 General works
By region or country
Class here works on cemeteries in their medical and public health aspects, and administrative reports, regulations, by-laws, etc.
For historical and descriptive works, see classes D and F
United States
629.A3 General works

Public health. Hygiene. Preventive medicine
Disposal of the dead
Burial. Interment
Cemeteries
By region or country
United States -- Continued
629.A4A-Z By region or state, A-Z
629.A5-Z By city, etc., A-Z
630.A-Z Other regions or countries, A-Z
*Under each country:*
*.x2* *General works*
*.x3A-Z* *By region or state, A-Z*
*.x4A-Z* *By city, etc., A-Z*
Cremation
Cf. GT3330+, Manners and customs
631 Periodicals. Societies. Serials
History
633 General works
634.A-Z By region or country, A-Z
635 General works
Crematories
Cf. NA6117, Architecture
636 General works
By region or country
636.5 United States
636.7.A-Z Other regions or countries, A-Z
637 Exhumation
638 Immunity and immunization in relation to public health
Cf. QR180+, Immunology
Cf. RJ240, Pediatrics
Cf. RM270+, Immunotherapy
For vaccination in individual diseases, see RA644.A+
Prevention of disease (General), see RA425
Transmission of disease
Cf. RA565+, Environmental health
Transmission by animals. Zoonoses
Cf. QL99, Medical zoology (Systematic works)
Cf. RC113.5, Internal medicine
Cf. SF740+, Veterinary medicine
639 General works
639.3 Vector control
For control of particular vectors, see RA639.5
639.5 Insects
640 Mosquitoes
641.A-Z Other, A-Z
641.A65 Arachnida
641.A7 Arthropods
641.B38 Bats
641.B5 Birds
641.C45 Chiggers
641.C6 Cockroaches
641.D6 Dogs
641.F5 Fleas

Public health. Hygiene. Preventive medicine
Transmission of disease
Transmission by animals. Zoonoses
Other, A-Z -- Continued

641.F6 Flies
Flies, Tsetse, see RA641.T7
641.G3 Gasteropoda. Snails
641.G7 Ground squirrels
641.L6 Lice
641.M5 Mites
641.M6 Mollusks
641.P7 Primates
641.R15 Raccoons
641.R2 Rats
641.R6 Rodents
641.S55 Simuliidae
641.S59 Skunks
Snails, see RA641.G3
641.T5 Ticks
641.T7 Tsetse flies
641.5 Transmission by humans. Carrier state
642.A-Z Other means of transmission, A-Z
642.A5 Airborne infection
642.B56 Bloodborne infection
Foodborne infection, see RA601.5
642.S6 Soilborne infection
642.W3 Waterborne infection

Communicable diseases and public health
Including preventive measures and vaccination in individual diseases
Cf. RA638, Immunization
Cf. RA648.5+, Epidemics
Cf. RA655+, Quarantine
Cf. RA761+, Disinfection
For diagnosis and treatment, see RC1+

643 General works
By region or country
United States
643.5 General works
643.6.A-Z By region or state, A-Z
643.7.A-Z Other regions or countries, A-Z
644.A-Z Individual diseases or groups of diseases, A-Z
Acquired immune deficiency syndrome, see RA644.A25
644.A25 AIDS. HIV infections
644.A57 Amebiasis
644.A6 Anthrax
644.A82 Ascariasis
644.B32 Bacterial diseases
644.B7 Brucellosis
Cerebrospinal meningitis, see RA644.M6
644.C26 Chagas' disease
644.C3 Cholera
644.C74 Creutzfeldt-Jakob disease

Public health. Hygiene. Preventive medicine
Communicable diseases and public health
Individual diseases
or groups of diseases, A-Z -- Continued

644.D4 Dengue
Diarrhea, see RA644.D9
644.D6 Diphtheria
644.D64 Distomatosis
644.D75 Dracunculiasis
644.D9 Dysentery. Diarrhea
644.E34 Echinococcosis
644.E52 Encephalitis, Epidemic. Equine encephalomyelitis in humans
644.E54 Enterovirus diseases
Equine encephalomyelitis in humans, see RA644.E52
644.E83 Escherichia coli infections
644.F5 Filiariasis
644.G53 Giardiasis
Gonorrhea, see RA644.V4
644.H32 Hantavirus infections
644.H38 Helminthiasis
644.H4 Hepatitis
644.H45 Herpes virus diseases
HIV infections, see RA644.A25
644.H65 Hookworm disease
644.H85 Human monkeypox
Infectious hepatitis, see RA644.H4
644.I6 Influenza
644.I65 Intestinal parasites
644.L23 Legionnaires' disease
644.L25 Leishmaniasis
644.L3 Leprosy
644.L4 Leptospirosis
644.L94 Lyme disease
644.M2 Malaria
644.M5 Measles
644.M6 Meningitis, Cerebrospinal
644.M8 Mumps
644.M92 Mycoses
644.N66 Nosocomial infections
644.O53 Onchocerciasis
644.P18 Parasitic diseases
Parrot fever, see RA644.P95
644.P7 Plague
644.P8 Pneumonia
644.P9 Poliomyelitis
644.P93 Prion diseases
644.P95 Psittacosis. Parrot fever
644.Q25 Q fever
644.R3 Rabies
644.R4 Respiratory infections
644.R5 Rheumatic fever
644.R53 Rickettsial diseases

Public health. Hygiene. Preventive medicine
Communicable diseases and public health
Individual diseases
or groups of diseases, A-Z -- Continued

644.R54 Rift Valley fever
644.R8 Rubella
644.S15 Salmonellosis
644.S2 Scarlet fever
644.S3 Schistosomiasis
Serum hepatitis, see RA644.H4
Sexually transmitted diseases, see RA644.V4
644.S6 Smallpox
644.S7 Spirochetosis
644.S75 Streptococcal infections
Syphilis, see RA644.V4
644.T4 Tetanus
644.T66 Treponematoses
644.T69 Trypanosomiasis
644.T7 Tuberculosis
644.T75 Tularemia
644.T8 Typhoid fever
644.T9 Typhus fever
644.U73 Urethritis
644.V4 Venereal diseases. Sexually transmitted diseases
644.V5 Verruga peruana
644.V55 Virus diseases
644.W6 Whooping cough
644.Y4 Yellow fever

Chronic and noninfectious diseases and public health
Cf. RA790+, Mental health
Cf. RA973.5, Hospital care
Cf. RA997+, Nursing homes. Long-term care facilities
Cf. RJ380+, Pediatrics
Cf. RT120.C45, Nursing
For diagnosis and treatment, see RC1+

644.5 General works
By region or country
United States
644.6 General works
644.7.A-Z By region or state, A-Z
644.8.A-Z Other regions or countries, A-Z
645.A-Z Individual diseases or groups of diseases, A-Z
645.A24 Abnormalities. Birth defects
645.A44 Allergy
645.A49 Alzheimer's disease
645.A53 Anemia
645.A83 Asthma
645.A86 Atherosclerosis
645.B32 Backache
Birth defects, see RA645.A24
645.B54 Blindness
645.B73 Brain injuries

Public health. Hygiene. Preventive medicine
Chronic and noninfectious diseases and public health
Individual diseases
or groups of diseases, A-Z -- Continued

645.C3 Cancer
645.C34 Cardiovascular diseases
645.C47 Cerebral palsy
645.C49 Cerebrovascular disease
645.C66 Communicative disorders
645.C67 Contact dermatitis
645.C68 Coronary heart disease
645.D5 Diabetes
645.D54 Digestive disorders
645.E64 Epilepsy
645.G34 Gallstones
645.G4 Genetic disorders
645.G64 Goiter
645.H4 Heart diseases
645.H63 Hodgkin's disease
645.H87 Hypercholesteremia
645.H9 Hypertension
645.H94 Hypokinesia
645.I53 Inflammatory bowel diseases
645.I55 Iodine deficiency diseases
Cf. RA645.G64, Goiter
645.I75 Iron deficiency anemia
645.K5 Kidney diseases
645.L58 Liver cirrhosis
645.L84 Lung diseases
645.M45 Melanoma
645.M68 Mountain sickness
645.M82 Multiple sclerosis
645.M85 Musculoskeletal disorders
645.N48 Neurological diseases
645.N87 Nutrition disorders
Including malnutrition and nutritionally induced diseases
645.O23 Obesity
645.O26 Occupational diseases
645.O74 Osteoarthritis
645.O75 Osteoporosis
645.P4 Pellagra
645.P46 Peptic ulcer
645.P48 Peripheral vascular diseases
645.P76 Prostate diseases
645.R35 Renal insufficiency
645.R4 Respiratory diseases
645.R5 Rheumatic diseases
645.S53 Sickle cell anemia
Smoking, see RA645.T62
645.S66 Spinal cord injuries
645.S68 Sports injuries
645.T62 Tobacco habit. Smoking

Public health. Hygiene. Preventive medicine
Chronic and noninfectious diseases and public health
Individual diseases
or groups of diseases, A-Z -- Continued
645.T73 Traumatology. Wounds and injuries (General)
Cf. RA645.S68, Sports injuries
Cf. RA772.A25, Accidents
645.V56 Vitamin A deficiency
Wounds and injuries, see RA645.T73
Home health care services
Cf. RA973, Hospital-based home care programs
Cf. RT120.H65, Home nursing
645.3 General works
By region or country
United States
645.35 General works
645.36.A-Z By region or state, A-Z
645.37.A-Z Other regions or countries, A-Z
Emergency medical services
Cf. RA975.D57, Disaster hospitals
Cf. RA975.5.E5, Hospital emergency services
Cf. RA975.5.T83, Trauma centers
Cf. RA995+, Ambulance service
Cf. RB36.3.E54, Emergency laboratory services
645.5 General and United States
645.6.A-Z By region or state, A-Z
645.7.A-Z Other regions or countries, A-Z
645.8 Emergency medical services at large gatherings, festivals, meetings, etc.
645.9 Natural disasters
War and public health
646 General works
647 Bacterial warfare
Cf. UG447.8, Military aspects
648 Chemical warfare
Cf. UG447+, Military aspects
648.3 Nuclear warfare
Epidemics. Epidemiology
For atlases, see G1046
For works limited to chronic and noninfectious diseases, see RA644.5+
For works limited to infectious and parasitic diseases, see RA643+
648.5 Periodicals. Societies. Serials
648.6 Congresses
649 History
Biography
649.4 Collective
649.5.A-Z Individual, A-Z
By region or country
America
650 General works
650.5 United States

Public health. Hygiene. Preventive medicine
Epidemics. Epidemiology
By region or country
America -- Continued
650.55.A-Z Other American regions or countries, A-Z
*Under each country:*
.x *General works*
.x2 *Local. By province, department, etc., A-Z*
Europe
650.6.A1 General works
650.6.A2-Z By region or country, A-Z
Apply table at RA650.55.A-Z
Asia
650.7.A1 General works
650.7.A2-Z By region or country, A-Z
Apply table at RA650.55.A-Z
Africa
650.8.A1 General works
650.8.A2-Z By region or country, A-Z
Apply table at RA650.55.A-Z
Australia and Pacific islands, A-Z
650.9.A1 General works
650.9.A2-Z By region or country, A-Z
Apply table at RA650.55.A-Z
650.9.A8 Australia
Apply table at RA650.55.A-Z
651 General works
652 General special
652.2.A-Z Special aspects of the subject as a whole, A-Z
652.2.C55 Clinical aspects
652.2.C6 Codes
652.2.D38 Data processing
652.2.M3 Mathematical models
652.2.P82 Public health surveillance
Statistical methods, see RA652.2.M3
Surveillance, see RA652.2.P82
Telegraph codes, see RA652.2.C6
652.4 Technique
652.7 Problems, exercises, examinations
653 Popular works
653.5 Juvenile works
654 Study and teaching
Quarantine (Land, maritime, and air)
655 General works
661 General special
663 International
By region or country
North America
664 General works
United States
665 General works
667.A-Z By region or state, A-Z

Public health. Hygiene. Preventive medicine
Quarantine (Land, maritime, and air)
By region or country
North America -- Continued

671 Canada
673 Mexico
675.A-Z Central America, A-Z
677.A-Z West Indies, A-Z

South America

678 General works
679 Argentina
681 Bolivia
683 Brazil
685 Chile
687 Colombia
689 Ecuador
691 Guianas
693 Paraguay
695 Peru
697 Uruguay
699 Venezuela

Europe

700 General works
701 Great Britain. England
703 Scotland
704 Wales
705 Northern Ireland
706 Ireland
707 Austria
709 Belgium
711 Denmark
713 France

Germany

Including West Germany

715 General works
716.A-Z German states, A-Z
716.5 East Germany
717 Greece
719 Netherlands
721 Italy
723 Norway
725 Portugal
727 Russia
729 Spain
731 Sweden
733 Switzerland
737.A-Z Other European regions or countries, A-Z

Asia

738 General works
739 China
740 Pakistan
741 India
742 Sri Lanka

Public health. Hygiene. Preventive medicine
Quarantine (Land, maritime, and air)
By region or country
Asia -- Continued
742.5 Burma
743 Japan
745 Iran
747 Turkey
749 Former Soviet Union in Asia
751.A-Z Other Asian regions or countries, A-Z
751.A5 Arabia
751.P6 Philippines
Africa
753 General works
754 Egypt
755.A-Z Other African regions or countries, A-Z
756 Australia
756.5 New Zealand
758.A-Z Pacific islands, A-Z
Disinfection. Fumigation. Sterilization.
Decontamination
Cf. R857.C6, Clean air systems
Cf. RD91+, Surgery
Cf. RG730, Obstetrics
Cf. RK506+, Dentistry
Cf. RS199.S73, Pharmacy
761 General works
762 Disinfection of objects
Physical agents of disinfection
763 General works
Special, see RA766.A+
765 Chemical agents of disinfection (General)
766.A-Z Individual disinfectants or germicides, A-Z
766.C48 Chlorhexidine
766.C5 Chlorine compounds
766.E8 Ethylene oxide
766.F6 Formaldehyde
766.H4 Heat
Cf. RA766.S8, Steam
766.H8 Hydrocyanic acid
766.M5 Mercury compounds
766.P43 Peroxyacetic acid
766.R2 Radiation
766.R3 Refrigeration
766.S8 Steam
Cf. RA766.H4, Heat
766.S9 Sulphur dioxide
767.A-Z Individual contaminants, A-Z
767.A35 Aflatoxins
767.N58 Nitrosoamines
770 Housing and public health
Cf. RA564.9.A+, Public health of homeless persons

Public health. Hygiene.
Preventive medicine -- Continued
770.5 Household hygiene
Cf. TX301+, The house (Home economics)
Rural health and hygiene. Rural health services
Cf. R729.5.R87, Rural medical practice
Cf. RA975.R87, Rural hospitals
771.A1 Periodicals. Societies. Serials
771.A2 Congresses
771.A3-Z General works
By region or country
United States
771.5 General works
771.6.A-Z By region or state, A-Z
771.7.A-Z Other regions or countries, A-Z
772.A-Z Other subjects of public health, A-Z
772.A25 Accidents
772.F57 Firearms accidents
772.F6 Floods
772.H65 Home accidents
772.I5 Inflammable materials
772.N7 Noises
Cf. RF293.5, Otology
772.T7 Traffic accidents
Cf. HE5613.5+, Motor vehicles
Personal health and hygiene
773 Periodicals. Societies. Serials
773.6 Communication in health
General works
775 Through 1900
776 1901-
776.5 General special
776.7 Problems, exercises, examinations
Study and teaching, see RA440+
776.75 Longevity. Rejuvenation. Youth extension
Health behavior and habits
776.9 General works
776.95 Health self-care
776.98 Grooming (General)
Including the use of cosmetics
Cf. GT2340+, Manners and customs
Cf. TP983+, Cosmetics manufacture
Cf. TT950+, Hairdressing
Personal health and grooming guides for classes of people
Children. Youth
Cf. RJ101+, Health care of children
777 General works
777.2 Boys
777.25 Girls
777.3 College students
777.5 Middle aged

Public health. Hygiene. Preventive medicine
Personal health and hygiene
Personal health and grooming guides for classes of people -- Continued

777.6 Aged
Cf. RC952+, Care and treatment of the aged
777.65 Executives
777.7 Family
777.75 Medical personnel
777.8 Men
Women
Including beauty and use of cosmetics
Cf. RG121, Gynecology
Cf. TP983+, Cosmetics manufacture
Cf. TT950+, Hairdressing, beauty culture, etc.
778.A1 Periodicals. Societies. Serials
778.A2-Z General works
778.2 Lesbians
778.4.A-Z By ethnic group, A-Z
778.4.A36 Afro-Americans
778.4.H57 Hispanic Americans
778.5 Hygiene products
779 Clothing. Shoes
Cf. TS989+, Boot and shoe making
Cf. TT490+, Clothing manufacture, dressmaking, and tailoring
780 Cleanliness. Bathing
Cf. RA606, Bathing beaches, baths, and swimming pools
Cf. RM801+, Hydrotherapy
780.5 Massage
Cf. RM721+, Therapeutic massage
Exercise for health
Cf. RG558.7, Exercise in pregnancy
Cf. RJ133, Pediatrics
Cf. RM725+, Exercise therapy
For exercises on muscular development and specific activities, see GV1+
781 General works
781.15 Aerobic exercises
781.17 Aquatic exercises
781.2 Isometric exercises
781.5 Posture
Including the Alexander technique
Cf. BF172, Psychology
781.6 Reducing exercises. Figure control
781.63 Stretching
781.65 Walking
781.68 Aṣṭāṅga yoga

Public health. Hygiene. Preventive medicine
Personal health and hygiene
Exercise for health -- Continued
781.7 Haṭha yoga
Including prânayâmaq
Cf. BL1238.56.H38, Hinduism
Cf. RM727.Y64, Therapeutics
781.75 Breema
781.8 Ch'i kung
781.85 Tao yin
782 Breathing
Cf. QP121+, Physiology
Cf. RM733, Respiration as cure
783 Outdoor life. Vacations
Cf. GV191.2+, Recreation
Cf. HD5260+, Employee vacations
783.5 Travel hygiene
784 Nutrition
Cf. QP141+, Physiology
Cf. RM214+, Diet therapy
Cf. TX341+, Home economics
784.5 Detoxification. Detox
785 Relaxation. Rest. Stress management
Cf. RC455.4.S87, Psychiatry
Cf. RC489.R45, Psychiatry
Sleep
Cf. BF1068+, Psychology of the unconscious
Cf. QP425+, Physiology of sleep
Cf. RC547+, Sleep disturbances
786 General works
786.3 Snoring
788 Sex hygiene
Cf. HQ56+, Sex instruction
Cf. HQ763+, Birth control
Cf. RC881, Diseases of genital organs (Popular works)
Cf. RG121, Female hygiene
Cf. RT87.S49, Nursing
Mental health. Mental illness prevention
Cf. BF636+, Applied psychology
Cf. BF710, Emotional maturity
Cf. BL65.M45, Mental health and religion
Cf. RC435+, Psychiatry
Cf. RJ499+, Mental health of children
For the mental health care of specific groups of people, see RC451.4.A+
For the mental health care of specific groups of people, see RJ499+
790.A1 Periodicals. Societies. Serials
790.A2 Congresses
790.A3-Z General works
790.5 General special
790.53 Mental health promotion

Public health. Hygiene. Preventive medicine
Mental health. Mental illness prevention -- Continued
790.55 Community psychology
Cf. RC455, Community psychiatry
By region or country
United States
790.6 General works
790.65.A-Z By region or state, A-Z
790.7.A-Z Other regions or countries, A-Z
790.75 Mental health as a profession
Study and teaching
790.8 General works
790.85 Audiovisual aids
For catalogs of materials, see RA790.Z9A-Z
790.87 Mental health education of the public
790.95 Mental health consultation
Cf. RC455.2.C65, Psychiatric consultation
Medical geography. Climatology. Meteorology
Including weather and disease
791 Periodicals. Societies. Serials
791.2 Congresses
Medical geography (General)
792 General works
792.5 Cartography. Mapping
For collections of maps and atlases, see G1046
793 Medical climatology and meteorology
794 Health resorts, spas, etc.
Including seashore resorts
Cf. GB1198+, Hot springs
Cf. TN923+, Mineral waters
Cf. TP625, Artificial mineral waters
By region or country
For the tropics and Arctic regions, see RC955+
801 America
For health and diseases of American Indians (Modern medicine only), see RA448.5.I5
For tribal medicine, see E-F
North America
802 General works
803 Health resorts. Mineral waters (General)
United States
804 General works
805 Health resorts. Mineral waters (General)
807.A-Z By region or state, A-Z
*Under each state:*
*.x* *General works*
*.x2A-Z* *Local, A-Z*
Canada
809 General works
809.5 Health resorts. Mineral waters (General)
810.A-Z Local, A-Z
Mexico

Medical geography. Climatology. Meteorology
By region or country
Mexico -- Continued
811 General works
811.5 Health resorts. Mineral waters (General)
812.A-Z Local, A-Z
Central America
813 General works
813.5 Health resorts. Mineral waters (General)
814.A-Z Local, A-Z
West Indies
815 General works
815.5 Health resorts. Mineral waters (General)
816.A-Z Local, A-Z
South America
817 General works
819-820 Argentina
819 General works
819.5 Health resorts. Mineral waters (General)
820.A-Z Local, A-Z
821-822 Bolivia
821 General works
821.5 Health resorts. Mineral waters (General)
822.A-Z Local, A-Z
823-824 Brazil
823 General works
823.5 Health resorts. Mineral waters (General)
824.A-Z Local, A-Z
825-826 Chile
825 General works
825.5 Health resorts. Mineral waters (General)
826.A-Z Local, A-Z
827-828 Colombia
827 General works
827.5 Health resorts. Mineral waters (General)
828.A-Z Local, A-Z
829-830 Ecuador
829 General works
829.5 Health resorts. Mineral waters (General)
830.A-Z Local, A-Z
831-832 Guianas
831 General works
831.5 Health resorts. Mineral waters (General)
832.A-Z Local, A-Z
837-838 Paraguay
837 General works
837.5 Health resorts. Mineral waters (General)
838.A-Z Local, A-Z
839-840 Peru
839 General works
839.5 Health resorts. Mineral waters (General)
840.A-Z Local, A-Z
841-842 Uruguay

Medical geography. Climatology. Meteorology
By region or country
South America
Uruguay -- Continued
841 General works
841.5 Health resorts. Mineral waters (General)
842.A-Z Local, A-Z
843-844 Venezuela
843 General works
843.5 Health resorts. Mineral waters (General)
844.A-Z Local, A-Z
Europe
845 General works
846 Health resorts. Mineral waters (General)
Great Britain
847 General works
848 Health resorts. Mineral waters (General)
England
849 General works
849.5 Health resorts. Mineral waters (General)
850.A-Z Local, A-Z
850.B3 Bath, England. Hot Springs
Scotland
851 General works
851.5 Health resorts. Mineral waters (General)
852.A-Z Local, A-Z
Wales
853 General works
853.5 Health resorts. Mineral waters (General)
854.A-Z Local, A-Z
Northern Ireland
855 General works
855.5 Health resorts. Mineral waters (General)
856.A-Z Local, A-Z
Ireland
856.2 General works
856.25 Health resorts. Mineral waters (General)
856.3.A-Z Local, A-Z
Austria
857 General works
857.5 Health resorts. Mineral waters (General)
858.A-Z Local, A-Z
Belgium
859 General works
859.5 Health resorts. Mineral waters (General)
860.A-Z Local, A-Z
Denmark
861 General works
861.5 Health resorts. Mineral waters (General)
862.A-Z Local, A-Z
France
863 General works
863.5 Health resorts. Mineral waters (General)

Medical geography. Climatology. Meteorology
By region or country
Europe
France -- Continued
864.A-Z Local, A-Z
864.R6 Riviera
864.V6 Vichy. Vichy water
Germany
Including West Germany
865 General works
865.5 Health resorts. Mineral waters (General)
866.A-Z Local, A-Z
East Germany
866.2 General works
866.25 Health resorts. Mineral waters (General)
866.3.A-Z Local, A-Z
Greece
867 General works
867.5 Health resorts. Mineral waters (General)
868.A-Z Local, A-Z
Netherlands
869 General works
869.5 Health resorts. Mineral waters (General)
870.A-Z Local, A-Z
Italy
871 General works
871.5 Health resorts. Mineral waters (General)
872.A-Z Local, A-Z
Riviera, see RA864.R6
872.53 Malta
Norway
873 General works
873.5 Health resorts. Mineral waters (General)
874.A-Z Local, A-Z
Portugal
875 General works
875.5 Health resorts. Mineral waters (General)
876.A-Z Local, A-Z
Russia
877 General works
877.5 Health resorts. Mineral waters (General)
878.A-Z Local, A-Z
Spain
879 General works
879.5 Health resorts. Mineral waters (General)
880.A-Z Local, A-Z
Sweden
881 General works
881.5 Health resorts. Mineral waters (General)
882.A-Z Local, A-Z
Switzerland
883 General works
883.5 Health resorts. Mineral waters (General)

Medical geography. Climatology. Meteorology
By region or country
Europe
Switzerland -- Continued
884.A-Z Local, A-Z
887.A-Z Other European regions or countries, A-Z
887.R8 Romania
Asia
891 General works
China
901 General works
901.5 Health resorts. Mineral waters (General)
902.A-Z Local, A-Z
Pakistan
909 General works
909.5 Health resorts. Mineral waters (General)
910.A-Z Local, A-Z
India
911 General works
911.5 Health resorts. Mineral waters (General)
912.A-Z Local, A-Z
Sri Lanka
913 General works
913.5 Health resorts. Mineral waters (General)
914.A-Z Local, A-Z
Vietnam
916 General works
916.5 Health resorts. Mineral waters (General)
917.A-Z Local, A-Z
Burma
918 General works
918.5 Health resorts. Mineral waters (General)
919.A-Z Local, A-Z
Japan
921 General works
921.5 Health resorts. Mineral waters (General)
922.A-Z Local, A-Z
Iran
924 General works
924.5 Health resorts. Mineral waters (General)
925.A-Z Local, A-Z
Former Soviet Union in Asia
For Transcaucasia, see RA878.A+
927 General works
927.5 Health resorts. Mineral waters (General)
928.A-Z Local, A-Z
Turkey
931 General works
931.5 Health resorts. Mineral waters (General)
932.A-Z Local, A-Z
934.A-Z Other Asian regions or countries, A-Z
934.D9 Dutch East Indies. Indonesia
Indonesia, see RA934.D9

Medical geography. Climatology. Meteorology
By region or country
Asia
Other Asian regions or countries, A-Z -- Continued
934.P5 Philippines
Africa
943 General works
Egypt
947 General works
947.5 Health resorts. Mineral waters (General)
948.A-Z Local, A-Z
949.A-Z Other African regions or countries, A-Z
949.A4 Algeria
949.A9 Azores
949.C3 Cameroon
Australia
951 General works
951.5 Health resorts. Mineral waters (General)
952.A-Z Local, A-Z
952.5 New Zealand
Pacific islands
953 General works
953.5 Health resorts. Mineral waters (General)
954.A-Z Local, A-Z
Tropics, tropical hygiene, see RC960+
Arctic regions, see RC955+
Medical centers. Hospitals. Dispensaries. Clinics
For reports of cases, see RC31.A+
960 Periodicals. Societies. Serials
961 Congresses
Collected works (nonserial)
962 Several authors
962.12 Individual authors
962.2 Nomenclature. Terminology. Abbreviations
963 General works
963.5 Juvenile works
964 History
964.5 Research. Experimentation
965 Sociological aspects
965.3 Psychological aspects
965.5 Public relations. Hospital and community
Cf. RA999.P8, Nursing homes
965.6 Hospital patients. Hospital-patient relations
Including patient representative services
Cf. RA975.5.P38, Patient education programs
Cf. RA975.5.P39, Patient escort services
Hospitals and the law, see K3604
965.8 Accreditation of health facilities
Medical centers, clinics, etc.
966 General works
Individual centers, see RA980+

Medical centers. Hospitals.
Dispensaries. Clinics -- Continued
Health facilities. Hospital buildings
Cf. NK2195.H43, Interior decoration
For special hospitals, see RA975.A+
For special hospitals, see RA982.A+
967 Architectural planning and construction
967.5.A-Z Specifications. By place, A-Z
967.7 Location. Grounds
Environmental services
Cf. RA975.5.H6, Housekeeping
Cf. RA975.5.L3, Laundry services
967.75 General works
967.8 Hospital engineering. Maintenance and repair
967.9 Energy consumption. Energy conservation
968 Hospital equipment and furnishings. Fixtures and supplies
Cf. RD63, Operating rooms, equipment, and supplies
969 Sanitation
Cf. RA999.S36, Long-term care facilities
969.3 Water supply
969.33 Bathing facilities
969.35 Toilet facilities
Air conditioning. Ventilation. Heating
969.4 General works
969.43 Clean air systems
Including laminar flow
969.45 Waste disposal
969.48 Electric power
969.49 Communication systems
969.5 Lighting
969.6 Odor control
969.7 Noise control
969.9 Safety measures
Cf. TH9445.H7, Fires and fire prevention
969.95 Security measures
Hospital and health facility administration
971 General works
Communication
971.2 General works
971.23 Computer networks. Computer network resources
Including the Internet
Finance and business management
Cf. HF5686.H7, Accounting
Cf. RA410.58, Hospital-physician joint ventures
971.3 General works
971.32 Prospective payment
Cf. RA974.3, Prospective payment for outpatient services
971.33 Materials management. Purchasing of equipment, furnishings, supplies, etc.

Medical centers. Hospitals. Dispensaries. Clinics
Hospital and health
facility administration -- Continued
971.35 Personnel management. Labor-management relations
971.38 Risk management
971.6 Administrative records and reports
Including data processing
For medical records departments, see RA976+
For medical reports, see RC31.A+
971.8 Admission and discharge of patients
971.85 Waiting lists
971.9 Hospital-physician relations
Cf. RA410.58, Hospital-physician joint ventures
972 Medical management of hospitals. Hospital staff (Medical and surgical). Interns' and resident physicians' manuals
Hospital employees (Non-medical and non-surgical)
Cf. RA971.35, Labor-management relations
972.5 General works
972.55 Clerical staff
Including hospital admitting clerks, insurance clerks, ward clerks, etc.
972.7 Volunteer services in hospitals
Cf. RA999.V64, Nursing homes
973 Convalescent care. Home care programs
Cf. RA645.3+, Home care services
Cf. RA975.C64, Convalescent hospitals
973.5 Care of chronic patients
Outpatient services. Hospital-based ambulatory medical care
Including hospital day
Cf. RC439.2, Psychiatric hospitals
Cf. RD110+, Outpatient surgery. Ambulatory surgery
974 General works
974.3 Prospective payment
974.5 Outpatient clinics. Dispensaries
Clinical and pathological laboratories, see RB36+
975.A-Z Special types of hospitals, A-Z
For hospitals in special fields of medicine, see the field, e.g. RC439, and RC443+, Psychiatric hospitals
975.C37 Catholic hospitals and health facilities
975.C64 Convalescent hospitals. Subacute care facilities
Day hospitals, see RA974+
975.D57 Disaster hospitals
Hospices, see RA1000+
Military hospitals, see UH460+
Naval hospitals, see VG410+
975.P74 Proprietary hospitals
975.R44 Religious hospitals and health facilities
975.R87 Rural hospitals
975.S49 Seventh-Day Adventist health facilities

Medical centers. Hospitals. Dispensaries. Clinics
Special types of hospitals, A-Z -- Continued
Subacute care facilities, see RA975.C64
975.T43 Teaching hospitals
975.U5 University hospitals
975.U72 Urban hospitals
975.5.A-Z Other special services and departments, A-Z
Ambulance service, see RA995+
975.5.A5 Anesthesia services
Blood banks, see RM172
975.5.B87 Burn care units
975.5.C3 Cardiovascular services
975.5.C36 Case management services
975.5.C4 Central service departments
975.5.C45 Child care services
975.5.C6 Coronary care units
Delivery rooms (Obstetrics), see RG500+
Dental service, see RK51.7
975.5.D47 Diagnostic services
975.5.D5 Diet kitchens. Food service
Cf. RA999.F65, Nursing homes
Cf. RM219+, Dietic cookbooks
975.5.E5 Emergency services
975.5.E65 Encephalography departments
Escort services for patients, see RA975.5.P39
975.5.E9 Extended care units
Cf. RA997+, Nursing homes. Long-term care facilities
Food service, see RA975.5.D5
975.5.G37 Gastroenterology services
975.5.H4 Health promotion services
975.5.H6 Housekeeping
Including housekeepers' manuals
Inhalation therapy units, see RA975.5.R47
975.5.I56 Intensive care units
975.5.I85 Isolation services
975.5.L3 Laundry services
Maternity services, see RG500+
Medical records departments, see RA976+
975.5.N4 Nephrological services
Operating rooms, see RD63, RG500+
975.5.P38 Patient education programs
975.5.P39 Patient escort services
Patient representatives service, see RA965.6
975.5.P5 Pharmacies
Cf. RA999.P45, Nursing homes
Cf. RS152, Hospital pharmacy
975.5.P6 Physical therapy departments
975.5.R3 Radiological services
975.5.R43 Rehabilitation services
975.5.R47 Respiratory services
Including inhalation and respiratory therapy services

Medical centers. Hospitals. Dispensaries. Clinics
Other special services
and departments, A-Z -- Continued
975.5.S92 Substance abuse services
975.5.T83 Trauma centers
X-ray departments, see RA975.5.R3
Medical records departments. Medical records administration
Cf. R864, Medical records
Cf. RA999.M43, Nursing homes
Cf. RC65, Case history taking and recording
976 General works
976.5 Medical records personnel
Hospital libraries, see Z675.H7
Directories
976.9 General works
By region or country
United States
977 General works
977.5.A-Z By region or state, A-Z
978.A-Z Other regions or countries, A-Z
By region or country
980 America
United States
981.A2 General works
Government hospitals
981.A3 General works
981.A35 Indian hospitals
981.A4 Public Health Service hospitals
Military hospitals, see UH473+
Naval hospitals, see VG410+
981.A45 Afro-American hospitals
981.A5-Z By region or state, A-Z
982.A-Z By city, A-Z
*Under each:*
*.x* *General works*
*.x2A-Z* *Special institutions. By name, A-Z*
983.A-Z Canada
983.A1 General works
983.A4A-Z Provinces and territories, A-Z
983.A5-Z By city, A-Z
Apply table at RA982.A-Z
984.A-Z Other American regions or countries, A-Z
*Under each country:*
*.x* *General works*
*.x2* *Government hospitals. By author*
*.x3* *By state, province, etc., A-Z*
*.x4* *By city, A-Z*
984.4 Atlantic Ocean islands
984.5.A-Z Individual islands or groups of islands, A-Z
Apply table at RA984.A-Z
Europe
985 General works

Medical centers. Hospitals. Dispensaries. Clinics
By region or country
Europe -- Continued
Great Britain. England
986 General works
987.A-Z By country (British Isles), A-Z
987.N67 Northern Ireland
987.S4 Scotland
987.W2 Wales
988.A-Z By city, A-Z
Apply table at RA982.A-Z
Ireland
988.3 General works
988.4.A-Z By province, etc., A-Z
988.5.A-Z By city, A-Z
989.A-Z Other European regions or countries, A-Z
Apply table at RA984.A-Z
Asia
990.A1 General works
990.A2-Z By region or country
Apply table at RA984.A-Z
990.5 Arab countries (Collectively)
For individual countries, see RA990.A2+
Africa
991.A1 General works
991.A2-Z By region or country
Apply table at RA984.A-Z
991.5 Indian Ocean islands
Australia
992.A1 General works
992.A2-Z By state or territory, A-Z
Apply table at RA984.A-Z
992.3.A-Z By city, A-Z
New Zealand
992.5 General works
992.6.A-Z By provincial district or territory, A-Z
992.7.A-Z By city, A-Z
Pacific islands
993.A1 General works
993.A2-Z By island or group of islands, A-Z
Apply table at RA984.A-Z
Ambulance service
Including ambulance service for children
995.A1 Periodicals. Societies. Serials
995.A2 Congresses
995.A6-Z General works
By region or country
United States
995.5.A1 General works
995.5.A2-Z By region or state, A-Z
Apply table at RA807.A-Z
996.A-Z Other regions or countries, A-Z
Apply table at RA413.5.A-Z

Medical centers. Hospitals.
Dispensaries. Clinics -- Continued
Aeronautics in medicine
Including flying doctors and ambulances
Cf. TL722.8, Aeronautical engineering
996.5 General works
996.55.A-Z By region or country, A-Z
996.56 Helicopter ambulances
Nursing homes. Long-term care facilities
Cf. RA975.C64, Subacute care facilities
Cf. RA975.5.E9, Hospitals
Cf. RC954.3+, Nursing home care
Cf. RT120.L64, Nursing
By region or country
General and United States
997.A1 Periodicals. Societies. Serials
997.A15 Congresses
997.A2 Directories
997.A3-Z General works
997.5.A-Z By region or state, A-Z
998.A-Z Other regions or countries, A-Z
998.5 Design and construction
999.A-Z Special services and departments, A-Z
999.A35 Administration
999.F65 Food service
999.I5 In-service training
999.M43 Medical records
999.P39 Personnel management
999.P45 Pharmaceutical services
999.P8 Public relations
999.R42 Recreational activities
999.R57 Risk managment
999.S34 Safety measures
999.S36 Sanitation
999.V64 Volunteer services
Hospices. Terminal care facilities
Cf. R726.8, Terminal care
Cf. RT87.T45, Nursing
1000 General works
By region or country
United States
1000.3 General works
1000.4.A-Z By region or state, A-Z
1000.5.A-Z Other regions or countries, A-Z
Forensic medicine. Medical jurisprudence. Legal medicine
For medical toxicology, see RA1228
1001 Periodicals. Societies. Serials
Collected works (nonserial)
1011 Several authors
1012 Individual authors
1016 Congresses
1017 Dictionaries and encyclopedias

Forensic medicine.
Medical jurisprudence.
Legal medicine -- Continued
1018 Handbooks, manuals, etc.
Statistics and surveys
1018.5 General works
By region or country
United States
1018.55 General works
1018.56.A-Z By region or state, A-Z
1019 Atlases. Pictorial works
History
1021 General works
1022.A-Z By region or country, A-Z
Biography
1025.A1 Collective
1025.A3-Z Individual, A-Z
Study and teaching
1027 General works
1027.5.A-Z By region or country, A-Z
Research. Experimentation
1027.8 General works
1027.9.A-Z By region or country, A-Z
1028 Outlines, syllabi, etc.
Laboratories, institutes, etc.
1032 General works
1034 Laboratory technique
1038 Instruments, apparatus, and appliances
Museums. Exhibitions
1042 General works
1042.2.A-Z By region or country, A-Z
Apply table at RA438.A-Z
General works
1050 Through 1850
1051 1851-
1053 General special
1054 Addresses, essays, lectures
1055 Medicolegal examination. Identification of persons, living or dead
1055.4 Industrial medicine
1055.5 Disability evaluation
Cf. RC470, Psychiatry
Cf. RC963.4, Industrial medicine
Cf. RD734.3, Orthopedic disability evaluation
For disability evaluation in specific diseases, see RA1170.A+
1056 Medical evidence (Expert testimony)
1056.5 Malpractice
Cf. R729.8, Medical errors
Cf. R730, Quackery
1057 Forensic chemistry
Cf. HV8073+, Investigation of crimes (Social pathology)

Forensic medicine.
Medical jurisprudence.
Legal medicine -- Continued
1057.5 Forensic genetics
1057.55 DNA fingerprints
(1058) Forensic pathology
see RA1063.4
1058.5 Forensic radiography
1058.7 Forensic thermography
1059 Forensic examination of the skeleton and bones.
Forensic osteology
Cf. GN69.8, Forensic anthropology
Forensic examination of blood, hair, skin, etc.
Cf. HV8077.5.B56, Bloodstain patterns
Cf. RB145, Pathology of the blood
1061 General works
1061.5 Intoxication tests. Blood alcohol determination
1061.6 Forensic serology
1062 Forensic examination of teeth. Forensic dentistry
1062.5 Forensic examination of eyes. Forensic ophthalmology
1062.8 Forensic examination of ears. Forensic audiology
Death determination and certification
Including recognition of apparent death and prevention of premature burial
Cf. HA38+, Registration of deaths
Cf. RA405.A+, Public health administration
1063 General works
1063.3 Brain death
Medicolegal investigation of death. Forensic pathology. Autopsy
1063.4 General works
1063.45 Forensic entomology
1063.47 Forensic taphonomy
1063.5 Destruction or attempted destruction of the human body
Forensic obstetrics
1064 General works
1065 Tests of live birth. Docimasia pulmonum, etc.
1067 Abortion. Infanticide
Cf. RG631+, Fetal and neonatal death
Cf. RG648, Spontaneous abortion
Cf. RG734+, Induced abortion
Asphyxia
1071 General works
1076 Drowning and suffocation
1081 Hanging and strangulation
1082 Autoerotic asphyxia
Cf. RC560.A97, Psychiatry
Newborn infants, see RJ256
1085 Burns. Fire
1091 Electricity
Including lightning
1101 Cold
1116 Starvation

Forensic medicine.
Medical jurisprudence.
Legal medicine -- Continued
1121 Wounds and injuries. Accidents
Cf. RD92+, Surgery
Assault and battery
Including family violence
1122 General works
1122.5 Battered child syndrome
Cf. RC569.5.C55, Child abuse
Cf. RD93.5.C4, Treatment of injuries
Cf. RJ375, Pediatrics
1122.8 Torture
1123 Homicide
Cf. RC569.5.H65, Psychiatry
Euthanasia, see R726
Suicide
Cf. HV6543+, Suicide as a crime
1136 General works
1137 Psychological autopsy
1138 Medicolegal aspects of consanguinity, maternity, paternity, pregnancy, etc.
1141 Sexual offenses, diseases, etc.
Cf. HV6556+, Sex crimes
Cf. RC560.S47, Psychiatry
1146 Malingering. Feigned diseases. Self injuries
Cf. RC569.5.F27, Factitious disorders
1147 Forensic neurology
1147.5 Forensic neuropsychology
1148 Forensic psychology
Cf. RA1137, Psychological autopsy
Forensic psychiatry
1151 General works
1152.A-Z Specific conditions, A-Z
1152.M84 Multiple personality
1152.P67 Post-traumatic stress disorder
1155 Forensic nursing
1160 Forensic pharmacology
Cf. RA1061.5, Intoxication tests
Cf. RA1228, Forensic toxicology
1165 Forensic epidemiology
1170.A-Z Medicolegal aspects of specific diseases, A-Z
1170.A78 Arthritis
1170.B33 Backache. Back injuries
1170.C35 Cancer
Forensic cardiology, see RA1170.H4
1170.H4 Heart disease. Forensic cardiology
1170.S54 Sleep disorders
1171 Other special
e.g. Medicolegal aspects of the use of X-ray, hypnotism, etc.; surgeon's liability in connection with foreign substances in operations
Cf. HV6110, Hypnotism and crime

Toxicology
Cf. RC347.5, Neurotoxicology
Cf. RC365, Central nervous system
Cf. RC528.T6, Toxic psychoses
Cf. RC582.17, Immunotoxicology
Cf. RC677, Cardiovascular toxicology
Cf. RC720, Inhalation toxicology. Pulmonary toxicology
Cf. RC848.H48, Hepatotoxicology
Cf. RC918.N45, Nephrotoxicology
Cf. RE901.T67, Ophthalmology
Cf. RF285.O83, Ototoxic effects
Cf. RL803, Dermatotoxicology

1190 Periodicals. Societies. Serials
1191 Congresses
1193 Dictionaries and encyclopedias
Communication in toxicology
1193.3 General works
1193.4 Information centers
1193.7 Directories
History
1195 General works
By region or country
United States
1196 General works
1196.5.A-Z By region or state, A-Z
1197.A-Z Other regions or countries, A-Z
1197.M3 Malaysia
Biography
1197.5 Collective
1197.52.A-Z Individual, A-Z
Study and teaching
1198 General works
1198.2 Audiovisual aids
1198.3.A-Z By region or country, A-Z
Research. Experimentation
1199 General works
1199.4.A-Z Special topics, A-Z
1199.4.A38 Acute toxicity testing
1199.4.A54 Animal models
1199.4.D66 Dose-response relationship
1199.4.H85 Human cells
1199.4.I5 In vitro
1199.4.I53 In vivo
1199.4.L57 Liver cells
1199.4.M37 Mathematical models
1199.4.M53 Microbiological assay (Toxicology)
Mutagenicity testing, see RA1224.4.M86
1199.4.S73 Statistical methods
1199.4.S77 Structure-activity relationships
1199.4.T37 Target organs
1199.5.A-Z By laboratory animal, A-Z
1199.5.I57 Invertebrates

Toxicology
Research. Experimentation
By laboratory animal, A-Z -- Continued
1199.5.P74 Primates
1199.5.R36 Rats
General works
1201 Through 1900
1211 1901-
1213 Popular works
1214 Juvenile works
1215 Handbooks, manuals, etc.
Statistics and surveys
1215.5 General works
1215.52.A-Z By region or country, A-Z
1216 General special
1218 Addresses, essays, lectures
1219 Clinical cases
1219.3 Chemical toxicology
1219.5 Biochemical toxicology
1220 Metabolism. Physiological effect of poisons
1220.3 Molecular toxicology
1220.5 Toxicological interactions
Analytic toxicology. Examination for poisons
1221 General works
Popular works, see RA1213
1223.A-Z Special tests or methods, A-Z
1223.B54 Biological monitoring
1223.B56 Biopsy
1223.C45 Chromatography
Chromatography, Gas, see RA1223.G37
1223.G37 Gas chromatography
1223.H58 Histochemistry
1223.I45 Immunoassay
1223.R33 Radiography
1224 Behaviorial toxicology
1224.2 Reproductive toxicology
Genetic toxicology
For specific poisons, see RA1230+
1224.3 General works
1224.4.A-Z Special topics, A-Z
Ionizing radiation, see RA1224.4.R34
1224.4.M86 Mutagenicity testing
1224.4.R34 Radioisotopes. Ionizing radiation
1224.45 Developmental toxicology
1224.5 Toxicological emergencies
1225 Pediatric toxicology
1226 Environmental toxicology
1228 Medicolegal toxicology
Including cases
Cf. HV6549+, Poisoning and poisoners (Crimes against the person)
Cf. RA1160, Forensic pharmacology

Toxicology -- Continued
Industrial toxicology
For general toxicology in specific industries, see RC965.A+
For specific poisons or industries limited to specific poisons, see RA1230+
1229 General works
1229.3 Handbooks, manuals, etc.
1229.4 Biological monitoring
1229.5 Threshold limit values
Special poisons and groups of poisons
Cf. RC268.6+, Carcinogens
Inorganic poisons
1230 General works
1231.A-Z Special, A-Z
1231.A5 Aluminum
1231.A6 Ammonia
1231.A65 Antimony
1231.A7 Arsenic and arsenic compounds
1231.A8 Asbestos
1231.B4 Beryllium
1231.C3 Cadmium
1231.C43 Cerium
1231.C44 Cesium
1231.C5 Chromium
1231.C7 Copper
Cyanide, see RA1242.H9
1231.F4 Ferro-silicon
1231.F55 Fluorine and fluorine compounds
Cf. RC627.F57, Fluorosis
1231.G6 Gold
Heavy metals, see RA1231.M52
1231.L4 Lead and lead compounds
Cf. RA577.L4, Air pollution
1231.L5 Lithium
1231.M4 Manganese
1231.M5 Mercury and mercury compounds
1231.M52 Metals
Including heavy metals
Metals, Platinum group, see RA1231.P53
Metals, Rare earth, see RA1231.R27
1231.M55 Minerals
Including mineral dusts
1231.M6 Molybdenum
1231.N37 Neptunium
1231.N44 Nickel
1231.N47 Nitrates
1231.N5 Nitrogen oxide
1231.P5 Phosphorus
1231.P52 Phyllosilicates
1231.P53 Platinum group metals
1231.P55 Plutonium
1231.P6 Potassium cyanide

Toxicology
Special poisons and groups of poisons
Inorganic poisons
Special, A-Z -- Continued
1231.Q37 Quartz
1231.R2 Radioactive substances
Cf. RA569, Public health
Cf. RC93+, Internal medicine
1231.R23 Radium
1231.R27 Rare earth metals
1231.S45 Selenium
1231.S5 Silver
1231.S76 Strontium
1231.T4 Tellurium
1231.T45 Thallium
1231.T5 Thorium
1231.T55 Tin
1231.T57 Titanium
1231.T7 Trace elements
1231.T73 Transuranium elements
1231.T75 Tritium
1231.U7 Uranium
1231.V3 Vanadium
Organic poisons
1235 General works
1238 Drugs (General)
1242.A-Z Special, A-Z
1242.A26 Acesulfame-K
1242.A29 Acetaminophen
1242.A3 Acetates
1242.A32 Acetone
1242.A33 Acrylamide
1242.A333 Acrylates
1242.A34 Acrylonitrile
1242.A344 Aflatoxins
1242.A347 Alachlor
1242.A35 Alcohol
Cf. HV5001+, Temperance
Cf. QP801.A3, Physiological effect
Cf. RC564.7+, Alcoholism
1242.A353 Aldicarb
1242.A36 Algae
1242.A38 Alkaloids
1242.A43 Amanita phalloides
1242.A46 Aminodiphenylamine
1242.A5 Amphetamine
1242.A54 Amyl acetate
1242.A57 Anethole
1242.A6 Aniline
Animal foodstuffs, see RA1259
1242.A65 Anthraquinones
1242.A72 Arachnida
1242.A73 Aspartame

Toxicology
Special poisons and groups of poisons
Organic poisons
Special, A-Z -- Continued

1242.A74 Asphalt
1242.A79 Atrazine
1242.A8 Atropine
1242.A9 Azaconazole
1242.A94 Azo compounds. Azo dyes
1242.B3 Barbiturates
1242.B4 Benzene
1242.B42 Benzenedicarbonitrile
1242.B425 Benzidine
1242.B43 Benzodiazepines
1242.B76 Butadiene
1242.B8 Butane
1242.B86 Butyl methyl ether
1242.C17 Cannabis. Marijuana
1242.C19 Carbamates
1242.C2 Carbolic acid
1242.C23 Carbon disulphide
1242.C24 Carbon tetrachloride
1242.C26 Castor bean
1242.C37 Chloranil
1242.C4 Chlordan
1242.C43 Chlordecone
1242.C435 Chlorinated paraffin
Chlorodinitrobenzene, see RA1242.D53
1242.C437 Chloroaniline
1242.C439 Chlorobenzene
1242.C4394 Chlorocresol
1242.C44 Chlorofluorocarbons
1242.C45 Chloroform
1242.C46 Chloronitrobenzenes
1242.C47 Chlorophenols
1242.C49 Chlorotoluenes
1242.C69 Coal
1242.C7 Coal-tar derivatives
1242.C75 Cocaine
1242.C8 Coriaria
1242.C82 Cotton dust
1242.C84 Crotalaria
1242.C87 Crotonaldehyde
1242.D35 DDT
1242.D4 Detergents, Synthetic
1242.D43 Diaminodiphenylmethane
1242.D44 Diazepam
1242.D443 Dibutylphthalate
1242.D446 Dichlorobenzidine
1242.D45 Dichloroethane
1242.D452 Dichloroethyl ether
1242.D453 Dichloroethylene
1242.D457 Dichloromethane

Toxicology
Special poisons and groups of poisons
Organic poisons
Special, A-Z -- Continued

1242.D4574 Dichloromethyl ether
1242.D458 Dichloronitrobenzene
1242.D46 Dichlorophenoxyacetic acid
1242.D47 Dieldrin
1242.D474 Diethyl phthalate
1242.D476 Diethylaniline
1242.D48 Diethylstilbestrol
1242.D49 Digoxin
1242.D498 Dimethyl sulphate
1242.D5 Dimethylaniline
1242.D52 Dinitrobenzenes
1242.D53 Dinitrochlorobenzene
1242.D535 Dinitrotoluenes
1242.D54 Dioxane
1242.D55 Dioxins
Cf. RA1242.T44, Tetrachlorodibenzodioxin
1242.D57 Diphenylamine
1242.D58 Diphenylguanidine
1242.E45 Endosulfan
1242.E5 Enzymes
1242.E55 Epichlorohydrin
1242.E6 Ergot
1242.E64 Estrogen. Estrogen antagonists
1242.E66 Ether
1242.E67 Ethoxylates
1242.E69 Ethyl acrylate
1242.E7 Ethylaniline
1242.E718 Ethylene glycol
1242.E72 Ethylene oxide
1242.E75 Ethylhexyl acrylate
1242.F45 Fenitrothion
1242.F56 Fish
Food, see RA1258+
1242.F6 Formaldehyde
1242.F86 Fusarium
1242.G3 Gasoline
Cf. RA577.A9, Air pollution (Automobile exhaust gas)
Cf. RA577.L4, Air pollution (Lead)
1242.H35 Halocarbons
Hashish, see RA1242.C17
Hemp, see RA1242.C17
1242.H45 Heptachlor
1242.H47 Hexachlorobenzene
1242.H474 Hexachlorobutadiene
1242.H476 Hexachloroethane
1242.H48 Hexane
1242.H5 Hexone
1242.H87 Hydrocarbons

Toxicology
Special poisons and groups of poisons
Organic poisons
Special, A-Z -- Continued

| | |
|---|---|
| 1242.H9 | Hydrocyanic acid and salts |
| 1242.I55 | Iodochlorhydroxyquin |
| 1242.I77 | Isoprene |
| 1242.I8 | Isopropyl alcohol |
| 1242.K44 | Kelevan |
| 1242.L3 | Lacquer |
| 1242.L35 | Lathyrus |
| 1242.L5 | Linseed oil |
| 1242.L96 | Lysergic acid diethylamide |
| | MSG, see RA1242.S63 |
| 1242.M28 | Malathion |
| 1242.M3 | Maleic hydrazide |
| | Marijuana, see RA1242.C17 |
| 1242.M34 | Marine phytoplankton |
| 1242.M36 | Methacrylic acid |
| 1242.M38 | Methanesulfonates |
| | Methanol, see RA1242.W8 |
| 1242.M4 | Methaqualone |
| | Methyl butyl ether, see RA1242.B86 |
| 1242.M45 | Methyl ethyl ketone |
| 1242.M46 | Methyl methacrylate |
| 1242.M47 | Methylnaphthalenes |
| 1242.M55 | Mirex |
| | Monosodium glutamate, see RA1242.S63 |
| 1242.M6 | Morphine |
| 1242.M9 | Mushrooms |
| 1242.M94 | Mycotoxins |
| 1242.N28 | Naphthalene |
| 1242.N3 | Narcotics |
| 1242.N5 | Nicotine |
| 1242.N57 | Nitrilotriacetic acid |
| 1242.N58 | Nitro compounds |
| 1242.N584 | Nitroaniline |
| 1242.N586 | Nitrobenzene |
| 1242.N59 | Nitropropanes |
| 1242.N62 | Nitrotoluene |
| 1242.N65 | Nonylphenol |
| 1242.O25 | Ochratoxins |
| 1242.O7 | Opium |
| 1242.O9 | Oxalic acid |
| 1242.P34 | Paraquat |
| 1242.P35 | Parathion |
| 1242.P4 | Pentachlorophenol |
| 1242.P413 | Pentaerythritol tetranitrate |
| 1242.P42 | Petroleum chemicals |
| 1242.P45 | Phenyldichlorarsine |
| 1242.P47 | Phenylenediamines |
| 1242.P54 | Phenytoin |
| 1242.P56 | Phosphorus organic compounds |

Toxicology
  Special poisons and groups of poisons
    Organic poisons
      Special, A-Z -- Continued

1242.P58 Phthalate esters
1242.P6 Physostigmine
Plant foodstuffs, see RA1260
1242.P66 Plastics
Poison ivy and sumac, see RA1242.R4
1242.P69 Polybrominated biphenyls
1242.P7 Polychlorinated biphenyls
1242.P72 Polychlorinated dibenzodioxins
1242.P73 Polycyclic aromatic hydrocarbons
1242.P75 Polymers
1242.P78 Polyurethanes
1242.P79 Propylene oxide
1242.P95 Pyridine
1242.Q56 Quintozene
1242.R35 Rattlesnake venom
1242.R36 Resorcinol
1242.R37 Retinoids
1242.R4 Rhus. Poison ivy and sumac
1242.S3 Salicylates
1242.S4 Scilla
1242.S46 Scorpion venom
1242.S48 Seafood toxins
1242.S52 Shellfish
1242.S53 Snake venom
1242.S63 Sodium glutamate
1242.S72 Starches
1242.S73 Steroid hormones
1242.S8 Strychnine
1242.S85 Styrene
Synthetic detergents, see RA1242.D4
1242.S9 Systox
TNT, see RA1242.T7
1242.T37 Tannins
1242.T42 Tetrachlorobenzene
1242.T44 Tetrachlorodibenzodioxin
1242.T447 Tetrachloroethane
1242.T45 Tetrachloroethylene
1242.T46 Tetrachloronitrobenzene
1242.T47 Tetradifon
1242.T48 Tetrahydronaphthalene
1242.T5 Thalidomide
1242.T53 Thiaarenes
1242.T6 Tobacco components
  Including cigarette smoke
  Cf. RA1242.N5, Nicotine
1242.T62 Tolidine
1242.T63 Toluene
1242.T64 Toxaphene
1242.T642 Triazines

Toxicology
Special poisons and groups of poisons
Organic poisons
Special, A-Z -- Continued

1242.T643 Tributylamine
1242.T645 Tributyltin oxide
1242.T65 Trichlorobenzene
1242.T66 Trichloroethane
1242.T67 Trichloroethylene
1242.T68 Trichothecenes
1242.T685 Triethyl phosphate
1242.T69 Trifluoromethylaniline
1242.T7 Trinitrotoluene (TNT)
1242.T74 Tris(2-chloroethyl) phosphate
1242.T78 Tryptophan
1242.U78 Urushiol
1242.V58 Vitamin E
1242.W3 Walnut wood
1242.W79 Wood
1242.W8 Wood alcohol
1242.X9 Xylene
1242.Z54 Zinc naphthenate

Gaseous poisons
Cf. RA576+, Air pollution

1245 General works
1247.A-Z Special, A-Z
1247.A3 Acrolein
Aerosols, see RA1270.A+
Ammonia, see RA1231.A6
1247.C15 Carbon dioxide. Carbonic acid
1247.C2 Carbon monoxide
Carbonic acid, see RA1247.C15
1247.C5 Chlorine
1247.C53 Chlorobenzylidene malononitrile
Cigarette smoke, see RA1242.T6
1247.C65 Combustion gases
1247.D53 Dichlorodifluoromethane
1247.E68 Ethyl bromide
1247.G2 Gas, Illuminating
Gasoline, see RA1242.G3
1247.H8 Hydrogen sulphide
Illuminating gas, see RA1247.G2
1247.M36 Methane
1247.M38 Methyl bromide
1247.M4 Methyl chloride
1247.M43 Methyl ether
1247.M45 Methyl isocyanate
1247.M8 Mustard gas
1247.O9 Oxygen
1247.O96 Ozone
1247.R33 Radon
Toluene, see RA1242.T63
1247.V54 Vinyl chloride

Toxicology
Special poisons and groups of poisons -- Continued
1250 Vegetable poisons (General)
For special poisons, see RA1242.A+
1255 Animal poisons (General)
For special poisons, see RA1242.A+
Food poisons
Cf. RC143, Bacterial food poisoning
Cf. RC596, Food allergies
For special poisons, see RA1242.A+
1258 General works
1259 Poisons from animal foodstuffs
1260 Poisons from plant foodstuffs
1270.A-Z Other poisons and groups of poisons, A-Z
1270.A34 Aerosols
1270.A4 Agricultural chemicals
1270.A53 Anesthetics
1270.A7 Arrow poisons
Chemical warfare agents, see RA648
1270.C63 Composite materials
1270.C65 Cosmetics
1270.D46 Dental materials
1270.E93 Explosives
1270.F4 Feed additive residues
1270.F52 Fibers
Including organic and inorganic fibers
1270.F56 Flavoring essences
1270.F6 Food additives
1270.F86 Fungicides
1270.H3 Herbicides
1270.I5 Insecticides
1270.L37 Latex paint
1270.L83 Lubricating oils
1270.M64 Molluscicides
1270.N58 Nitrogen fertilizers
1270.P37 Perfumes
1270.P39 Pesticide residues
1270.P4 Pesticides
1270.S48 Sewage
1270.S6 Solvents
Including organic and inorganic solvents
1270.S84 Sugar substitutes
1270.S87 Surface active agents
1270.S9 Synthetic poisons
1270.V47 Veterinary drug residues
1270.X46 Xenobiotics

Pathology
Cf. R134.8, Paleopathology
1 Periodicals. Societies. Serials
3 Congresses
Collected works (nonserial)
6 Several authors
6.2 Individual authors
Nomenclature. Terminology. Abbreviations, see RB115
10 Directories
Museums. Exhibitions, see R871+
History
15 General works
15.2.A-Z By region or country, A-Z
Biography
Cf. RA1025.A+, Forensic pathologists
16 Collective
17.A-Z Individual, A-Z
Pathological anatomy and histology
General works
24 Through 1900
25 1901-
27 General special
30 Handbooks, manuals, etc.
31 Problems, exercises, examinations
32 Outlines, syllabi, etc.
33 Atlases. Pictorial works
35 Moulage. Molding and casting of anatomical models
Cf. NB1180, Sculpture
Laboratories, institutes, etc.
Cf. R860+, Medicine (General)
Cf. RA428+, Public health laboratories
36 General works
36.2 Equipment
36.3.A-Z Special aspects, A-Z
Design, see RB36.3.P55
36.3.E54 Emergency laboratory services
36.3.F55 Finance and business management
36.3.P55 Planning and design
36.3.Q34 Quality control
36.5.A-Z Individual, A-Z
Clinical pathology. Laboratory technique
Class here works on chemical and microscopic diagnosis in general.
For works on the diagnosis of individual diseases, or diseases of systems or organs, see RC, RA, etc.
37.A1 Periodicals. Societies. Serials
37.A2 Congresses
37.A25 Dictionaries and encyclopedias
37.A3-Z General works
37.5 Study and teaching
Research. Experimentation, see RB125
37.6 Medical laboratory technology as a profession

Clinical pathology.
Laboratory technique -- Continued
38 Computer applications
Cf. RA427.6, Multiphasic screening
38.2 Handbooks, manuals, etc.
38.25 Problems, exercises, examinations
38.3 Mathematics. Statistical methods
40 Chemical examination
Cf. QD71+, Analytical chemistry
Cf. QP501+, Animal biochemistry
Cf. RB112.5, Clinical biochemistry
Cf. RS400+, Pharmaceutical chemistry
40.7 Chromatography
41 Electrochemical analysis
42 Radioactive techniques in laboratory examination
Microscopial examination. Cytodiagnosis
Cf. QM550+, Normal histology
Cf. QR1+, Microbiology
43 General works
43.5 Electron microscopy
Cf. RB46.7, Electron microscopic immunocytochemistry
43.6 Microprobe analysis. X-ray microanalysis
Molecular diagnosis
Including molecular probes in general
43.7 General works
43.8.A-Z Special methods, A-Z
43.8.C36 Capillary electrophoresis
43.8.D63 DNA probes
43.8.F58 Fluorescence in situ hybridization
43.8.P64 Polymerase chain reaction
44 Examination of chromosomes
Cf. RB155, Medical genetics
45 Examination of the blood
Cf. RB145, Pathology of the blood
45.15 Phlebotomy. Blood collection
45.2 Examination of blood gases
45.3 Blood coagulation tests
45.5 Examination of blood groups
46 Examination of serum
Immunological examination. Immunodiagnosis
46.5 General works
46.6 Immunohistochemistry
46.7 Immunocytochemistry
Including electron microscopic immunocytochemistry
47 Examination of the gastric contents
Cf. RC803+, Gastroenterology
47.5 Examination of hair
48 Examination of enzymes. Clinical enzymology
48.5 Examination of hormones
Cf. RC648+, Endocrine diseases
49 Examination of the feces
51 Examination of the sputum

Clinical pathology.
Laboratory technique -- Continued
52 Examination of body fluids
52.5 Examination of saliva
52.7 Examination of serous fluids
52.8 Examination of synovial fluid
53 Examination of the urine
Cf. QP551+, Animal biochemistry
Cf. SF773, Veterinary medicine
54 Examination of semen
55 Examination of cerebrospinal fluid
55.2 Examination of bone marrow
Examination for drugs
Cf. RS189+, Pharmaceutical drug assay
56 General works
56.5.A-Z Special drugs, A-Z
56.5.A43 Amiodarone
56.5.A45 Amphetamines
56.5.A56 Anti-inflammatory agents
56.5.A58 Antibiotics and anti-infective agents
56.5.B45 Benzodiazepines
57 Post-mortem examination. Autopsies
Cf. RA1063.4+, Forensic pathology
General pathology
For pathology of individual diseases, diseases of systems, or organs, see RC, RE, etc.
General works
110 Through 1900
111 1901-
112 General special
112.5 Clinical biochemistry
113 Physiological pathology. Clinical physiology
114 Comparative pathology
115 Nomenclature. Terminology. Abbreviations
118 Handbooks, manuals, etc.
119 Problems, exercises, examinations
120 Outlines, syllabi, etc.
121 Addresses, essays, lectures
Study and teaching
123 General works
123.5 Audiovisual aids
For catalogs of materials, see RB123.5.Z9
123.6.A-Z By region or country, A-Z
124.A-Z Individual schools. By name, A-Z
125 Experimental pathology
For experimental animals, see QL55
Manifestations of disease
For general pathology, see RB110+
For symptoms referable to individual diseases, diseases of systems or organs, see the disease in RC, RE, etc.

Manifestations of disease -- Continued

127 Pain
Cf. RD98.4, Postoperative pain
Cf. RT87.P35, Nursing

128 Headache
Cf. RC392, Migraine

129 Fever
Cf. RC106, Eruptive fevers

131 Inflammation. Suppuration

131.5 Granuloma

132 Pathologic pigmentation
Cf. RL790, Dermatology

133 Necrosis. Gangrene
Cf. RD628, Surgery

135 Atrophy
Cf. RL391, Dermatology

Mineral infiltrates, concrements, etc.

137 General works

138 Calcification

Disorders of growth. Hypertrophy, hyperplasia, etc.
Cf. RC648+, Endocrinology
Cf. RJ135, Pediatrics
Cf. RJ482.G76, Pediatrics
Cf. RL401+, Dermatology

140 General works

140.3 Dwarfism
Cf. CT9992, Biography
Cf. GN69.3, Anthropology

140.5 Gigantism
Cf. GN69+, Anthropology

Emaciation, see RC627.E5

Obesity, see RC628+

Disorders or circulation and fluid balance
Including dropsy, edema, embolism, hemorrhage, hyperemia, infarction, ischemia, thrombosis
Cf. RC630, Metabolic diseases
Cf. RC666+, Diseases of the circulatory system

144 General works

144.5 Reperfusion injury

145 Pathology of the blood
Cf. QP91+, Physiology
Cf. RB45, Examination of the blood
Cf. RC636, Diseases of the blood
Cf. SF769.5, Veterinary hematology

Disorders of metabolism
Cf. RC627.5+, Metabolic diseases

147 General works

147.5 Mitochondrial pathology

148 Periodicity of diseases. Clinical chronobiology

149 Sequelae

150.A-Z Other manifestations of disease, A-Z

Manifestations of disease
Other manifestations of disease, A-Z -- Continued

150.A65 Anorexia
Cf. RC552.B84, Anorexia nervosa
Cf. RJ399.A6, Pediatrics
150.A67 Anoxemia
150.A87 Asthenia
150.C6 Coma
Consciousness, Loss of, see RB150.L67
150.F37 Fatigue
Including chronic fatigue syndrome
150.L67 Loss of consciousness
150.M84 Multiple organ failure
150.N38 Nausea
150.S5 Shock
Cf. RD59, Surgical and traumatic shock
150.S84 Sudden death
150.S9 Syncope
150.T7 Tremor
150.V4 Vertigo

Theories of disease. Etiology. Pathogenesis
151 General works
152 General special
Environmentally induced diseases
Cf. RA1226, Environmental toxicology
152.5 General works
152.6 Multiple chemical sensitivity
152.7 Persian Gulf Syndrome
Infection and resistance to infection
153 General works
154 Focal infection
155 Heredity. Medical genetics
Cf. RA1224.3+, Genetic toxicology
Cf. RC268.4+, Cancer genetics
Cf. RC627.8, Inborn errors of metabolism
Cf. RJ47.3+, Pediatrics
155.5 Genetic disorders. Human chromosome abnormalities
Cf. RA645.G64, Public health
Cf. RE661.G45, Retinal diseases
Cf. RG580.G45, Genetic disorders in pregnancy
Diagnosis
155.6 General works
155.65 Genetic screening
155.7 Genetic counseling
155.8 Gene therapy
156 Chronic disease
Cf. RC108, Internal medicine
157 Acquired disease
170 Oxidation. Free radicals
171 Maillard reaction
Special factors in the production of disease
Physical and chemical agents, see RC91+
Physical agents, see RC102+

Theories of disease. Etiology. Pathogenesis
Special factors in
the production of disease -- Continued
Chemical agents, see RA1190+
Bacteria, see QR74.8+, QR74.8, RC115+
Fungi, see QR245+, RC117.A+
Spirochetes and protozoa, see QR251+, RC118+
Viruses and rickettsia, see QR353+, RC114+
Parasites, see RC119+
Psychiatric factors, see RC435+
Immunologic factors, see RC581+
Allergic disturbances, see RC583+
Endocrine disturbances, see RC648+
Nutritional and metabolic disturbances, see RC620+
210 Influence of age
Cf. RC952+, Geriatrics
Cf. RJ1+, Pediatrics
212 Influence of sex
Cf. RC875+, Diseases of the genital organs
214 Other factors in the production of disease

Internal medicine
Including clinical family medicine
For works on medicine for nurses, see RT65
Periodicals, societies, serials, see R5+
31.A-Z Medical reports of hospitals. By place of hospital, A-Z
Subarranged by name of hospital
Cf. RA971.6, Hospital administrative reports
Cf. RC65, Case history taking and recording
Collected works (nonserial)
39 Several authors
40 Individual authors
41 Dictionaries and encyclopedias
46 General works
48 General special
Special aspects of the subject as a whole
48.5 Diseases of men
Cf. RC875+, Andrology
48.6 Diseases of women
Cf. RG1+, Gynecology
48.8 Rare diseases
Psychosomatic medicine
Cf. RC435+, Psychiatry
For psychosomatic aspects of individual diseases or diseases of an organ, region, or system, see the disease
49 General works
52 Research. Experimentation
55 Handbooks, manuals, etc.
58 Problems, exercises, examinations
59 Outlines, syllabi, etc.
60 Addresses, essays, lectures
Study and teaching, see R735+
64 Medical protocols
Class here works on the design and use of protocols for patient evaluation and treatment
65 Case history taking and recording
Cf. R864, Medical records
Cf. RA976+, Medical record departments and administration
66 Clinical cases
67 Clinical indications
Practice of internal medicine, see R728+
69 Semiology. Symptomatology
Examination. Diagnosis
Cf. RA427.6, Multiphasic screening
Cf. RB37.A1+, Diagnosis by laboratory methods
Cf. RT48, Nursing
For diagnosis of individual diseases, or diseases of an organ, region, or system, see the disease
71.A1-A19 Periodicals. Societies. Serials
71.A2-Z General works
Collected works (nonserial)
71.2 Several authors

Examination. Diagnosis
Collected works (nonserial) -- Continued
71.22 Individual authors
71.3 General special
71.4 Periodic health examination
71.5 Differential diagnosis
71.6 Noninvasive diagnosis
71.8 Function tests
Cf. RC683.5.H4, Heart function tests
Cf. RC734.P84, Pulmonary function tests
Cf. RC804.G26, Gastrointestinal function tests
Cf. RJ51.F9, Pediatrics
72 Basal metabolism
Cf. QP171+, Physiology
Pain (Diagnostic significance)
Cf. RB127, Pain pathology and treatment (General)
73 General works
73.2 Acupuncture points
73.3 Mouth. Tongue
73.4 Face. Facial expression
73.5 Eye
73.55 Iridology. Iridodiagnosis
73.6 Hands. Fingernails
73.7 Skin
74 Pulse. Blood pressure
Including sphygmographs and sphygmomanometers
Cf. RC683.5.A43, Ambulatory blood pressure monitoring
75 Temperature. Thermometry
Physical diagnosis
76 General works
76.3 Auscultation and percussion
Including stethoscope and phonendoscope
76.5 Palpation
Electrodiagnosis
77 General works
77.5 Electromyography
Radiography. Roentgenography
Cf. RM845+, Radiotherapy
For particular applications, see the subject, e.g., RE79.R3, Ophthalmology; RG107.5.R3, Gynecology; RJ51.R3, Pediatrics, etc.
78.A1 Periodicals. Societies. Serials
78.A2 Congresses
78.A3 Nomenclature. Terminology. Abbreviations
78.A6-Z General works
78.15 Problems, exercises, examinations
78.17 Outlines, syllabi, etc.
78.2 Atlases. Pictorial works
78.3 Accidents and complications
78.4 Positioning

Examination. Diagnosis
Radiography. Roentgenography -- Continued
78.5 Equipment and supplies
Including catalogs
Microscopic diagnosis, see RB37.A1+
Chemical examination, see RB40
Urine analysis, see RB53
Examination of the blood, see RB45
Autopsies, see RA1063.4+, RB57
78.7.A-Z Other special, A-Z
78.7.A7 Arterial catheterization
Blood cells, Radiolabeled, see RC78.7.R43
78.7.B74 Breath tests
78.7.C65 Contrast media
Cytologic diagnosis, see RB43+
78.7.D35 Data processing
78.7.D53 Diagnostic imaging
78.7.D86 Duplex ultrasonography
Emission tomography, see RC78.7.T62
78.7.E45 Electrical impedance tomography
78.7.E48 Endoscopic ultrasonography
78.7.E5 Endoscopy
78.7.F5 Fluoroscopic diagnosis
Imaging, Diagnostic, see RC78.7.D53
Imaging, Microwave, see RC78.7.M53
Immunoelectrophoresis, see RB46.5+
78.7.L9 Lymphangiography
78.7.M5 Microradiography
78.7.M53 Microwave imaging
78.7.N65 Nonionic contrast media
78.7.N83 Nuclear magnetic resonance
78.7.R38 Radioimmunoimaging
78.7.R4 Radioisotope scanning
78.7.R43 Radiolabeled blood cells
78.7.R5 Reflex testing
78.7.S65 Spectroscopy
78.7.S72 Stable isotopes
78.7.T5 Thermography
78.7.T6 Tomography
78.7.T62 Tomography, Emission
78.7.U4 Ultrasonics
Cf. RC78.7.E48, Endoscopic ultrasonography
78.7.X4 Xeroradiography
80 Prognosis
Popular medicine
81.A1 Periodicals. Societies. Serials
81.A2 Dictionaries and encyclopedias
81.A3-Z General works
82 General special

Medical emergencies. Critical care. Intensive care. First aid
Cf. RA645.5+, Emergency medical services
Cf. RA1224.5, Toxicology
Cf. RC270.9, Cancer critical care
Cf. RC350.N49, Neurological intensive care
Cf. RC675, Cardiovascular emergencies
Cf. RC684.C36, Cardiac intensive care
Cf. RC735.R48, Respiratory intensive care
Cf. RC926, Musculoskeletal emergencies
Cf. RD92+, Emergency surgery. Wounds and injuries
Cf. RD113+, Bandaging, dressings, etc.
Cf. RF89, Otolaryngologic emergencies
Cf. RG158, Gynecology
Cf. RJ370+, Pediatrics
Cf. RT120.E4, Emergency nursing
Cf. RT120.I5, Intensive care nursing
Cf. TN297, Mining
Cf. UH396, Soldiers' first-aid manuals

86 Periodicals. Societies. Serials
86.2 Congresses
86.3 Communication in emergency medicine
86.5 Juvenile works
86.7 General works
86.8 Handbooks, manuals, etc.
86.9 Problems, exercises, examinations
86.92 Outlines, syllabi, etc.
86.95 Moral and ethical aspects
87 Popular works
87.1 Heat prostration. Sunstroke
87.3 Hazardous substances
Including noxious gases
87.5 Electric shock
Cf. RD96.5, Surgery for injuries
87.9 Artificial respiration. CPR
88 Drowning
88.5 Cold injuries
Including frostbite, chilblains, and immersion
88.9.A-Z By activity or environment, A-Z
For the medical and physiological aspects of special sports and activities, see RC1220.A+
Backpacking, see RC88.9.H55
88.9.B6 Boating. Yachting
88.9.C3 Camping
88.9.C5 Civil defense
88.9.H55 Hiking. Backpacking
88.9.I5 Industry
88.9.M35 Martial arts
Military medical services, see UH396
88.9.M6 Mountaineering
Naval medical services, see VG466

Medical emergencies.
Critical care. Intensive care. First aid
By activity or environment, A-Z -- Continued
88.9.O95 Outdoor life (General)
Cf. RC88.9.B6, Boating
Cf. RC88.9.C3, Camping
Cf. RC88.9.H55, Hiking
Cf. RC88.9.M6, Mountaineering
88.9.P6 Polar regions
88.9.S94 Survivalism
88.9.T47 Terrorism
Including weapons of mass destruction
88.9.T7 Traffic
88.9.T76 Travel
Weapons of mass destruction, see RC88.9.T47
88.9.W5 Winter sports
Yachting, see RC88.9.B6
Pastoral medicine, see BV4335+
90 Iatrogenic diseases
Cf. RJ520.I28, Pediatrics
Diseases due to physical and chemical agents
91 General works
Diseases due to radioactive substances
Cf. RA569, Public health aspects
Cf. RA1231.R2, Toxicology
Cf. RD96.55, Radiation burns
Cf. RJ384, Pediatrics
Cf. RM845+, Radiotherapy
93.A1 Periodicals. Societies. Serials
93.A2 Dictionaries and encyclopedias
93.A3-Z General works
95.A-Z Special substances or forms of radiation, A-Z
95.A2 Actinium
95.A42 Alpha particles. Alpha rays
95.A46 Americium
95.G34 Gamma rays
95.R3 Radium
95.U7 Uranium
Diseases due to physical agents
Cf. RC955+, Arctic and tropical medicine
Cf. RC1050+, Aviation medicine
102 General works
103.A-Z Special, A-Z
Altitude sickness, see RC103.M63
103.A4 Anoxemia
103.C3 Caisson disease. Decompression sickness
Car sickness, see RC103.M6
Cold injuries, etc. (First aid aspects), see RC88.5
Decompression sickness, see RC103.C3
103.H4 Heat disorders
Cf. RC87.1, Heat prostration
103.L5 Light-induced diseases

Diseases due to physical and chemical agents
Diseases due to physical agents
Special, A-Z -- Continued
103.M6 Motion sickness
Including car sickness, seasickness
103.M63 Mountain sickness
Seasickness, see RC103.M6
Diseases due to chemical agents, see RA1190+
106 Eruptive fevers. Exanthemata
Cf. RB129, Fever as a manifestation of disease
For individual exanthematous diseases, see RC120+
108 Chronic diseases
Cf. RA644.5+, Public health
Cf. RC1045.C4, Automotive medicine
Cf. RJ380+, Pediatrics
Cf. RT120.C45, Nursing
Infectious and parasitic diseases
Cf. QR201.A+, Pathogenic microorganisms
Cf. RA643+, Public health
Cf. RC678, Cardiovascular infections
Cf. RC901.8, Urinary tract infections
Cf. RE96, Ophthalmology
Cf. RG218, Gynecology
Cf. RG578, Infectious diseases in pregnancy
Cf. RJ275, Newborn infants
Cf. RJ401+, Pediatrics
Cf. RL201+, Dermatology
Cf. RT95+, Nursing
For individual diseases, except tuberculosis, see RC120+
For tuberculosis, see RC306+
109 Periodicals. Societies. Serials
Collected works (nonserial)
110 Several authors
110.2 Individual authors
111 General works
112 General special
113 Popular works
113.2 Atlases. Pictorial works
113.3 Examination. Diagnosis
113.5 Zoonoses. Diseases communicable from animals to man
Cf. RA639+, Public health
Virus and rickettsial diseases
For individual diseases, see RC120+
114 General works
Virus diseases
Cf. RC685.V57, Heart diseases
Cf. RG580.V5, Virus diseases in pregnancy
114.5 General works
114.55 Enterovirus diseases
114.6 Slow virus disease
114.7 Rickettsial disease

| | |
|---|---|
| | Infectious and parasitic diseases -- Continued |
| | Bacterial diseases |
| | Cf. QR201.A+, Bacteria of individual diseases |
| 115 | General works |
| 116.A-Z | Special groups, A-Z |
| | For individual diseases, see RC120+ |
| 116.C5 | Clostridium diseases |
| | Cf. RC862.C47, Intestinal diseases |
| 116.E6 | Enterobacterial infections |
| 116.G677 | Gram-negative bacterial infections |
| 116.H44 | Haemophilus infections |
| 116.M8 | Mycobacterial diseases |
| 116.M85 | Mycoplasma diseases |
| 116.P7 | Pseudomonas aeruginosa disease |
| | Rickettsial diseases, see RC114.7 |
| | Salmonella infections, see RC182.S12 |
| 116.S8 | Staphylococcal infections |
| 116.S84 | Streptococcal diseases |
| | Mycotic diseases |
| | Cf. QK600+, Botanical works on fungi |
| | Cf. QR245+, Medical mycology |
| | Cf. RC776.F8, Fungous diseases of the lungs |
| | Cf. RL765+, Skin diseases |
| 117.A1 | Periodicals. Societies. Serials |
| 117.A2 | Congresses |
| 117.A5-Z | General works |
| | Spirochetal and protozoan diseases |
| 118 | General works |
| 118.5 | Spirochetal diseases |
| 118.7 | Protozoan diseases |
| | Cf. RA639+, Transmission of disease |
| | Parasitic diseases |
| | Cf. QL99, Medical zoology (Systematic works) |
| | Cf. QL392.A1+, Helminthology |
| | Cf. QL757, Parasitology |
| | Cf. RA639+, Transmission of disease |
| | For skin diseases due to parasites, see RL760+ |
| 119 | General works |
| 119.5 | Diseases due to ectoparasites |
| 119.7 | Diseases due to endoparasites. Intestinal parasites |
| | Individual diseases |
| | For diseases or manifestations of diseases of an organ, region, or system, see the organ, region, or system |
| 120 | Actinomycosis |
| | African trypanosomiasis, see RC186.T82 |
| 121.A3 | Alastrim |
| | Cf. RC183+, Smallpox |
| 121.A5 | Amebiasis (Amebic dysentery) |
| | Cf. RC140, Dysentery |
| | American trypanosomiasis, see RC124.4 |
| 121.A57 | Angiostrongylosis |
| | Ankylostomiasis, see RC199.95 |

Infectious and parasitic diseases
Individual diseases -- Continued
121.A6 Anthrax
121.A8 Ascariasis
121.A85 Aspergillosis
Bacillary dysentery, see RC140
122.B3 Balantidium coli
122.B4 Behcet's disease
Bilharziasis, see RC182.S24
Black death, see RC171+
123.B6 Blastomycosis
Bornholm disease, see RC179.5
Botulism, see RC143
Breakbone fever, see RC137
123.B7 Brucellosis. Undulant fever
Bubonic plague, see RC171+
California encephalitis, see RC141.E6
123.C3 Candidiasis
Cf. RG269.C35, Gynecology
Carrion's disease, see RC203.5
124 Cerebrospinal meningitis (Epidemic, Meningococcic)
Cf. RC376, Meningitis
124.4 Chagas' disease. American trypanosomiasis
Chancroid, see RC203.C5
124.5 Chlamydia infections
125 Chickenpox. Varicella
Cholera
126 General works
127 History
By region or country
United States
131.A2 General works
131.A3-Z By region or state, A-Z
132.A-Z Other American regions or countries, A-Z
*Under each country:*
*.x* *General works*
*.x2A-Z* *Local, A-Z*
Europe
133.A1 General works
133.A2-Z By region or country, A-Z
Apply table at RC132.A-Z
134.A-Z Other regions or countries, A-Z
Apply table at RC132.A-Z
Clostridium diseases, see RC116.C5
136.3 Coccidioidomycosis
136.35 Coccidiosis
Common cold, see RF361+
Coryza, see RF361+
136.5 Cryptosporidiosis
136.7 Cysticercosis
Cf. RC394.C87, Cerebrospinal cysticercosis
136.8 Cytomegalic inclusion
Deer-fly fever, see RC186.T85

Infectious and parasitic diseases
Individual diseases -- Continued
137 Dengue fever. Breakbone fever
Diphtheria
138 General works
History
138.1 General works
138.2 Ancient
138.3 Medieval
138.4 Modern
By region or country
United States
138.5.A2 General works
138.5.A3-Z By region or state, A-Z
138.55.A-Z Other American regions or countries, A-Z
Apply table at RC132.A-Z
138.6.A-Z Europe, A-Z
Apply table at RC132.A-Z
138.7.A-Z Asia, A-Z
Apply table at RC132.A-Z
138.8.A-Z Africa, A-Z
Apply table at RC132.A-Z
138.9.A-Z Australia and Pacific islands, A-Z
Apply table at RC132.A-Z
139 Distomatosis
Cf. RC848.F29, Fascioliasis
140 Dysentery
Cf. RC121.A5, Amebic dysentery
Cf. RC182.S47, Shigellosis
140.5 Ebola virus disease
Echinococcosis, see RC184.T6
Elephantiasis, see RC142.5
141.E6 Encephalitis lethargica. Epidemic encephalitis
Including California encephalitis, Japanese B encephalitis, Saint Louis encephalitis, and Tick-borne encephalitis
Cf. RC186.T82, Trypanosomiasis, African. Sleeping sickness
Cf. RC370, Encephalomyelitis
Cf. RC390, Encephalitis
Enterobacterial infections, see RC116.E6
141.5 Epstein-Barr virus disease
Ergotism, see RA1242.E6
142 Erysipelas
142.5 Filariasis
Including elephantiasis, onchocerciasis, etc.
143 Food poisoning (Infection and intoxication)
Including botulism
Cf. RA1258+, Food poisons
Cf. RC182.S12, Salmonella infections
Frambesia, see RC205
144.G3 Gas gangrene
German measles, see RC182.R8

Infectious and parasitic diseases
Individual diseases -- Continued
145 Giardiasis
146 Glanders
147.G6 Glandular fever. Infectious mononucleosis
Gonorrhea, see RC202
Grippe, see RC150+
Hansen's disease, see RC154+
147.H44 Hemorrhagic fever, Omsk
Herpes simplex, see RC147.H6
147.H6 Herpes zoster. Shingles. Herpes simplex
Cf. RC203.H45, Herpes genitalis
147.H7 Histoplasmosis
Cf. RE901.H5, Ocular histoplasmosis
Hookworm disease, see RC199.95
Hydatid disease, see RC184.T6
148 Hydrophobia. Rabies
Infantile paralysis, see RC180+
Infectious mononucleosis, see RC147.G6
Influenza. Grippe
150 General works
History
150.1 General works
150.2 Ancient
150.3 Medieval
150.4 Modern
By region or country
United States
150.5.A2 General works
150.5.A3-Z By region or state, A-Z
150.55.A-Z Other American regions or countries, A-Z
Apply table at RC132.A-Z
Europe
150.6.A1 General works
150.6.A2-Z By region or country, A-Z
Apply table at RC132.A-Z
Asia
150.7.A1 General works
150.7.A2-Z By region or country, A-Z
Apply table at RC132.A-Z
Africa
150.8.A1 General works
150.8.A2-Z By region or country, A-Z
Apply table at RC132.A-Z
Australia and Pacific islands
150.9.A1 General works
150.9.A2-Z By country, A-Z
Apply table at RC132.A-Z
Japanese B encephalitis, see RC141.E6
152 Kala-azar. Visceral leishmaniasis
152.5 Lassa fever
152.7 Legionnaires' disease
Cf. RA644.L23, Public health

Infectious and parasitic diseases
Individual diseases -- Continued
Leishmaniasis
Cf. RL764.C8, Cutaneous leishmaniasis
153 General works
153.5 Mucocutaneous leishmaniasis
Visceral leishmaniasis, see RC152
Leprosy. Hansen's disease
154.A1 Periodicals. Societies. Serials
154.A2 Congresses
154.A3-Z General works
History
154.1 General works
154.2 Ancient
154.3 Medieval
154.4 Modern
By region or country
United States
154.5.A2 General works
154.5.A3-Z By region or state, A-Z
*Under each state:*
*.x* *General works*
*.x2A-Z* *Local, A-Z*
154.55.A-Z Other American regions or countries, A-Z
Apply table at RC132.A-Z
Europe
154.6.A1 General works
154.6.A2-Z By region or country, A-Z
Apply table at RC132.A-Z
Asia
154.7.A1 General works
154.7.A2-Z By region or country, A-Z
Apply table at RC132.A-Z
Africa
154.8.A1 General works
154.8.A2-Z By region or country, A-Z
Apply table at RC132.A-Z
Australia and Pacific islands
154.9.A1 General works
154.9.A2-Z By region or country, A-Z
Apply table at RC132.A-Z
154.95 Leptospirosis
155 Listeriosis
155.5 Lyme disease
Lymphogranuloma venereum, see RC203.L9
Malaria
Cf. RA644.M2, Public health
Cf. RC152, Kala-azar
156.A1 Periodicals. Societies. Serials
156.A3-Z General works
157 General special
158 Examination. Diagnosis
159.A-Z Special therapies, A-Z

Infectious and parasitic diseases
Individual diseases
Malaria
Special therapies, A-Z -- Continued
159.A5 Antimalarials. Chemotherapy
Chemotherapy, see RC159.A5
159.Q8 Quinine
160 History
By region or country
United States
161.A2 General works
161.A3-Z By region or state, A-Z
162.A-Z Other American regions or countries, A-Z
Apply table at RC132.A-Z
Europe
163.A1 General works
163.A2-Z By region or country, A-Z
Apply table at RC132.A-Z
Asia
164.A1 General works
164.A2-Z By region or country, A-Z
Apply table at RC132.A-Z
Africa
165.A1 General works
165.A2-Z By region or country, A-Z
Apply table at RC132.A-Z
Australia and Pacific islands
166.A1 General works
166.A2-Z By region or country, A-Z
Apply table at RC132.A-Z
167 Marburg virus disease
168.M4 Measles. Morbilli
168.M45 Melioidosis
168.M6 Miliary fever. Sweating sickness
Moniliasis, see RC123.C3
Morbilli, see RC168.M4
168.M8 Mumps
Myalgia, Epidemic, see RC179.5
Mycobacterial diseases, see RC116.M8
Mycoplasma diseases, see RC116.M85
168.M95 Myiasis
Oidomycosis, see RC123.C3
Omsk hemorrhagic fever, see RC147.H44
Onchocerciasis, see RC142.5
Oroya fever, see RC203.5
168.P15 Papillomavirus diseases
168.P17 Paracoccidioidomycosis
Parasmallpox, see RC121.A3
168.P2 Paratyphoid fever
Cf. RC187+, Typhoid fever
Parrot fever, see RC182.P8
Pertussis, see RC204
Plague. Bubonic plague. Black death

Infectious and parasitic diseases
Individual diseases
Plague. Bubonic plague. Black death -- Continued
171 General works
172 History
By region or country
United States
176.A2 General works
176.A3-Z By region or state, A-Z
177.A-Z Other American regions or countries, A-Z
Apply table at RC132.A-Z
Europe
178.A1 General works
178.A2-Z By region or country, A-Z
Apply table at RC132.A-Z
179.A-Z Other regions or countries, A-Z
Apply table at RC132.A-Z
179.5 Pleurodynia, Epidemic
Pneumonia, see RC771+
Poliomyelitis
Cf. RJ496.P2, Pediatrics
180.A1 Periodicals. Societies. Serials
180.A2 Congresses
180.A3-Z General works
180.1 General special
180.2 Popular works
180.3 Pathology
180.4 Examination. Diagnosis
180.5.A-Z Special therapeutic methods and apparatus, A-Z
Iron lung, see RC180.5.R4
180.5.K4 Kenny method
180.5.P5 Physical therapy
180.5.R4 Respirators. Iron lung
180.5.S4 Serotherapy
180.6 Research. Experimentation
180.7 Clinical cases
180.8 Nursing
180.9 History
181.A-Z By region or country, A-Z
Cf. RA644.P9, Immunology and other preventive measures
Apply table at RC132.A-Z
Pseudomonas aeruginosa diseases, see RC116.P7
182.P8 Psittacosis. Parrot fever
Pyemia, see RC182.S4
182.Q35 Q fever
Rabbit fever, see RC186.T85
Rabies, see RC148
182.R3 Relapsing fever
182.R4 Rheumatic fever
182.R5 Rhinosporidiosis
182.R6 Rocky Mountain spotted fever. Tick fever
182.R8 Rubella. German measles

Infectious and parasitic diseases
Individual diseases -- Continued
Rubeola, see RA644.R8, RC168.M4
Saint Louis encephalitis, see RC141.E6
182.S12 Salmonella infections
Class here infections other than typhoid and paratyphoid fever
182.S14 Sarcoidosis
Scabies, see RL764.S28
182.S2 Scarlet fever. Scarlatina
182.S24 Schistosomiasis. Bilharziasis
Scrub typhus, see RC186.T83
182.S3 Septic sore throat. Streptococcal sore throat
182.S4 Septicemia and pyemia
Cf. RG220, Toxic shock syndrome
182.S47 Shigellosis
Shingles, see RC147.H6
Sleeping sickness, see RC186.T82
Slow virus diseases, see RC114.6
Smallpox
For parasmallpox (alastrim), see RC121.A3
183.A1 Periodicals. Societies. Serials
General works
183.A2 Through 1855
183.A3-Z 1856-
History
183.1 General works
183.2 Ancient
183.3 Medieval
183.4 Modern
By region or country
United States
183.49 General works
183.5.A-Z By region or state, A-Z
183.55.A-Z Other American regions or countries, A-Z
Europe
183.6.A1 General works
183.6.A2-Z By region or country, A-Z
Asia
183.7.A1 General works
183.7.A2-Z By region or country, A-Z
Africa
183.8.A1 General works
183.8.A2-Z By region or country, A-Z
Australia and Pacific islands
183.9.A1 General works
183.9.A2-Z By region or country, A-Z
184.S6 Sporotrichosis
Spotted fever of the Rocky Mountains, see RC182.R6
Staphylococcal diseases, see RC116.S8
Stomatitis, Ulceromembranous, see RC186.T8
Streptococcal diseases, see RC184.S84
Streptococcal sore throat, see RC182.S3

Infectious and parasitic diseases
Individual diseases -- Continued
184.S84 Strongyloidiasis
Sweating sickness, see RC168.M6
Syphilis, see RC201+
Tapeworm infestation
Cf. RC136.7, Cysticercosis
184.T5 General works
184.T6 Hydatid disease. Echinococcosis
185 Tetanus
Tick-borne encephalitis, see RC141.E6
Tick fever, see RC182.R6
186.T7 Torula infection
186.T75 Toxoplasmosis
Cf. RE901.T69, Ocular toxoplasmosis
Trachoma, see RE321+
186.T8 Trench mouth. Vincent's angina. Ulceromembranous stomatitis
186.T815 Trichinosis
186.T82 Trypanosomiasis, African. Sleeping sickness
Trypanosomiasis, American, see RC124.4
186.T83 Tsutsugamushi disease. Scrub typhus
Tuberculosis, see RC306+
186.T85 Tularemia
Typhoid fever
187 General works
History
188 General works
189 Ancient
190 Medieval
191 Modern
By region or country
United States
192.A2 General works
192.A3-Z By region or state, A-Z
193.A-Z Other American regions or countries, A-Z
Apply table at RC132.A-Z
Europe
194.A1 General works
194.A2-Z By region or country, A-Z
Apply table at RC132.A-Z
Asia
195.A1 General works
195.A2-Z By region or country, A-Z
Apply table at RC132.A-Z
Africa
196.A1 General works
196.A2-Z By region or country, A-Z
Apply table at RC132.A-Z
Australia and Pacific islands
197.A1 General works
197.A2-Z By country, A-Z
Apply table at RC132.A-Z

Infectious and parasitic diseases
Individual diseases -- Continued
Typhus
199 General works
History
199.1 General works
199.2 Ancient
199.3 Medieval
199.4 Modern
By region or country
United States
199.5.A2 General works
199.5.A3-Z By region or state, A-Z
199.55.A-Z Other American regions or countries, A-Z
Apply table at RC132.A-Z
Europe
199.6.A1 General works
199.6.A2-Z By region or country, A-Z
Apply table at RC132.A-Z
Asia
199.7.A1 General works
199.7.A2-Z By region or country, A-Z
Apply table at RC132.A-Z
Africa
199.8.A1 General works
199.8.A2-Z By region or country, A-Z
Apply table at RC132.A-Z
Australia and Pacific islands
199.9.A1 General works
199.9.A2-Z By country, A-Z
Apply table at RC132.A-Z
Ulceromembranous stomatitis, see RC186.T8
199.95 Uncinariasis. Ankylostomiasis. Hookworm disease
Undulant fever, see RC123.B7
Varicella, see RC125
Sexually transmitted diseases. Venereal diseases
Cf. RA644.V4, Public health
Cf. RC870+, Diseases of the genitourinary system
Periodicals, societies, serials, see RC201.A1
Congresses, see RC201.A2
History, see RC201.4+
General works
200.A2 Through 1900
200.A3-Z 1901-
200.1 General special
200.2 Popular works
200.25 Juvenile works
200.3 Addresses, essays, lectures
200.35 Immunological aspects
200.4 Pathology
Examination. Diagnosis
200.5 General works

Infectious and parasitic diseases
Individual diseases
Sexually transmitted diseases. Venereal diseases
Examination. Diagnosis -- Continued

200.55.A-Z Special diagnostic methods, A-Z
For prophylaxis, see RA644.V4
200.55.M64 Molecular diagnosis
200.55.S4 Serum diagnosis
200.6.A-Z Special therapies, A-Z
200.6.P4 Penicillin
200.7.A-Z By age group, class, etc.
200.7.C45 Children
200.7.G38 Gay men
200.7.S55 Single people
200.8 Venereal disease and marriage
Syphilis
201.A1 Periodicals. Societies. Serials
201.A2 Congresses
201.A3A-Z General works
201.1 General special
201.15 Pathology
Examination. Diagnosis
201.2 General works
Special diagnostic methods, see RC200.55.A+
Special therapies, see RC200.6.A+
201.3 Congenital syphilis
History
201.4 General works
201.43 Ancient
201.45 Medieval
201.47 Modern
By region or country
United States
201.5.A2 General works
201.5.A3-Z By region or state, A-Z
201.55.A-Z Other American regions or countries, etc. A-Z
Apply table at RC132.A-Z
Europe
201.6.A1 General works
201.6.A2-Z By region or country, A-Z
Apply table at RC132.A-Z
Asia
201.63.A1 General works
201.63.A2-Z By region or country, A-Z
Apply table at RC132.A-Z
Africa
201.65.A1 General works
201.65.A2-Z By region or country, A-Z
Apply table at RC132.A-Z
Australia and Pacific islands
201.67.A1 General works
201.67.A2-Z By country, A-Z
Apply table at RC132.A-Z

Infectious and parasitic diseases
Individual diseases
Sexually transmitted diseases. Venereal diseases
Syphilis -- Continued
201.7.A-Z By region, system, or organ of the body, A-Z
201.7.N4 Nervous system. Neurosyphilis
Neurosyphilis, see RC201.7.N4
201.8.A-Z By age group, class, A-Z
201.9.A-Z By ethnic groups, A-Z
202 Gonorrhea
203.A-Z Other venereal diseases, A-Z
203.C5 Chancroid
203.H45 Herpes genitalis
Locomotor ataxia, see RC203.T3
203.L9 Lymphogranuloma venereum
203.T3 Tabes dorsalis. Locomotor ataxia
203.5 Verruga peruana
Vincent's angina, see RC186.T8
203.7 Weil's disease
204 Whooping cough
205 Yaws
Yellow fever
206 General works
History
207 General works
208 Ancient
209 Medieval
210 Modern
By region or country
United States
211.A2 General works
211.A3-Z By region or state, A-Z
212.A-Z Other American regions or countries, A-Z
Apply table at RC132.A-Z
Europe
213.A1 General works
213.A2-Z By region or country, A-Z
Apply table at RC132.A-Z
Asia
214.A1 General works
214.A2-Z By region or country, A-Z
Apply table at RC132.A-Z
Africa
215.A1 General works
215.A2-Z By region or country, A-Z
Apply table at RC132.A-Z
Australia and Pacific islands
216.A1 General works
216.A2-Z By country, A-Z
Apply table at RC132.A-Z
251 Constitutional diseases (General)
Cf. RB155, Medical genetics
Cf. RX241+, Homeopathy

Neoplasms. Tumors. Oncology
Cf. RD651+, Surgery
254.A1 Periodicals. Societies. Serials
254.A7-Z General works
254.5 General special
254.6 Pathology
255 Examination. Diagnosis
Therapeutics
256 General works
257.A-Z Special therapies, A-Z
258 Classification
259 Benign neoplasms. Paraneoplastic syndromes
260 Unspecified neoplasms. Mixed neoplasms
Cancer and other malignant neoplasms
Cf. RA1170.C35, Medical jurisprudence
Cf. RD651+, Surgery
Cf. RG580.C3, Cancer in pregnancy
Cf. RK651.5.C35, Prosthodontics
261.A1 Periodicals. Societies. Serials
261.A2 Congresses
261.A7-Z General works
262 General special
263 Popular works
264 Juvenile literature
265 Addresses, essays, lectures
Biography of cancer patients
For biography of patients with cancer of a specific part of the body, see RC280.A+
265.5 Collective
265.6.A-Z Individual, A-Z
266 Nursing
266.5 Study and teaching
267 Research. Experimentation
Reporting. Registries
267.5 General works
By region or country, see RC276+
Prevention
268 General works
268.15 Chemoprevention
268.2 Endocrine aspects
Cf. RC271.H55, Hormone therapy
Cf. RC280.A+, Endocrine gland neoplasms
268.25 Environmental aspects
268.3 Immunological aspects
Cf. QR188.6, Tumor immunology
Cf. RC271.I45, Immunotherapy
Genetic aspects
268.4 General works
268.415 Proto-oncogenes
268.42 Oncogenes
268.43 Antioncogenes
268.44.A-Z Individual marker genes, oncogenes, antioncogenes, and gene families, A-Z

Neoplasms. Tumors. Oncology
Cancer and other malignant neoplasms
Genetic aspects
Individual marker genes, oncogenes, antioncogenes, and gene families, A-Z -- Continued

268.44.C43 CEA genes
268.44.F67 Fos oncogenes
268.44.M93 Myc oncogenes
268.44.P16 p53 antioncogene
268.44.R37 Ras oncogenes
268.45 Nutritional aspects
Cf. RC271.D52, Diet therapy
268.48 Etiology
Carcinogenesis
268.5 General works
268.52 Cocarcinogenesis
268.55 Radiation carcinogenesis
268.57 Microbial carcinogenesis. Viral carcinogenesis
Cf. QR201.T84, Tumor microorganisms
Cf. QR372.O6, Oncoviruses
Chemical carcinogenesis. Carcinogens
268.6 General works
268.65 Carcinogenicity testing
268.7.A-Z Special carcinogens, A-Z
268.7.A23 Acetylaminofluorene
268.7.A42 Alcohol
268.7.A44 Alkylating agents
268.7.A74 Aromatic amines
268.7.A75 Aromatic compounds
268.7.A76 Arsenic
268.7.A78 Asbestos
268.7.A94 Azo dyes
268.7.B42 Benzanthracenes
268.7.B44 Benzopyrene
Chemicals (General), see RC268.6+
268.7.C56 Chloroacetic acids
268.7.C62 Coal tar dyes
268.7.C64 Coffee
268.7.C93 Cyclamates
268.7.C95 Cyclopentaphenanthrenes
268.7.D48 Dichloroethylene
268.7.D5 Dichloromethyl ether
268.7.D53 Diesel motor exhaust gas
268.7.E43 ELF electromagnetic fields
268.7.F55 Fluoride
268.7.F6 Food additives
268.7.H34 Haloethers
268.7.H88 Hydrazines
268.7.H9 Hydrocarbines
Inorganic fibers, see RC268.7.M54
268.7.M45 Metals
Mineral fibers, see RC268.7.M54

Neoplasms. Tumors. Oncology
Cancer and other malignant neoplasms
Carcinogenesis
Chemical carcinogenesis. Carcinogens
Special carcinogens, A-Z -- Continued

268.7.M5 Mineral oils
268.7.M54 Minerals. Mineral fibers. Inorganic fibers
268.7.N52 Nickel compounds
268.7.N54 Nitrites
268.7.N55 Nitrofurans
268.7.N57 Nitroquinoline oxide
268.7.N58 Nitroso compounds
268.7.N59 Nitrosoamines
268.7.O72 Oral contraceptives
268.7.P47 Pesticides
268.7.P5 Phenanthrene
268.7.P64 Polycyclic aromatic hydrocarbons
268.7.P74 Printing ink
268.7.S23 Saccharin
268.7.S7 Steroid hormones
268.7.T62 Tobacco
268.7.T74 Trihalomethanes
268.7.U73 Urethane
268.7.V54 Vinyl chloride
Vinylidene chloride, see RC268.7.D48
269 Pathology
269.5 Metastasis
269.7 Cell biology. Cytology
Examination. Diagnosis
270 General works
270.3.A-Z Special diagnostic methods, A-Z
270.3.C97 Cytodiagnosis. Cytopathology
270.3.D53 Diagnostic imaging
270.3.E43 Electron microscopy
270.3.F56 Flow cytometry
270.3.F58 Fluorescent probes
270.3.H56 Histopathology
270.3.I44 Immunocytochemistry
270.3.I45 Immunodiagnosis
270.3.I46 Immunohistochemistry
270.3.M33 Magnetic resonance imaging
Markers, Tumor, see RC270.3.T84
270.3.M65 Monoclonal antibodies
270.3.N44 Needle biopsy
270.3.R33 Radioimmunoimaging
270.3.R35 Radionuclide imaging
270.3.T65 Tomography
270.3.T84 Tumor markers
270.5 Spontaneous cancer regression
270.8 Therapeutics
270.9 Critical care
271.A-Z Special therapies, A-Z
Cf. RD651+, Surgery

Neoplasms. Tumors. Oncology
Cancer and other malignant neoplasms
Therapeutics
Special therapies, A-Z -- Continued

| | |
|---|---|
| 271.A35 | Adjuvant treatment |
| | Adriamycin, see RC271.D68 |
| 271.A59 | Aldehydes |
| 271.A62 | Alternative treatment |
| 271.A63 | Anthracyclines |
| 271.A65 | Antibiotics |
| 271.A66 | Antibody-directed enzyme prodrug therapy |
| 271.A67 | Antibody-toxin conjugates |
| 271.A68 | Antimetabolites |
| 271.A69 | Antisense nucleic acids |
| 271.A78 | Ascorbic acid |
| 271.A8 | Asparagin |
| 271.A84 | Asparaginase |
| 271.B2 | BCG |
| 271.B4 | Beet juice |
| 271.B45 | Bestatin |
| 271.B53 | Biological response modifiers |
| 271.B57 | Bleomycin |
| 271.B59 | Blood transfusion |
| 271.B8 | Busulfan |
| 271.C35 | Camptothecins |
| 271.C44 | Cellular therapy |
| 271.C48 | Chemokines |
| 271.C5 | Chemotherapy |
| 271.C55 | Cisplatin |
| 271.C6 | Colchicine |
| 271.C7 | Cruzin |
| 271.C9 | Cyclophosphamide |
| 271.C95 | Cytokines |
| 271.D52 | Diet therapy |
| 271.D53 | Differentiation therapy |
| 271.D54 | DNA topoisomerase inhibitors |
| 271.D68 | Doxorubicin |
| 271.E4 | Electrocoagulation (Cancer therapy) |
| 271.E43 | Electrons (Cancer therapy) |
| 271.E68 | Essiac |
| 271.E7 | Estrogen antagonists |
| 271.E76 | Etoposide |
| | Fast neutrons, see RC271.N48 |
| 271.F55 | Fluoropyrimidines |
| 271.F6 | Folic acid and derivatives |
| 271.G45 | Gene therapy |
| 271.G56 | Ginseng |
| 271.G72 | Grapes |
| | Heat, see RC271.T5 |
| 271.H47 | Herbs |
| 271.H53 | Holistic therapy |
| 271.H55 | Hormones |
| 271.I2 | Ibenzmethyzin |

Neoplasms. Tumors. Oncology
Cancer and other malignant neoplasms
Therapeutics
Special therapies, A-Z -- Continued

| | |
|---|---|
| 271.I45 | Immunotherapy |
| 271.I46 | Interferon |
| 271.I47 | Interleukin-2 |
| 271.K54 | Killer cells |
| 271.K7 | Krebiozen |
| 271.L3 | Laetrile |
| 271.L65 | Lonidamine |
| 271.L87 | Luteinizing hormone releasing hormone agonists |
| 271.M32 | Marijuana |
| 271.M35 | Medroxyprogesterone |
| 271.M4 | Mental healing |
| 271.M44 | Methotrexate |
| 271.M5 | Mistletoe |
| 271.M53 | Mitomycin C |
| 271.M55 | Mitotane |
| 271.M57 | Mitoxantrone hydrochloride |
| 271.M65 | Monoclonal antibodies |
| 271.M8 | Mucorhicin |
| | Natulan, see RC271.I2 |
| 271.N46 | Neovascularization inhibitors |
| 271.N48 | Neutrons. Fast neutrons |
| 271.N56 | Nitrosoureas |
| 271.N83 | Nucleosides |
| 271.O25 | Octreotide acetate |
| 271.O7 | Organometallic compounds |
| 271.O73 | Organotin compounds |
| 271.P27 | Paclitaxel |
| 271.P33 | Palliative treatment |
| 271.P38 | Peroxidase |
| 271.P4 | Petroleum |
| 271.P43 | Photochemotherapy |
| 271.P44 | Physical therapy |
| 271.P45 | Pituitary extract |
| 271.P54 | Plasma exchange |
| 271.P55 | Platinum organic compounds |
| 271.P6 | Podophyllum |
| 271.P79 | Psychotherapy |
| 271.R24 | Radiesthesia |
| 271.R26 | Radioimmunotherapy |
| 271.R27 | Radioisotope brachytherapy |
| 271.R3 | Radiotherapy |
| 271.S55 | Shark cartilage |
| 271.S66 | Somatostatin derivatives |
| | Surgery, see RD651+ |
| 271.T15 | T cells |
| 271.T36 | Tamoxifen |
| (271.T38) | Taxol<br>see RC271.P27 |
| 271.T4 | Tecoma impetiginosa |

Neoplasms. Tumors. Oncology
Cancer and other malignant neoplasms
Therapeutics
Special therapies, A-Z -- Continued
271.T5 Thermotherapy. Heat
Transfusion, Blood, see RC271.B59
271.T68 Triazenes
271.T7 Triethylenethiophosphoramide
271.V56 Vindesine
271.V57 Vitamin A
Vitamin C, see RC271.A78
Vitamin M, see RC271.F6
271.V58 Vitamins
271.Z55 Zinostatin
275 History
By region or country
Including hospitals
United States
276 General works
277.A-Z By region or state, A-Z
279.A-Z Other regions or countries, A-Z
Biography
Cf. RC265.5+, Biography of cancer patients
279.5 Collective
279.6.A-Z Individual, A-Z
280.A-Z By region, system, or organ of the body, or type of tumor, A-Z
280.A2 Abdomen
280.A26 Acoustic nerve
280.A28 Adipose tissues
280.A3 Adrenal gland
280.A4 Alimentary canal
280.B48 Bile ducts. Biliary tract
Biliary tract, see RC280.B48
280.B5 Bladder
Blood-forming organs, see RC280.H47
280.B6 Bones
280.B7 Brain
280.B8 Breast. Mammary glands
280.B9 Bronchi
280.C3 Cardia
Central nervous system, see RC280.N43
280.C4 Cerebellum
Cervix uteri, see RC280.U8
280.C5 Chest
280.C6 Colon
Including colorectal neoplasms
280.C65 Connective tissues
280.D5 Digestive organs
Duodenum, see RC280.S8
280.E2 Ear
280.E55 Endocrine glands
Endometrium, see RC280.U8

Neoplasms. Tumors. Oncology
By region, system, or organ of the body, or type of tumor, A-Z -- Continued

280.E6 Endothelium
Epiglottis, see RC280.T5
280.E66 Epithelium
280.E8 Esophagus
280.E9 Eye
280.F32 Face
280.F66 Foot
280.G3 Gall bladder
Gastrointestinal system, see RC280.D5
Genital organs
For individual organs, see the organ, e.g. RC280.P37, Penis
280.G4 General works
280.G5 Female
280.G52 Male
280.H35 Hand
280.H4 Head
280.H45 Heart
280.H47 Hematopoietic system. Blood-forming organs
280.I5 Intestines
280.J3 Jaws
280.K5 Kidneys
Larnyx, see RC280.T5
280.L46 Lips
280.L5 Liver
280.L8 Lungs
280.L9 Lymphatics. Lymphomas
Mammary glands, see RC280.B8
280.M35 Mediastinum
280.M37 Melanoma
280.M4 Meninges
280.M6 Mouth
280.M8 Muscles
280.M83 Musculoskeletal system
Nasopharynx, see RC280.P4
280.N35 Neck
Nervous system
280.N4 General works
280.N43 Central nervous system
280.N58 Nonchromaffin paraganglia
280.N6 Nose
280.O8 Ovaries
280.P25 Pancreas
280.P3 Parathyroid glands
Parotid glands, see RC280.S3
280.P35 Pelvis
280.P37 Penis
280.P38 Peritoneum
280.P4 Pharynx. Nasopharynx

Neoplasms. Tumors. Oncology
By region, system, or organ of the body, or type of tumor, A-Z -- Continued
280.P45 Pineal body
280.P5 Pituitary gland
280.P6 Placenta
280.P7 Prostate gland
280.R37 Rectum
Cf. RC280.C6, Colorectal neoplasms
280.R38 Respiratory organs
280.R4 Reticulo-endothelial systems
280.S28 Sacrococcygeal region
280.S3 Salivary glands
280.S5 Skin
Cf. RD655, Surgery
Cf. RD677, Dermoid cysts (Surgery)
280.S66 Soft tissue
280.S7 Spinal cord
280.S72 Spine
280.S75 Spleen
280.S8 Stomach and duodenum
280.S9 Synovial membrane
280.T4 Testicle
280.T5 Throat. Epiglottis. Larynx. Trachea. Vocal cords
280.T55 Thymus gland
280.T6 Thyroid gland
280.T69 Tongue
280.T7 Tonsils
Trachea, see RC280.T5
280.U74 Urinary organs
280.U8 Uterus. Cervix uteri. Endometrium
Vocal cords, see RC280.T5
280.V8 Vulva
281.A-Z By age group, class, etc.
281.A34 Aged. Geriatric oncology
281.C4 Children
Geriatric oncology, see RC281.A34
281.V48 Veterans
281.W65 Women
282.A-Z By ethnic group, A-Z
Afro-Americans, see RC282.B55
282.B55 Blacks
282.H57 Hispanic Americans
282.J4 Jews
282.N37 Navajo
Tuberculosis
Including tuberculosis of the lungs
Cf. QR189.5.T7+, Bacteriology
Cf. RA644.T7, Public health
306 Periodicals. Societies. Serials
Collected works (nonserial)
306.5 Several authors

| | |
|---|---|
| | Tuberculosis |
| | Collected works (nonserial) -- Continued |
| 306.52 | Individual authors |
| 307.A2 | Museums. Exhibitions |
| 307.A4-Z | Congresses |
| | Hospitals, clinics, etc. |
| 309.A1 | General works |
| 309.A2 | Directories |
| | By region or country |
| | United States |
| 309.A5 | General works |
| 309.A6-Z | By region or state, A-Z<br>Assign second cutter for author only |
| 309.5.A-Z | Other regions or countries, A-Z<br>Assign second cutter for author only |
| 310 | History |
| | General works |
| 310.5 | Through 1900 |
| 311 | 1901- |
| 311.1 | General special |
| 311.19 | Pathology. Pathogenesis |
| 311.2 | Examination. Diagnosis |
| 311.3.A-Z | Special therapies, A-Z<br>For surgical therapeutics, see the region of the body in RD |
| 311.3.C3 | Capparis moonii |
| 311.3.C45 | Chemotherapy |
| 311.3.C6 | Collapse therapy |
| 311.3.D5 | Diet |
| 311.3.I8 | Isoniazid |
| 311.3.M4 | Methazid |
| 311.3.P6 | Pneumothorax |
| 311.3.Q54 | Quinolones |
| 311.3.R54 | Rifamycins |
| 311.3.S4 | Serotherapy |
| 311.3.S7 | Streptomycin |
| 311.3.T4 | Thiosemicarbazones |
| 311.3.V5 | Vitamins |
| 311.4 | Research. Experimentation |
| 311.6 | Home care and rehabilitation |
| 311.8 | Nursing |
| 312 | Popular works |
| 312.2 | Clinical cases |
| 312.5.A-Z | By region, system, or organ of the body, A-Z |
| 312.5.B6 | Bones |
| 312.5.B7 | Breast |
| 312.5.E3 | Ear |
| 312.5.E9 | Eye |
| | Genital organs |
| 312.5.G4 | General and male |
| 312.5.G5 | Female |
| 312.5.H4 | Heart |
| 312.5.H5 | Hip joint |

| | |
|---|---|
| | Tuberculosis |
| | By region, system, or organ of the body, A-Z -- Continued |
| 312.5.J6 | Joints |
| 312.5.K5 | Kidneys |
| | Lungs |
| | see RC310+ |
| 312.5.L9 | Lymphatics |
| 312.5.M45 | Meninges |
| 312.5.N4 | Nervous system |
| 312.5.N6 | Nose |
| 312.5.P55 | Pleura |
| 312.5.R4 | Respiratory system |
| 312.5.S5 | Skin |
| 312.5.S6 | Spine |
| 312.5.T5 | Throat |
| 312.6.A-Z | By age group, class, etc., A-Z |
| | Class here general works only |
| | For country subdivisions, see RC313+ |
| 312.6.A3 | Adolescents |
| 312.6.A4 | Aged |
| 312.6.C4 | Children |
| 312.6.P7 | Prisoners |
| 312.7.A-Z | By ethnic group, A-Z |
| | Class here general works only |
| | For country subdivisions, see RC313+, e.g., RC313.A55, U.S. Indians; RC313.A57, Afro-Americans |
| | Afro-Americans, see RC313.A57 |
| 312.7.B55 | Blacks |
| | By region or country |
| 313.A-Z | United States |
| 313.A1-A16 | Periodicals. Societies. Serials |
| 313.A2 | General works |
| | By region |
| 313.A3 | New England |
| 313.A4 | South |
| 313.A5 | West |
| | By ethnic group |
| 313.A55 | Indians |
| 313.A57 | Afro-Americans |
| 313.A58A-Z | Other, A-Z |
| 313.A6-W | By state, A-W |
| | Canada |
| 314 | General works |
| 314.23.A-Z | By province, A-Z |
| 314.5.A-Z | West Indies, A-Z |
| | Apply table at RC132.A-Z |
| 314.5.C8 | Cuba |
| 315.A-Z | Other American regions or countries, A-Z |
| | Apply table at RC132.A-Z |
| | Europe |
| 316.A1 | General works |

Tuberculosis
By region or country
Europe -- Continued
316.A2-Z By region or country, A-Z
Apply table at RC132.A-Z
Asia
317.A1 General works
317.A2-Z By region or country, A-Z
Apply table at RC132.A-Z
Africa
318.A1 General works
318.A2-Z By region or country, A-Z
Apply table at RC132.A-Z
Australia
319.A1 General works
319.A2-Z By region or country, A-Z
319.5 New Zealand
Pacific islands
320.A1 General works
320.A2-Z By island or group of islands, A-Z
Apply table at RC132.A-Z
Arctic regions
320.5.A1 General works
320.5.G7 Greenland
Neurosciences. Biological psychiatry. Neuropsychiatry
Cf. QM451+, Human neuroanatomy
Cf. QP351+, Neurophysiology and neuropsychology
Cf. RJ486.5+, Biological child psychiatry. Pediatric psychiatry
Cf. RM315+, Neuropsychopharmacology
321 Periodicals. Societies. Serials
326 Societies
327 Congresses
328 Hospitals, clinics, etc.
Cf. RC439, Psychiatric hospitals
329 Yearbooks
331 Serials. Monographic series
Collected works (nonserial)
332 Several authors
333 Individual authors
334 Dictionaries and encyclopedias
335 Directories
336 Study and teaching
337 Research. Experimentation
337.8 Documentation
History
Cf. RC438+, History of psychiatry
338 General works
By region or country
United States
339.A1 General works
339.A2A-Z By region or state, A-Z
339.A3-Z Other regions or countries, A-Z

Neurosciences.
Biological psychiatry.
Neuropsychiatry -- Continued
Biography
Cf. RC438.5+, Biography of psychiatrists, psychotherapists
Cf. RD592.8+, Biography of neurosurgeons
339.5 Collective
339.52.A-Z Individual, A-Z
General works
Cf. RC346+, Neurology
Cf. RC454, Psychiatry
340 Through 1900
341 1901-
343 General special
343.4 Handbooks, manuals, etc.
343.5 Problems, exercises, examinations
343.6 Outlines, syllabi, etc.
344 Addresses, essays, lectures
Neurology. Diseases of the nervous system
Including manifestations of diseases
Cf. QM451+, Anatomy
Cf. QP351+, Physiology
Cf. RA1147, Forensic neurology
Cf. RB127+, Pain (General)
Cf. RD592.5+, Neurosurgery
Cf. RG580.N47, Diseases in pregnancy
Cf. RJ486+, Pediatric neurology
346 General works
346.3 Neurological errors
346.4 Genetic aspects
346.5 Immunological aspects
347 Pathology
347.5 Neurotoxicology
Cf. RC365, Central nervous system
Examination. Diagnosis
Cf. RC386.5+, Diseases of the brain
348 General works
349.A-Z Special diagnostic procedures, A-Z
349.D52 Diagnostic imaging
349.E53 Electrodiagnosis
Electroencephalography, see RC386.6.E43
349.E55 Electrophoresis (Neurology)
Evoked potentials, see RC386.6.E86
Imaging, Diagnostic, see RC349.D52
349.M34 Magnetic resonance imaging
349.N48 Neural conduction measurement
349.R3 Radiography
349.R33 Radioisotope scanning
349.T65 Tomography
349.U47 Ultrasonic imaging
Therapeutics
349.8 General works

Neurosciences.
Biological psychiatry. Neuropsychiatry
Neurology. Diseases of the nervous system
Therapeutics -- Continued

350.A-Z Special therapies, A-Z
For surgical therapeutics, see the region of the body in RD

350.B3 Balneotherapy
350.B56 Biofeedback training
350.B72 Brain stimulation
350.C54 Chemotherapy
350.D78 Drug infusion pumps
350.E5 Electrotherapy
350.E85 Exercise
350.G45 Gene therapy
350.G75 Growth factors
350.H47 Herbs
350.I4 Impletol
Intensive care, Neurological, see RC350.N49
350.I45 Interferon
350.N48 Neural stimulation
350.N49 Neurological intensive care
350.P48 Physical therapy
350.S73 Steroids
350.4 Aftercare. Rehabilitation
350.5 Neurological nursing
Cf. RD596, Neurosurgical nursing
350.7 Neurological emergencies
Cf. RC350.N49, Neurological intensive care
351 Popular works
Cf. RA790+, Mental health
355 Handbooks, manuals, etc.
356 Problems, exercises, examinations
357 Outlines, syllabi, etc.
358 Addresses, essays, lectures
358.8 Atlases
359 Clinical cases
359.5 Infections. Neurovirology
Diseases of the central nervous system
360 General works
361 General special
361.5 Examination. Diagnosis
For special diagnostic techniques, see RC349.A+
362 Congenital malformations. Dysraphia
363 Inflammatory diseases (General)
365 Metabolic, toxic, and degenerative diseases (General)
366 Myelin sheath pathology
367 Vascular lesions (General)
Central pain
368 General works
368.3 Deafferentation pain syndrome
370 Encephalomyelitis

Neurosciences.
Biological psychiatry. Neuropsychiatry
Neurology. Diseases of the nervous system
Diseases of the
central nervous system -- Continued
Epilepsy
Cf. RA645.E64, Public health
Cf. RJ496.E6, Pediatrics
372.A1 Periodicals. Societies. Serials
372.A2 Congresses
372.A3A-Z Individual institutions. By name, A-Z
Cf. HV3006+, Institutions for the mentally handicapped
372.A4-Z General works
372.2 Juvenile works
372.3 Epilepsy literature
372.5 Pathology
373 Examination. Diagnosis
374.A-Z Special therapies, A-Z
Cf. RD593, Neurosurgery
374.C48 Chemotherapy (General)
374.L35 Lamotrigine
374.M48 Metindione
374.P48 Phenytoin
374.P75 Progabide
374.5 Petit mal epilepsy
375 Tourette syndrome
376 Meningitis
Cf. RC124, Cerebrospinal meningitis
Cf. RC312.5.M45, Tuberculosis meningitis
376.5 Movement disorders. Basal ganglia diseases. Extra-pyramidal disorders
377 Multiple sclerosis
378 Myoclonus
Neoplasms (General), see RC280.N43
Neurosyphilis, see RC201.7.N4
382 Parkinson's disease
Including postencephalitic Parkinson's disease and symptomatic Parkinson's disease
382.2 Perception disorders
Cf. RC394.A37, Agnosia
Cf. RC394.S93, Synesthesia
Cf. RE91+, Vision disorders
Cf. RF290, Hearing disorders
Tourette's syndrome, see RC375
Tuberculosis, see RC312.5.N4
385 Other diseases (not A-Z)
Class here diseases not limited to the brain or spinal cord
Diseases of the brain
Including manifestations of diseases
386 General works
386.2 General special

Neurosciences.
Biological psychiatry. Neuropsychiatry
Neurology. Diseases of the nervous system
Diseases of the central nervous system
Diseases of the brain -- Continued
Examination. Diagnosis

386.5 General works
386.6.A-Z Special diagnostic procedures, A-Z
386.6.A45 Ambulatory electroencephalography
386.6.A54 Angiography
386.6.B46 Bender-Gestalt Test
386.6.B55 Biopsy
386.6.B65 Booklet Category Test
386.6.B7 Brain mapping
386.6.B73 Brain microdialysis
386.6.D52 Diagnostic imaging
Cf. RC473.B7, Psychiatry
386.6.E43 Electroencephalography
Electroencephalography, Ambulatory, see RC386.6.A45
Emission tomography, see RC386.6.T65
Encephalography, see RC386.6.R3
Encephalography, Ultrasonic, see RC386.6.U45
386.6.E86 Evoked potentials
Cf. RF294.5.E87, Evoked response audiometry
386.6.H34 Halstead-Reitan Neuropsychological Test Battery
Imaging, see RC386.6.D52
386.6.L87 Luria-Nebraska Neuropsychological Battery
386.6.M32 Magnetic brain stimulation
386.6.M34 Magnetic resonance imaging
386.6.M36 Magnetoencephalography
386.6.M44 Mental status examination
386.6.N48 Neuropsychological tests
386.6.N83 Nuclear magnetic resonance spectroscopy
386.6.P57 Pneumoencephalography
Cf. RC473.P6, Psychiatry
386.6.R3 Radiography
386.6.R33 Radioisotope scanning
386.6.R48 Rheoencephalography
386.6.T64 Tomography
386.6.T65 Tomography, Emission
386.6.U45 Ultrasonic encephalography
387 Brain abscess
387.5 Brain damage
388 Cerebral palsy
Cf. RA645.C47, Public health
Cf. RJ496.C4, Pediatrics
388.5 Cerebrovascular disease. Stroke
Including carotid artery diseases, cerebral ischemia, vertebrobasilar insufficiency

Neurosciences.
Biological psychiatry. Neuropsychiatry
Neurology. Diseases of the nervous system
Diseases of the central nervous system
Diseases of the brain -- Continued

389 Chorea (St. Vitus' dance)
Cf. RC394.H85, Huntington's chorea
390 Encephalitis
Cf. RC141.E6, Epidemic encephalitis
Cf. RC370, Encephalomyelitis
Cf. RJ496.E5, Pediatrics
391 Hydrocephalus
Cf. RJ496.H9, Pediatrics
392 Headache. Migraine
Cf. RB128, Headache as a manifestation of disease
Cf. RJ496.H3, Pediatrics
Neoplasms, see RC280.B7
394.A-Z Other diseases, A-Z
394.A37 Agnosia
394.A43 Akinetic mutism
Alexia, see RC394.W6
394.A5 Amnesia
Aphasia, see RC425+
Apoplexy, see RC394.H37
394.A75 Apraxia
394.A85 Attention-deficit disorder in adults
Basal ganglia diseases, see RC376.5
Brain dysfunction, Minimal, see RC394.M55
394.B7 Brain stem diseases
394.C3 Calcification
394.C47 Cerebellar degeneration
Cerebrospinal cysticercosis, see RC394.C87
Chorea, Huntington's, see RC394.H85
394.C64 Cognition disorders
394.C7 Concussion
394.C77 Convulsions
Cf. RC372+, Epilepsy
Cf. RJ496.C7, Pediatrics
394.C83 Creutzfeldt-Jakob disease
394.C87 Cysticercosis, Cerebrospinal
394.D35 Degeneration (General)
394.D4 Dementia paralytica. Paresis
Dyskinesia, Tardive, see RC394.T37
Dyslexia, see RC394.W6
394.E3 Edema
Extrapyramidal disorders, see RC376.5
394.F37 Fatal familial insomnia
394.H35 Hematoma
394.H37 Hemorrhage
394.H4 Hepatolenticular degeneration
394.H85 Huntington's chorea
394.I5 Infarction

| | |
|---|---|
| | Neurosciences. |
| | Biological psychiatry. Neuropsychiatry |
| | Neurology. Diseases of the nervous system |
| | Diseases of the central nervous system |
| | Diseases of the brain |
| | Other diseases, A-Z -- Continued |
| (394.J34) | Jakob-Creutzfeldt disease |
| | see RC394.C83 |
| 394.K6 | Korsakoff's syndrome |
| 394.K8 | Kuru |
| 394.L37 | Learning disabilities |
| 394.L4 | Leucodystrophy |
| 394.M46 | Memory disorders |
| | Cf. BF376, Psychology |
| 394.M48 | Metabolic disorders |
| 394.M55 | Minimal brain dysfunction |
| | Cf. RJ496.B7, Pediatrics |
| | Mutism, Akinetic, see RC394.A43 |
| 394.N47 | Neuroleptic malignant syndrome |
| 394.O45 | Olivopontocerebellar atrophies |
| | Paresis, see RC394.D4 |
| | Presenile dementia, see RC522+ |
| 394.P76 | Progressive supranuclear palsy |
| 394.R34 | Radiation damage |
| | Senile dementia, see RC524 |
| | Stroke, see RC388.5 |
| 394.S7 | Sturge-Weber syndrome |
| 394.S93 | Synesthesia |
| | Cf. BF495+, Psychology |
| 394.S95 | Syringobulbia |
| 394.T37 | Tardive dyskinesia |
| 394.T5 | Thrombosis |
| 394.T7 | Transient global amnesia |
| 394.V57 | Visual agnosia |
| 394.W47 | Wernicke-Korsakoff syndrome |
| 394.W6 | Word-blindness. Alexia. Dyslexia |
| 394.W63 | Word deafness |
| 395 | Congenital anomalies |
| | Epilepsy, see RC372+ |
| | Diseases of the spinal cord |
| | Including cerebrospinal fluid |
| 400 | General works |
| | Examination. Diagnosis |
| 402 | General works |
| 402.2.A-Z | Special diagnostic procedures, A-Z |
| 402.2.E94 | Evoked potentials |
| 402.2.M94 | Myelography |
| 402.2.R33 | Radiography |
| 403 | Landry's paralysis |
| 405 | Myelitis |
| | Cf. RC370, Encephalomyelitis |
| | Tabes dorsalis and locomotor ataxis, see RC203.T3 |
| 406.A-Z | Other, A-Z |

Neurosciences.
Biological psychiatry. Neuropsychiatry
Neurology. Diseases of the nervous system
Diseases of the central nervous system
Diseases of the spinal cord
Other, A-Z -- Continued
406.A24 Amyotrophic lateral sclerosis
406.C66 Compression
406.F7 Friedreich's ataxia
406.H45 Hemiplegia
406.P25 Paralysis of upper extremities
406.P3 Paraplegia
406.Q33 Quadriplegia
Spina bifida, see RJ496.S74
406.S9 Syringomyelia
Tetraplegia, see RC406.Q33
Tumors, see RC280.S7
406.V3 Vascular diseases
407 Diseases of the autonomic (vegetative) nervous system (General)
Including the sympathetic and parasympathetic nervous system
Diseases of the nerves and peripheral ganglia
409 General works
410 Cranial nerves
411 Spinal nerves
412 Neuralgia
416 Neuritis
418 Facial movement disorders. Facial paralysis
420 Sciatica
422.A-Z Other diseases, A-Z
422.C26 Carpal tunnel syndrome
422.C3 Causalgia
422.C4 Cervical syndrome
422.D52 Diabetic neuropathies
422.E56 Entrapment neuropathies
422.P4 Perineurial cysts
422.P64 Polyneuropathies
422.R43 Reflex sympathetic dystrophy
Speech and language disorders
Including neurological and psychoneurotic disorders
Cf. RF510+, Laryngology
Cf. RJ496.S7, Pediatrics
423.A1 Periodicals. Societies. Serials
423.A2-Z General works
424 Stuttering
Cf. RJ496.S8, Pediatrics
424.5 Cluttering
424.7 Articulation disorders
Aphasia
Cf. RJ496.A6, Pediatrics
425 General works

Neurosciences.
Biological psychiatry. Neuropsychiatry
Neurology. Diseases of the nervous system
Speech and language disorders
Aphasia -- Continued
425.3 Conduction aphasia
425.5 Agrammatism
425.6 Anomia
425.7 Paragrammatism
426 Echolalia
427 Speech clinics
428 Study and teaching of speech therapy
428.5 Speech therapy as a profession
428.8 Psychological aspects
429 Other (not A-Z)
Wounds and injuries of the nervous system and foreign bodies, see RD593
Psychiatry
Cf. HV7936.P75, Psychiatrists in police work
Cf. RA790+, Mental health
Cf. RA1151+, Forensic psychiatry
Cf. RC967.5, Industrial psychiatry
Cf. RJ499+, Child psychiatry
Cf. RZ400+, Mental healing
Periodicals, societies, see RC321
Serials, see RC331
Hospitals, clinics, etc , see RC439
Congresses, see RC327
Collected works (nonserial)
435 Several authors
435.2 Individual authors
436 Yearbooks
436.5 Nomenclature. Terminology. Abbreviations
437 Dictionaries and encyclopedias
437.2 Communication in psychiatry
437.25 Directories
Study and teaching, see RC459+
Research, experimentation, see RC337
437.5 Philosophy. Methodology
History
438 General works
By region or country, see RC443+
Biography
Including psychiatrists, psychotherapists, and clinical psychologists
For biography of patients, see RC464.A+
438.5 Collective
438.6.A-Z Individual, A-Z
Hospitals and hospital treatment
Cf. RC443+, Specific psychiatric institutions
Cf. RC475+, Psychotherapy
Cf. RJ504.5, Psychiatric hospital care of children

Neurosciences.
Biological psychiatry. Neuropsychiatry
Psychiatry
Hospitals and hospital treatment -- Continued
By region or country, see RC443+
439 General works
Emergency services, see RC480.6
439.2 Partial hospitalization. Psychiatric day treatment. Outpatient services
439.3 Discharge planning
439.4 Violence in psychiatric hospitals
Including violence in outpatient psychiatric settings
Cf. RC569.5.V55, Psychopathology of violence in general
439.5 Aftercare of hospitalized patients. Rehabilitation. Home care
Alternatives to psychiatric hospitalization
439.53 General works
439.55 Group homes
440 Psychiatric nursing
Allied mental health personnel. Mental health associates
440.2 General works
440.5 Psychiatric aides
440.6 Volunteer workers
440.7 Mental health care teams
Psychiatry as a profession
440.8 General works
440.82 Women in psychiatry. Women psychiatrists. Women psychotherapists
440.84 Gay psychiatrists. Gay psychotherapists. Lesbian psychiatrists. Lesbian psychotherapists
440.9 Certification
By region or country
443-445 United States
443 General works
445.A-Z By region or state, A-Z
*Under each state:*
*.x* *Periodicals. Societies*
*.x2* *General works*
*.x3A-Z* *Institutions. Hospitals, clinics, etc. By place, A-Z*
447-448 Canada
447 General works
448.A-Z By region or province, A-Z
Apply table at RC445.A-Z
Europe
450.A1 General works

| | |
|---|---|
| | Neurosciences. |
| | Biological psychiatry. Neuropsychiatry |
| | Psychiatry |
| | By region or country |
| | Europe -- Continued |
| 450.A2-Z | By region or country, A-Z |
| | *Under each country:* |
| | *.xA1-.xA5 Periodicals. Serials* |
| | *.xA6-.xZ General works* |
| | *.x2A-Z Local, A-Z* |
| 451.A-Z | Other regions or countries, A-Z |
| | Apply table at RC450.A2-Z |
| 451.4.A-Z | By age group, profession, etc. |
| | Adolescents, see RJ503 |
| 451.4.A5 | Aged. Geriatric psychiatry |
| | Cf. RC480.54, Psychotherapy for the aged |
| | Cf. RC524, Senile psychosis |
| | Cf. RC537.5, Depression |
| | Aliens, see RC451.4.E45 |
| 451.4.A68 | Armenian massacres survivors |
| 451.4.A7 | Artists |
| | Astronauts, see RC1090 |
| 451.4.A83 | Athletes |
| 451.4.A96 | Authors |
| | Aviators, see RC1090 |
| 451.4.B73 | Brain injured |
| 451.4.C44 | Celebrities |
| | Children, see RJ499+ |
| | Children of holocaust survivors, see RC451.4.H62 |
| | Children of Nazis, see RC451.4.N37 |
| | College students, see RC451.4.S7 |
| 451.4.C65 | Concentration camp inmates |
| | Criminals, see RC451.4.P68 |
| 451.4.D4 | Deaf |
| 451.4.D57 | Disaster victims |
| 451.4.E42 | Electronic data processing personnel |
| 451.4.E45 | Emigrants and immigrants |
| 451.4.E57 | Entertainers |
| 451.4.G39 | Gay men and lesbians |
| 451.4.H35 | Handicapped |
| | Cf. RC451.4.M47, Mentally handicapped |
| 451.4.H62 | Holocaust survivors. Children of holocaust survivors |
| 451.4.H64 | Homeless persons |
| 451.4.H67 | Hospital staff |
| 451.4.H68 | Housewives |
| | Immigrants, see RC451.4.E45 |
| | Infants, see RJ502.5 |
| | Lesbians, see RC451.4.G39 |
| 451.4.M44 | Medical personnel |
| 451.4.M45 | Men |

Neurosciences.
Biological psychiatry. Neuropsychiatry
Psychiatry
By age group, profession, etc. -- Continued

451.4.M47 Mentally handicapped
Cf. RC569.7+, Care and treatment of the mentally handicapped
451.4.M54 Middle aged
451.4.M543 Middle aged women
Minorities (Ethnic), see RC451.5.A2
451.4.M57 Minorities (Non-ethnic)
Minority students, see RC451.4.S7
451.4.M58 Minority women
451.4.N37 Nazis. Children of Nazis
451.4.N85 Nurses
451.4.N87 Nursing home patients. Spouses of nursing home patients
Overweight persons, see RC552.O25
451.4.P47 Pharmacists
451.4.P5 Physicians
451.4.P56 Political prisoners
451.4.P57 Political refugees
Politicians, see RC451.4.S64
451.4.P6 Poor
Cf. RC451.4.R87, Rural poor
451.4.P68 Prisoners. Criminals
Cf. RA1151+, Forensic psychiatry
Cf. RJ506.J88, Juvenile delinquency
451.4.P7 Prisoners of war
Cf. RC451.4.H62, Holocaust survivors
451.4.P75 Professional employees
451.4.P78 Psychologists
451.4.P79 Psychotherapists. Psychoanalysts. Psychiatrists
451.4.R43 Refugees
Cf. RC451.4.H62, Holocaust survivors
Cf. RC451.4.P57, Political refugees
451.4.R87 Rural poor
451.4.S55 Single people
451.4.S62 Socially handicapped
Soldiers, see RC550
Spouses of nursing home patients, see RC451.4.N87
451.4.S64 Statesmen. Politicians
451.4.S7 Students
Including college students, minority students
Cf. LB3430, Mental hygiene
451.4.T47 Terminally ill
451.4.T67 Torture victims
Tourists, see RC451.4.T73
451.4.T73 Travelers. Tourists
451.4.T85 Twins
451.4.U53 Unemployed

Neurosciences.
Biological psychiatry. Neuropsychiatry
Psychiatry
By age group, profession, etc. -- Continued
451.4.V48 Veterans
Cf. RC550, War neuroses
Cf. RC552.P67, Post-traumatic stress disorder
451.4.V53 Victims
451.4.W53 Widowed persons
451.4.W6 Women
Cf. RC451.4.M543, Middle aged women
Workers, see RC967
451.4.Y67 Young adults
Youth, see RJ503
451.5.A-Z By ethnic group, A-Z
451.5.A2 General works
Afro-Americans, see RC451.5.N4
451.5.A75 Asian Americans
Blacks, see RC451.5.N4
451.5.C45 Chinese Americans
451.5.C82 Cubans
451.5.F54 Filipino Americans
451.5.H57 Hispanic Americans
451.5.I5 Indians
451.5.I52 Indochinese in the United States. Indochinese Americans
451.5.I53 Irish Americans
451.5.J36 Japanese
451.5.J4 Jews
451.5.M48 Mexican Americans
451.5.N4 Negroes
451.5.P84 Puerto Ricans
General works
Through 1900, see RC340+
454 1901-
454.4 General special
455 Social psychiatry. Community psychiatry
455.2.A-Z Special aspects of the subject as a whole, A-Z
455.2.A28 Abuse of mental patients
Certification, see RC440.9
455.2.C4 Classification
455.2.C65 Consultation. Consultation-liaison psychiatry
455.2.D38 Data processing
455.2.D42 Decision making
455.2.E64 Epidemiology
455.2.E76 Errors in diagnosis and treatment
455.2.E8 Ethics
455.2.F35 False memory syndrome
455.2.F67 Forecasting
455.2.M38 Medical records
Methodology. Philosophy, see RC437.5
455.2.P43 Peer review

Neurosciences.
Biological psychiatry. Neuropsychiatry
Psychiatry
Special aspects of
the subject as a whole, A-Z -- Continued

455.2.P5 Photography
Cf. RC489.P56, Photography in psychotherapy
Practice, see RC465.5+
Prevention of mental illness, see RA790+
Psychiatric ethics, see RC455.2.E8
Psychiatry as a profession, see RC440.8+
455.2.P85 Public opinion
455.2.R43 Referral
Research, see RC337
455.2.T45 Television. Video tapes
Video tapes, see RC455.2.T45
455.4.A-Z Special aspects of mental illness, A-Z
Adjustment, see RC455.4.S87
Adjustment disorders, see RC455.4.S87
455.4.A35 Adoption
Affect (Psychology), see RC455.4.E46
455.4.A54 Animal models
455.4.A77 Art and mental illness
455.4.A84 Attachment behavior
455.4.A85 Attention
455.4.A86 Attitude. Thought and thinking
Bereavement, see RC455.4.L67
455.4.B5 Biological aspects. Physiological aspects of mental illness
455.4.B54 Birth order
(455.4.B64) Body image
see RC569.5.B65
455.4.B66 Boredom
455.4.B76 Brothers and sisters
455.4.C6 Comparative psychiatry
Cf. BF660+, Comparative psychology
Cf. QL750+, Animal behavior
Cf. RC455.4.A54, Animal models
455.4.C65 Conflict (Psychology)
Cultural psychiatry, see RC455.4.E8
455.4.D43 Defense mechanism
455.4.D45 Denial
455.4.D83 Dual-brain psychology
455.4.E35 Ego
455.4.E46 Emotions. Affect (Psychology)
455.4.E54 Endocrine aspects of mental illness
455.4.E58 Environmental aspects of mental illness
455.4.E8 Ethnopsychiatry. Cultural psychiatry. Transcultural psychiatry

Neurosciences.
Biological psychiatry. Neuropsychiatry
Psychiatry
Special aspects
of mental illness, A-Z -- Continued

455.4.F3 Family relationships. Problem families. Adult children of dysfunctional families
Cf. RC455.4.B76, Brothers and sisters
Cf. RC455.4.M37, Marriage and mental illness
Cf. RC488.5+, Family psychotherapy
Cf. RC489.F33, Family dynamics in psychotherapy
Cf. RC569.5.A3, Adult children of divorced parents
Cf. RC569.5.F3, Family violence
Cf. RJ507.D59, Divorced parents (Child psychiatry)

Gender role, see RC455.4.S45

455.4.G4 Genetic aspects of mental illness

Genius and mental illness, see BF423

Grief, see RC455.4.L67

Helplessness, see RC455.4.S43

455.4.I54 Inhibition

455.4.L53 Life change events

455.4.L64 Loneliness

455.4.L67 Loss. Bereavement. Grief
Including grief therapy

455.4.M37 Marriage and mental illness

455.4.N3 Narcissistic injuries

455.4.N8 Nutritional aspects of mental illness and mental health

455.4.O23 Object relations
Cf. RC489.O25, Object relations in therapy

455.4.P35 Paradox
Cf. RC489.P37, Paradox in psychotherapy

455.4.P47 Person schemas

Physiological aspects of mental illness, see RC455.4.B5

Pregnancy and mental illness, see RG588

455.4.P75 Projection

455.4.P78 Psycholinguistic aspects of mental illness
Cf. RC489.P73, Psychotherapy
Cf. RC514, Schizophrenia

455.4.R4 Religion and psychiatry

455.4.R42 Repetition compulsion

455.4.R43 Repression

455.4.R56 Risk factors of mental illness

455.4.S36 Schemas (Psychology)

455.4.S42 Self. Self-perception. Self-respect
Cf. RC489.S43, Self and psychotherapy
Cf. RC553.S45, Selflessness

455.4.S43 Self-defeating behavior. Helplessness

Neurosciences.
Biological psychiatry. Neuropsychiatry
Psychiatry
Special aspects
of mental illness, A-Z -- Continued
455.4.S44 Sex. Sexual behavior
455.4.S45 Sex-role aspects of mental illness. Gender role
Cf. RC451.4.W6, Women
Cf. RC455.4.M37, Marriage and mental illness
455.4.S53 Shame
Sisters and brothers, see RC455.4.B76
455.4.S67 Social adjustment
455.4.S87 Stress. Adjustment. Adjustment disorders
Cf. RA785, Stress management
455.4.T45 Temperament
Thought and thinking, see RC455.4.A86
Transcultural psychiatry, see RC455.4.E8
456 Handbooks, manuals, etc.
457 Problems, exercises, examinations
457.2 Outlines, syllabi, etc.
458 Addresses, essays, lectures
458.5 Atlases. Pictorial works
Psychiatry as a profession, see RC440.8+
Study and teaching
459 General works
459.5.A-Z By region or country, A-Z
Research, see RC337
460 Popular works
460.2 Juvenile works
Biography of mental patients and psychotherapy patients
464.A1 Collective
464.A2-Z Individual, A-Z
465 Clinical cases
Practice of psychiatry and psychotherapy.
Psychiatric and psychotherapeutic economics
Including business methods and employment surveys
465.5 General works
By region or country
United States
465.6 General works
465.7.A-Z By region or state, A-Z
465.8.A-Z Other regions or countries, A-Z
466 Mental health counseling
466.3 Mass media in counseling
Clinical psychology
Cf. R726.7, Clinical health psychology
Cf. RJ503.3, Pediatrics
466.8 History
466.83.A-Z By region or country, A-Z
467 General works
467.2 Handbooks, manuals, etc.

Neurosciences.
Biological psychiatry. Neuropsychiatry
Psychiatry
Clinical psychology -- Continued

467.7 Study and teaching
467.8 Research. Experimentation
467.95 Practice of clinical psychology. Clinical psychology economics
Including group practice, business methods and employment surveys
467.97 Prescription privileges

Examination. Diagnosis
Cf. BF698.4, Personality assessment
Cf. RC455.2.E76, Diagnostic errors
Cf. RJ503.5+, Pediatrics

469 General works
470 Psychiatric disability evaluation
For specific conditions, see RA1152.A+
471 Electrodiagnosis
473.A-Z Other diagnostic tests and procedures, A-Z
473.B43 Behavioral assessment
473.B46 Bender-Gestalt Test
473.B7 Brain imaging
473.C37 Case formulation
473.C45 Childhood Hand that Disturbs Test
473.C64 Cognitive Diagnostic Battery
473.C65 Cognitive Synthesis Test
473.D43 Defense Mechanisms Inventory
473.D54 Differential diagnosis
473.D72 Draw-a-Story
473.E36 Ego Function Assessment
473.F35 Family-Centered-Circle Drawings
473.G7 Graphology
473.H35 Hand Test
(473.H58) History taking
see RC480.7
473.I47 Interpersonal Relatedness Drawing
473.K47 Kestenberg Movement Profile
473.L32 Laboratory diagnosis
473.L64 Logotest
473.M44 Medical examinations
473.M47 Millon Clinical Multiaxial Inventory
473.M48 Millon Inventories
473.M5 Minnesota Multiphasic Personality Inventory
473.M84 Multiaxial Diagnostic Inventory
473.N48 Neuropsychological tests
473.N82 Nuclear magnetic resonance spectroscopy
473.P56 Personality Assessment Inventory
473.P6 Pneumoencephalography
473.P7 Projective techniques
473.P78 Psychiatric rating scales
473.P79 Psychological tests. Psychometrics
Psychometrics, see RC473.P79

Neurosciences.
Biological psychiatry. Neuropsychiatry
Psychiatry
Examination. Diagnosis
Other diagnostic tests
and procedures, A-Z -- Continued
473.R6 Rorschach test
473.S9 Szondi test
473.T48 Thematic Apperception Test
473.W34 Wada test
Therapeutics. Psychotherapy
Cf. RC439, Hospital treatment
Cf. RC455.2.E76, Treatment errors
Cf. RJ504+, Child psychotherapy
For psychotherapy in somatic diseases, see the disease, e.g., RC271.P79, Psychotherapy in cancer treatment
475 Periodicals. Societies. Serials
475.5 Congresses
475.7 Dictionaries and encyclopedias
Philosophy, see RC437.5
History, see RC438+
Biography of psychotherapists, see RC438.5+
Biography of psychotherapy patients, see RC464.A+
480 General works
480.5 General special
480.515 Popular works
Study and teaching, see RC459+
Research, see RC337
Clinical cases, see RC465
480.52 Differential therapeutics
Including differential therapeutics in psychotherapy
480.53 Chronic mental illness
For particular chronic mental illness, see the illness
Critical mental illness, see RC480.6
Practice of psychotherapy, see RC465.5+
480.54 Psychotherapy for the aged
480.55 Brief psychotherapy
Including single-session psychotherapy
480.6 Crisis intervention. Hospital emergency services
Including mobile emergency mental health services
For crisis intervention in specific problems or crises, see the problem or crisis
480.7 Interviewing in psychiatry and mental health. History taking
480.75 Outcome assessment
480.8 Psychotherapist and the patient. Mental health personnel and patient
481 Client-centered psychotherapy
482 Physical therapy

Neurosciences.
Biological psychiatry. Neuropsychiatry
Psychiatry
Therapeutics. Psychotherapy -- Continued
Chemotherapy
Cf. BF207, Psychological psychopharmacology
Cf. RC451.4.A+, Geriatric psychopharmacology
Cf. RM315+, Medical psychopharmacology

483 General works
483.3 Psychopharmacology consultation
483.5.A-Z Special chemotherapies, A-Z
483.5.A45 Alprazolam
483.5.A56 Anticonvulsants
483.5.B45 Benzamide
483.5.B48 Benzodiazepines
483.5.B77 Bromazepam
483.5.C45 Chlorpromazine
483.5.F55 Fluoxetine
483.5.F58 Flurothyl
483.5.H3 Hallucinogenic drugs
483.5.H33 Haloperidol
483.5.H6 Hormones
483.5.L5 Lithium
LSD, see RC483.5.L9
483.5.L9 Lysergic acid diethylamide. LSD
483.5.M44 Melatonin
Narcotics, see RC483.5.O64
483.5.N5 Nicotinic acid
483.5.N66 Nominfensine
Nutrition therapy, see RC455.4.N8
483.5.O64 Opioids. Narcotics
483.5.P74 Propranolol
483.5.T42 Thioridazine
483.5.T44 Thiothixene
483.5.T45 Thyroid hormones
483.5.T7 Trazodone
483.5.V5 Vitamin therapy
Shock therapy
483.9 General works
485 Electroconvulsive therapy
485.5 Insulin shock
487 Occupational therapy
Group therapy
Cf. RC510, Group psychoanalysis
488.A1 Periodicals. Societies. Serials
488.A2 Congresses
488.A3-Z General works

Neurosciences.
Biological psychiatry. Neuropsychiatry
Psychiatry
Therapeutics. Psychotherapy
Group therapy -- Continued
Family psychotherapy. Marital psychotherapy. Couples psychotherapy
Cf. RC455.4.F3, Family relations in mental illness
Cf. RC489.F33, Family dynamics in psychotherapy
Cf. RC569.5.F3, Family violence
488.5 General works
488.53 Family assessment
488.55 Contextual therapy
488.6 Divorce therapy
489.A-Z Other therapies and special aspects of therapy, A-Z
489.A34 Acting out. Enactment
Affect, see RC489.E45
489.A38 Adventure therapy
489.A7 Art therapy
489.A72 Arts
489.A77 Assertiveness training
Cf. BF575.A85, Psychology
489.B4 Behavior therapy
489.B45 Betrayal
489.B48 Bibliotherapy
489.B5 Bioenergetics
489.B53 Biofeedback
Cf. BF319.5.B5, Psychology
489.B57 Birth order
Body and mind therapies, see RC489.M53
489.C37 Catharsis
Character types, see RC489.T95
Client-centered psychotherapy, see RC481
489.C6 Cognitive-analytic therapy
489.C62 Cognitive-experiential psychotherapy
489.C63 Cognitive therapy. Cognitive-behavior therapy
489.C65 Communicative psychotherapy
Contracts, see RC489.T77
489.C68 Countertransference
489.C69 Covert conditioning
Creative writing, see RC489.W75
489.D3 Dance therapy
Including Authentic movement therapy
489.D35 Data processing
489.D45 Desensitization
489.D46 Developmental therapy
489.D5 Diaries. Journals
Differential therapeutics, see RC480.52
Drama, see RC489.P7
489.D74 Dream therapy. Dreams
489.E24 Eclectic psychotherapy

Neurosciences.
Biological psychiatry. Neuropsychiatry
Psychiatry
Therapeutics. Psychotherapy
Other therapies and special
aspects of therapy, A-Z -- Continued

489.E26 Ecopsychiatry
489.E3 Educational therapy
489.E35 Ego
489.E45 Emotions. Affect
489.E46 Empathy
Enactment, see RC489.A34
489.E7 Erhard seminars training
489.E75 Erotic aspects
est, see RC489.E7
489.E83 Ethical therapy
489.E9 Exercise
489.E93 Existential psychotherapy
489.E96 Experiential psychotherapy
489.E98 Eye movement desensitization and reprocessing
489.F27 Failure
489.F3 Fairy tales. Parables
489.F33 Family dynamics
489.F35 Fantasy. Imagery
489.F42 Feeling therapy
489.F44 Feldenkrais method
489.F45 Feminist therapy
489.F62 Focused expressive psychotherapy
489.F64 Folklore
489.F67 Forgiveness
489.G4 Gestalt therapy
Grief therapy, see RC455.4.L67
489.H64 Holding
Homeopathic treatment, see RX301.M45
489.H67 Horseback riding
489.H85 Humor
Imagery, see RC489.F35
489.I45 Impasse
489.I54 Internet (Computer network)
489.I55 Interpersonal psychotherapy
489.I57 Interpretation
For dream interpretation, see BF1074+
Jogging, see RC489.R86
Journals, see RC489.D5
Language, see RC489.P73
489.L4 Learning
Letter writing, see RC489.W75
489.L6 Logotherapy
489.M42 Mediation therapy
489.M43 Meditation
Cf. BF637.T68, Transcendental meditation
489.M47 Metaphor
489.M5 Milieu

Neurosciences.
Biological psychiatry. Neuropsychiatry
Psychiatry
Therapeutics. Psychotherapy
Other therapies and special aspects of therapy, A-Z -- Continued

489.M53 Mind and body therapies
489.M6 Modeling
489.M65 Morita psychotherapy
489.M654 Motion pictures
489.M655 Motivation
489.M66 Movement therapy
489.M84 Multimodal therapy
489.M85 Multiple psychotherapy
Music therapy, see ML3920
489.M96 Mythology
489.N3 Narcotherapy
489.N47 Neurolinguistic programming
489.N65 Nonverbal communication
489.N83 Nudity
489.O24 Object constancy
489.O25 Object relations
Parables, see RC489.F3
489.P37 Paradoxical psychotherapy
489.P46 Personal construct therapy
489.P47 Pet therapy
489.P54 Photocollage
489.P56 Photography
Play therapy, see RC489.R4, RJ505.P6
489.P6 Poetry
489.P67 Primal therapy
489.P68 Problem-solving therapy
489.P7 Psychodrama. Drama. Role playing
489.P72 Psychodynamic psychotherapy
489.P73 Psycholinguistics
Cf. RC455.4.P78, Psycholinguistic aspects of mental illness
Cf. RC514, Schizophrenia
489.P74 Psychological mindedness
489.P76 Psychosynthesis
489.P86 Puppets
489.R24 Radical therapy
489.R3 Rational-emotive therapy
489.R37 Reality therapy
489.R39 Reconstruction
489.R4 Recreational therapy
489.R42 Regression
489.R43 Reincarnation therapy
489.R44 Relapse prevention
489.R45 Relaxation
Cf. RA785, Personal health
489.R46 Religious aspects
489.R47 Remotivation therapy

Neurosciences.
Biological psychiatry. Neuropsychiatry
Psychiatry
Therapeutics. Psychotherapy
Other therapies and special aspects of therapy, A-Z -- Continued

489.R48 Reparation
489.R49 Resistance
Restricted environmental stimulation, see RC489.S44
Role playing, see RC489.P7
489.R64 Rolfing
489.R86 Running
489.S25 Sandplay
489.S43 Self. Self-esteem. Self-acceptance
489.S435 Semiotics
489.S44 Sensory deprivation. Restricted environmental stimulation
489.S45 Separation-individuation. Separation anxiety
489.S47 Sex between psychotherapist and patient
Sex therapy, see RC556+
489.S5 Sleep therapy
489.S62 Social interaction. Social structure
489.S63 Social skills
489.S65 Solution-focused therapy
489.S67 SpeyerMethod
489.S68 Sports therapy
489.S74 Storytelling
489.S76 Strategic therapy
489.S83 Subjectivity
489.S86 Supportive psychotherapy
Television, see RC455.2.T45
489.T45 Termination of psychotherapy
489.T66 Therapeutic alliance
489.T67 Therapeutic community
489.T68 Token economy
489.T69 Touch
489.T7 Transactional analysis
489.T73 Transference
489.T75 Transpersonal psychotherapy
489.T77 Treatment contracts
489.T82 Triangles
489.T95 Typology. Character types
489.V34 Values
Video tapes, see RC455.2.T45
489.V57 Virtual reality therapy
Wit and humor, see RC489.H85
489.W75 Writing. Written communication
Including creative writing, letter writing
Psychosurgery, see RD594+

Neurosciences.
Biological psychiatry. Neuropsychiatry
Psychiatry -- Continued
Hypnotism and hypnosis. Suggestion therapy
Cf. BF1111+, Hypnotism and suggestion
Cf. RD85.H9, Anesthesiology
Cf. RJ505.H86, Child psychotherapy
Cf. RZ400+, Mental healing
For works on hypnotism as a method of narcosis, and therapeutics is individual diseases, see the disease

490 Periodicals. Societies. Serials
490.5 Congresses
Biography
490.9 Collective
490.95.A-Z Individual, A-Z
General works
494 Through 1900
495 1901-
497 General special
498 Popular works
499.A-Z Special methods, A-Z
499.A8 Autogenic training. Self-hypnosis
499.D7 Dreaming
499.H94 Hypno-play therapy
499.H96 Hypnotic age regression
Self-hypnosis, see RC499.A8
499.S57 Sleep learning
499.S92 Subliminal perception
499.T68 Totems

Psychoanalysis
Cf. BF173+, Psychology
Cf. RJ504.2, Child analysis
For special aspects of clinical psychoanalysis, see RC489.A+

500 Periodicals. Societies. Serials
500.5 Congresses
Collected works (nonserial)
501 Several authors
501.2 Individual authors
501.4 Dictionaries and encyclopedias
502 Study and teaching
503 History
504 General works
506 General special
508 Popular works
509 Addresses, essays, lectures
509.7 Computer applications. Data processing
509.8 Clinical cases
510 Group psychoanalysis

Psychopathology
General works, see RC454
Psychoses

Neurosciences.
Biological psychiatry. Neuropsychiatry
Psychiatry
Psychopathology
Psychoses -- Continued
512 General works
514 Schizophrenia
Including all subtypes of schizophrenia
Cf. RC553.S34, Schizoaffective disorders
Cf. RC569.5.S36, Schizotypal personality disorder
516 Manic-depressive illness. Bipolar disorder
Cf. RC537+, Affective disorders in general
517 Involutional melancholia
520 Paranoia and paranoid states
520.7 Delirium
Dementia
521 General works
Presenile dementia
Cf. RC394.C83, Creutzfeldt-Jakob disease
522 General works
Alzheimer's disease
523 General works
523.2 Popular works
523.5 Binswanger's disease
524 Senile dementia. Senile psychosis
Alcoholic psychoses
Cf. RC564.7+, Alcoholism
525 General works
526 Delirium tremens
527.A-Z Other alcoholic psychoses, A-Z
528.A-Z Other psychoses, A-Z
528.F6 Folie a deux
Puerperal psychoses, see RG851
528.S9 Symptomatic psychoses
528.T6 Toxic psychoses
Neuroses
530 General works
531 Anxiety
Including anxiety sensitivity
532 Hysteria
533 Obsessive-compulsive neurosis. Compulsive behavior
Cf. RC455.4.R42, Repetition compulsion
Cf. RC552.C65, Compulsive eating
Cf. RC560.S43, Sexual addiction
Cf. RC569.5.E94, Exercise addiction
Cf. RC569.5.G35, Compulsive gambling
Cf. RC569.5.H34, Compulsive hair pulling
Cf. RC569.5.S56, Compulsive shopping
Cf. RC569.5.W67, Workaholism

Neurosciences.
Biological psychiatry. Neuropsychiatry
Psychiatry
Psychopathology
Neuroses -- Continued
535 Phobias. Fear. Terror
Including panic attacks and disorders
Cf. RC552.A44, Agoraphobia
Cf. RC552.F42, Fear of death
Cf. RC552.F423, Fear of failure
Cf. RC552.F43, Fear of success
Cf. RC552.S62, Social phobia
Depression. Affective disorders
Cf. BF575.G7, Psychological aspects of grief
Cf. RC455.4.L67, Psychiatric aspects of loss
Cf. RC516, Manic-depressive illness
Cf. RC553.S34, Schizoaffective disorders
Cf. RC569, Suicide
Cf. RG852, Postpartum depression
537 General works
537.5 Depression in old age
540 Alexithymia
541 Anhedonia
543 Lovesickness
545 Seasonal affective disorder
Paranoid states, see RC520
Psychosomatic disorders, see RC49+
Sleep disorders
Cf. RC569.5.E5, Enuresis
Cf. RC737.5, Sleep apnea syndrome
Cf. RJ506.S55, Child psychiatry
Cf. RM325, Hypnotics
547 General works
Insomnia
548 General works
548.5 Restless legs syndrome
549 Narcolepsy
550 War neuroses
Cf. RC451.4.P7, Prisoners of war
552.A-Z Other neuroses, A-Z
552.A43 Acrophobia
552.A44 Agoraphobia
552.A45 AIDS phobia
552.A5 Anorexia nervosa
Cf. RB150.A65, Anorexia
Appetite disorders, see RC552.E18
Artist's block, see RC552.W74
552.B84 Bulimia
552.C65 Compulsive eating
552.E18 Eating disorders

Neurosciences.
Biological psychiatry. Neuropsychiatry
Psychiatry
Psychopathology
Neuroses
Other neuroses, A-Z -- Continued
552.F42 Fear of death
Cf. BF789.D4, Psychological aspects of death
Cf. RC535, Psychopathological fear
552.F423 Fear of failure
552.F43 Fear of success
552.H8 Hypochondria
552.N5 Neurasthenia
Cf. BF482, Psychology of fatigue
552.O25 Obesity. Overweight persons
552.O3 Occupational neuroses
Cf. RC967.5, Industrial psychiatry
552.P67 Post-traumatic stress disorder
Cf. RA1152.P67, Forensic psychiatry
552.R44 Relationship addiction
552.S4 Self-mutilation
Sexual addiction, see RC560.S43
552.S62 Social phobia
Somatization disorder, see RC552.S66
Somatoform disorders. Somatization disorder
552.S66 Speech anxiety
552.S69 Tic disorders
552.T5 Cf. RJ496.T5, Pediatrics
Traumatic neuroses
552.T7 Writer's block. Artist's block
552.W74 Cf. PN171.W74, Authorship
Specific pathological states, A-Z
553.A-Z Adjustment disorders, see RC455.4.S87
Alienation
553.A4 Asperger's syndrome, see RC553.A88
Autism. Asperger's syndrome
553.A88 Cf. RJ506.A9, Pediatrics
Cognition disorders. Thought disorders
553.C64 Cf. RC473.C64, Cognitive Diagnostic Battery
Delusions
553.D35 Depersonalization
553.D4 Dissociation
553.D5 Erotomania
553.E76 Flight of ideas
553.F55 Fugue
553.F83 Guilt
(553.G8) see RC569.5.G84
Hallucinations
553.H3

Neurosciences.
Biological psychiatry. Neuropsychiatry
Psychiatry
Psychopathology
Specific pathological states, A-Z -- Continued
553.M36 Masochism
Cf. RC560.S23, Sadomasochism; sexual masochism
553.M43 Megalomania
Memory disorders, see RC394.M46
553.N36 Narcissism
553.N4 Negativism
553.S34 Schizoaffective disorders
553.S45 Selflessness
Thought disorders, see RC553.C64
553.T56 Time perception disorders
Personality disorders. Behavior problems
Cf. HV6080+, Criminal psychology
554 General works
555 Antisocial personality disorders
Sexual problems. Psychosexual disorders
Cf. HQ71+, Sociological aspects
Cf. HV42.5, Social services
Cf. RA1141, Forensic medicine
Cf. RC875+, Male functional disorders
Cf. RG159+, Female functional disorders
556 General works
Sexual therapy
557 General works
557.5.A-Z Specific aspects, A-Z
557.5.S94 Surrogates
Homosexuality
Class here works on homosexuality as a psychiatric disorder
Cf. RC451.4.G39, Mental health of gay men and lesbians
For general works on homosexuality, see HQ75+
558 General works
558.3 Male homosexuality
558.5 Female homosexuality. Lesbianism
560.A-Z Other special problems, A-Z
560.A56 Anorgasmy
560.A97 Autoerotic asphyxia
Cf. RA1082, Forensic medicine
560.B56 Bisexuality
Cf. HQ74+, Sociological aspects
(560.C4) Change of sex. Transsexualism
see RC560.G45

Neurosciences.
Biological psychiatry. Neuropsychiatry
Psychiatry
Psychopathology
Personality disorders. Behavior problems
Sexual problems. Psychosexual disorders
Other special problems, A-Z -- Continued

560.C46 Child molesting
Cf. RC569.5.A28, Adult child sexual abuse victims
Cf. RJ507.S49, Sexually abused children

560.E9 Exhibitionism

560.F4 Fetishism

560.F7 Frigidity

560.G45 Gender identity disorders. Transsexualism

560.I45 Impotence
Cf. RC889, Functional disorders

560.I53 Incest. Incest victims
Cf. HV6570.6+, Sociological aspects
Cf. RC569.5.E46, Emotional incest

560.J42 Jealousy

Masochism, see RC553.M36

Masochism, Sexual, see RC560.S23

560.M3 Masturbation
Cf. HQ447, Sociological aspects
Cf. RA1082, Autoerotic asphyxia

560.N4 Necrophilia

560.N63 Nocturnal emissions

560.N9 Nymphomania

560.P73 Premature ejaculation

560.R36 Rape. Rape victims. Rape trauma syndrome
Cf. HV6558+, Sociological aspects

560.S23 Sadomasochism. Sexual masochism
Cf. HQ79, Sociological aspects

(560.S35) Scopophilia
see RC560.V68

560.S43 Sex addiction
Cf. RC569.5.A32, Adult children of sex addicts

560.S44 Sexual abuse victims
Cf. RC569.5.A28, Adult child sexual abuse victim

560.S45 Sexual aversion disorders

560.S46 Sexual desire disorders

Sexual masochism, see RC560.S23

560.S47 Sexual offenses
Cf. RA1141, Forensic medicine

Transsexualism, see RC560.G45

560.V34 Vaginismus

560.V68 Voyeurism

Neurosciences.
Biological psychiatry. Neuropsychiatry
Psychiatry
Psychopathology
Personality disorders.
Behavior problems -- Continued
Drug abuse. Substance abuse
Cf. HV5800+, Social pathology
Cf. RA975.5.S92, Substance abuse services in hospitals
563 Periodicals. Societies. Serials
563.2 Congresses
563.6 Directories
564 General works
564.15 Handbooks, manuals, etc.
564.29 Popular works
564.3 Juvenile works
564.5.A-Z By age group, profession, etc., A-Z
564.5.A34 Aged
564.5.D46 Dentists
564.5.G39 Gay men and lesbians
564.5.H43 Health occupations students
Lesbians, see RC564.5.G39
564.5.M45 Medical personnel
Mentally ill, see RC564.68
564.5.N87 Nurses
564.5.P48 Physically handicapped
Pregnant women, see RG580.S75
564.5.P76 Professional employees
564.5.S83 Successful people
564.5.W65 Women
564.5.W66 Women physicians
564.6.A-Z By ethnic group, A-Z
564.6.A35 Afro-Americans
By region or country
United States
564.65 General works
564.66.A-Z By region or state, A-Z
564.67.A-Z Other regions or countries, A-Z
564.68 Dual diagnosis
Alcoholism
Cf. BF209.A43, Psychological aspects
Cf. HV5001+, Social pathology
Cf. QP801.A3, Physiological effect of alcohol
Cf. RC525+, Alcoholic psychoses
Cf. RC569.5.A29, Adult children of alcoholics
Cf. RC848.A42, Alcoholic liver diseases
Hospitals, clinics, etc.
564.7 General works
By region or country
United States

Neurosciences.
Biological psychiatry. Neuropsychiatry
Psychiatry
Psychopathology
Personality disorders. Behavior problems
Drug abuse. Substance abuse
Alcoholism
Hospitals, clinics, etc.
By region or country
United States -- Continued
564.73 General works
564.74.A-Z By region or state, A-Z
564.75.A-Z Other regions or countries, A-Z
565 General works
565.6.A-Z By ethnic group, A-Z
565.6.M56 Minorities
By region or country
United States
565.7 General works
565.8.A-Z By region or state, A-Z
565.9.A-Z Other regions or countries, A-Z
Medication abuse, see RM146+
Narcotic habit
For individual narcotics, see RC568.A+
566.A1 Periodicals. Societies. Serials
566.A2 Congresses
566.A3-Z General works
567 Nicotine. Tobacco habit
Cf. HV5725+, Sociology
567.5 Caffeine. Coffee habit
Food addiction, see RC552.O25
Food addiction, see RC552.C65
568.A-Z Other substances, A-Z
568.A45 Amphetamines
Angel dust, see RC568.P45
568.B3 Barbiturates
568.B45 Benzodiazepines
568.C2 Cannabis
568.C6 Cocaine. Crack
Crack, see RC568.C6
Hashish, see RC568.C2
568.H4 Heroin
Marijuana, see RC568.C2
568.M4 Methadone
568.M45 Methaqualone
568.O45 Opioids
568.O6 Opium
568.P45 Phencyclidine. Angel dust
568.Q37 Qat
568.S44 Sedatives
568.S64 Solvents
568.S74 Stimulants

Neurosciences.
Biological psychiatry. Neuropsychiatry
Psychiatry
Psychopathology
Personality disorders.
Behavior problems -- Continued

569 Suicide. Suicidal behavior
Cf. HV6543+, Social aspects
Cf. RA1136+, Forensic medicine
Cf. RC537+, Depression

569.5.A-Z Other personality disorders, behavior problems, situations, etc., A-Z

569.5.A24 Abrasiveness

569.5.A25 Acting out

569.5.A28 Adult child sexual abuse victims
Cf. RC455.2.F35, False memory syndrome

569.5.A29 Adult children of alcoholics

569.5.A3 Adult children of divorced parents

569.5.A32 Adult children of sex addicts

569.5.A34 Aggressiveness
Cf. RC569.5.V55, Violence

569.5.A53 Anger. Rage

Arson, see RC569.5.P9

569.5.A93 Avoidant personality disorder

569.5.B64 Body dysmorphic disorder

569.5.B65 Body image disturbance

569.5.B67 Borderline personality disorder

569.5.C55 Child abuse. Adult child abuse victims
Cf. RC569.5.M83, Munchausen syndrome by proxy
Cf. RC569.5.P75, Psychological child abuse
Cf. RJ507.A29, Abused children

569.5.C63 Codependency

569.5.C65 Commitment, Lack of
Cf. BF619, Psychology of commitment

569.5.C68 Complexes

Compulsive behavior, see RC533

Compulsive hair pulling, see RC569.5.H34

Compulsive shopping, see RC569.5.S56

Compulsive working, see RC569.5.W67

Criminal behavior, see HV6080+

569.5.D44 Deception

569.5.D47 Dependency

Email addiction, see RC569.5.I54

569.5.E46 Emotional incest

569.5.E48 Entitlement attitudes

569.5.E5 Enuresis
Cf. RJ476.E6, Pediatrics

569.5.E94 Exercise addiction

569.5.F27 Factitious disorders
Cf. RA1146, Malingering

569.5.F3 Family violence. Wife beating

Neurosciences.
Biological psychiatry. Neuropsychiatry
Psychiatry
Psychopathology
Personality disorders. Behavior problems
Other personality disorders, behavior problems, situations, etc., A-Z -- Continued

569.5.F5 Filicide
569.5.F67 Formes frustes
569.5.G35 Gambling. Compulsive gambling
569.5.G84 Guilt
569.5.H34 Hair pulling. Compulsive hair pulling. Trichotillomania
569.5.H65 Homicide. Homicidal behavior
Cf. HV6499+, Criminology
Cf. RA1123, Forensic medicine
569.5.I46 Impulsive personality
Cf. BF575.I46, Impulse
569.5.I54 Internet addiction
Including email addiction
569.5.K54 Kleptomania
Lack of commitment, see RC569.5.C65
569.5.M66 Money-related problems
569.5.M8 Multiple personality
569.5.M83 Munchausen syndrome by proxy
569.5.M9 Mythomania
569.5.N35 Nail-biting
569.5.P37 Passive-aggressive personality
569.5.P45 Perfectionism
569.5.P75 Psychological abuse. Psychological child abuse
Including psychologically abused adult and adult psychological child abuse victims
569.5.P9 Pyromania. Arson
Rage, see RC569.5.A53
Regret, see RC569.5.R45
569.5.R45 Remorse. Regret
569.5.R46 Remoteness (Personality trait)
569.5.R55 Rigidity
569.5.R58 Risk-taking
Cf. BF637.R57, Applied psychology
569.5.R59 Ritual abuse victims
569.5.S35 Schizoid personality
569.5.S36 Schizotypal personality disorder
569.5.S44 Self-containment
569.5.S45 Self-destructive behavior
Cf. RC552.S4, Self-mutilation
Cf. RC569, Suicidal behavior
Cf. RC569.5.S48, Self-injurious behavior

Neurosciences.
Biological psychiatry. Neuropsychiatry
Psychiatry
Psychopathology
Personality disorders. Behavior problems
Other personality disorders, behavior problems, situations, etc., A-Z -- Continued
569.5.S48 Self-injurious behavior
Cf. RC569.5.S45, Self-destructive behavior
569.5.S56 Shopping. Compulsive shopping
Speech disorders, see RC423+
569.5.S74 Stereotyped behavior
569.5.T47 Terrorism
Cf. HV6430+, Criminology
Trichotillomania, see RC569.5.H34
569.5.U53 Under achievement
Victims of violence, see RC569.5.V55
569.5.V55 Violence. Victims of violence
Cf. BF575.A3, Psychology
Cf. RC439.4, Violence in psychiatric hospitals
Cf. RJ506.A35, Child psychiatry
Violence, Family, see RC569.5.F3
Wife abuse, see RC569.5.F3
569.5.W67 Workaholism. Compulsive working
Mental retardation. Developmental disabilities
Cf. BF432.M37, Intelligence levels
Cf. HV3003.2+, Social and public welfare
Cf. RC451.4.M47, Psychopathology of the mentally handicapped
Cf. RJ506.D47, Developmental disabilities (Pediatrics)
Cf. RJ506.M4, Mental retardation (Pediatrics)
569.7 Periodicals. Societies. Serials
569.9 Congresses
569.95 Dictionaries
570 General works
570.2 General special
570.5.A-Z By region or country, A-Z
570.7 Sensory and communication disorders associated with mental retardation
571 Down syndrome
Cf. RJ506.D68, Pediatrics
574 X-linked mental retardation
Congenital disorders not associated with specific systems, functions, or infections
Cf. RC455.4.G4, Genetic aspects of mental illness
578 General works
580.A-Z Special syndromes, A-Z
580.E35 Ehlers-Danlos syndrome
580.M37 Marfan syndrome

| | |
|---|---|
| | Congenital disorders not associated with specific systems, functions, or infections |
| | Special syndromes, A-Z -- Continued |
| 580.P7 | Progeria |
| 580.W47 | Werner's syndrome |
| | Specialities of internal medicine |
| | Immunologic diseases |
| | Class here works emphasizing clinical immunology |
| | Cf. RJ385+, Pediatrics |
| | For works emphasizing basic aspects of immunology, see QR |
| | For works on the immune reponse to a particular disease or parasite, see the disease or parasite in RC - RL or SF |
| 581 | Periodicals. Societies. Serials |
| 581.2 | Congresses |
| 582 | General works |
| 582.15 | Immunopathology |
| 582.17 | Immunotoxicology |
| 582.2 | Examination. Diagnosis |
| | Cf. RB46.5, Immunodiagnosis |
| | Allergy. Hypersensitivity, Immediate and delayed |
| | Cf. RJ386+, Pediatrics |
| 583 | Periodicals. Societies. Serials |
| 583.2 | Congresses |
| 584 | General works |
| 585 | General special |
| 585.5 | Research |
| 585.9 | Pathology |
| | Examination. Diagnosis |
| 586 | General works |
| 587.A-Z | Special diagnostic procedures, A-Z |
| 587.P76 | Provocation tests |
| 587.R33 | Radioallergosorbent test |
| 587.S6 | Skin testing |
| 588.A-Z | Special therapies, A-Z |
| 588.A47 | Alternative treatment |
| 588.C45 | Chemotherapy |
| 588.D53 | Diet therapy |
| 588.H47 | Herbs |
| 588.I45 | Immunotherapy |
| | Respiratory allergy |
| 589 | General works |
| 590 | Hay fever |
| 591 | Asthma |
| | Cf. RJ436.A8, Pediatrics |
| (592-593) | Allergic diseases of the skin |
| | see RL242-RL249 |
| 594.A-Z | Other allergic disorders, A-Z |
| 594.A4 | Angioneurotic edema |
| 596 | Food allergies |
| | Cf. RC588.D53, Allergy diets |

Specialities of internal medicine
Immunologic diseases
Allergy. Hypersensitivity, Immediate and delayed -- Continued

| | |
|---|---|
| 598.A-Z | Hypersensitivity to other substances. By substance, A-Z |
| 598.A76 | Arthropod venom. Insect venom |
| 598.B4 | Bee proteins |
| 598.C56 | Cleaning compounds |
| 598.D7 | Drugs |
| 598.F4 | Feathers |
| 598.F57 | Fire ant venom |
| 598.F67 | Formaldehyde |
| | Imported fire ant venom, see RC598.F57 |
| | Insect venom, see RC598.A76 |
| 600 | Autoimmune diseases |
| | Immunodeficiency |
| | Cf. QR188.35, Immunology |
| | Cf. RJ387.D42, Pediatrics |
| 606 | General works |
| 607.A-Z | Individual diseases, A-Z |
| | Acquired immune deficiency syndrome, see RC607.A26 |
| 607.A26 | AIDS |
| | Cf. RA644.A25, Public health |
| 607.A83 | Ataxia telangiectasia |
| | Nutritional diseases |
| | Cf. RA645.N87, Public health |
| | Cf. RA784, Personal health |
| | Cf. RC455.4.N8, Nutritional aspects of mental illness |
| | Cf. RJ399.N8, Nutritional diseases of children |
| | Cf. RK281, Nutritional aspects of dental health |
| | Cf. RM214+, Diet therapy |
| | Cf. TX359, Nutrition policy |
| 620.A1 | Periodicals. Societies. Serials |
| 620.A2-Z | General works |
| 620.5 | General special |
| 620.6 | Nutrition disorders in old age |
| 620.9 | Pathology |
| 621 | Examination. Diagnosis |
| 622 | Nutritionally induced diseases |
| 623 | Malnutrition |
| | Deficiency diseases |
| 623.5 | General works |
| 623.7 | Avitaminosis |
| 627.A-Z | Special diseases, states, and factors in disease, A-Z |
| 627.B45 | Beriberi |
| 627.C37 | Carnitine deficiency |
| 627.C68 | Copper deficiency. Hypocupremia |
| | Cyanocobalamine, see RC627.V55 |
| 627.D9 | Dystrophy |
| 627.E5 | Emaciation |
| 627.E78 | Essential fatty acid deficiency |

Specialties of internal medicine
Nutritional diseases
Special diseases, states,
and factors in disease, A-Z -- Continued

627.F5 Fiber deficiency
627.F57 Fluorosis
Cf. RK341, Endemic dental fluorosis
627.F6 Folic acid deficiency
Hypocupremia, see RC627.C68
627.I63 Iodine deficiency
627.I75 Iron deficiency
Cf. RC641.7.I7, Iron deficiency anemia
Lipid metabolism disorders, see RC632.L54
627.M3 Magnesium deficiency
627.O7 Osteomalacia
627.P44 Pellagra
627.P6 Potassium deficiency
627.P7 Protein deficiency
627.R43 Refined carbohydrates
Saccharine disease, see RC627.R43
627.S24 Salt
627.S36 Scurvy. Vitamin C deficiency
627.S7 Starvation
627.T4 Thiamine deficiency
627.T5 Thirst
627.T7 Trace element deficiency
627.V54 Vitamin A deficiency
627.V543 Vitamin B deficiency
627.V55 Vitamin B12 deficiency
Vitamin C deficiency, see RC627.S36
Vitamin F deficiency, see RC627.E78
627.Z5 Zinc deficiency

Metabolic diseases
Cf. RB147+, Clinical pathology
Cf. RC931.M45, Bone diseases
Cf. RD605+, Surgery
Cf. RJ390, Pediatrics

627.5 Periodicals. Societies. Serials
627.54 General works
627.6 General special
627.8 Inborn errors of metabolism
For individual diseases, see RC632.A+

Obesity
Cf. RA645.O23, Public health
Cf. RC552.O25, Psychiatric aspects
Cf. RD87.3.O23, Obesity and anesthesia
Cf. RM222.2, Reducing diets

628 General works
628.5 Pickwickian syndrome

Gout
629 General works
629.3 Arthritis urica. Gouty arthritis
629.5 Podagra

Specialties of internal medicine
Metabolic diseases -- Continued
630 Water, electrolyte, and acid-base disorders
Cf. RB144+, Pathology
Cf. RJ268.6, Neonatology
632.A-Z Other metabolic diseases, A-Z
632.A32 Adenosine deaminase deficiency
632.A43 Alpha-1 antitrypsin deficiency
632.A45 Amino acid metabolism disorders
632.A5 Amyloidosis
632.A7 Aspartylglycosaminuria
632.C26 Calcium metabolism disorders
632.C64 Copper metabolism disorders
632.C8 Cystinosis
632.D87 Dyslipoproteinemias
632.F3 Fatty degeneration
632.G3 Galactosemia
632.G36 Gaucher's disease
632.G55 Glucosephosphate dehydrogenase deficiency
632.G57 Glycoprotein metabolism disorders
632.H4 Hemochromatosis
632.H45 Hemosiderosis
632.H65 Homocysteine metabolism disorders
632.H83 Hyperchloesteremia
632.H87 Hyperlipidemia
632.H88 Hyperlipoproteinemia
632.H888 Hypertriglyceridemia
632.H89 Hyperuricemia
632.H9 Hypervitaminosis
632.H92 Hypolipoproteinemia
632.H93 Hypophosphatasis
632.H94 Hypoproteinemia
632.I7 Iron metabolism disorders
632.L33 Lactose intolerance
632.L5 Lipid metabolism disorders
632.L54 Lipoprotein metabolism disorders
632.L94 Lysosomal storage diseases
632.M3 Magnesium disorders
632.M56 Mineral metabolism disorders
632.N47 Neuronal ceroid-lipofuscinosis
632.O73 Organic acid metabolism disorders
632.P56 Phosphorus metabolism disorders
632.P6 Porphyria
632.P64 Potassium metabolism disorders
632.P7 Protein metabolism disorders
632.P87 Purine metabolism disorders
632.S6 Sodium metabolism disorders
632.S67 Sphingolipidoses
632.T4 Tetany
Cf. RJ399.T4, Pediatrics
632.U73 Urea metabolism disorders

Specialties of internal medicine -- Continued
Diseases of the blood and blood-forming organs.
Hematologic diseases
Cf. RJ411+, Pediatrics
633.A1 Periodicals. Societies. Serials
633.A2 Congresses
633.A3-Z General works
636 Blood diseases (General)
Cf. QP91+, Physiology
Cf. RB45, Examination
Cf. RB145, Pathology
Leucopenia. Granulocytopenia
Including agranulocytosis
640 General works
640.5 Neutropenia. Febrile neutropenia
Anemia
641 General works
641.5 Pernicious anemia
641.7.A-Z Other anemias, A-Z
641.7.A6 Aplastic anemia
641.7.F36 Fanconi's anemia
641.7.H35 Hemoglobinopathy
641.7.H4 Hemolytic anemia
641.7.H9 Hypochromic anemia
641.7.H93 Hypovolemic anemia
641.7.I7 Iron deficiency anemia
641.7.M4 Megaloblastic anemia
641.7.P37 Paroxysmal hemoglobinuria
641.7.P87 Pure red cell aplasia
641.7.R44 Renal anemia
641.7.S5 Sickle cell anemia
Cf. RD87.3.S53, Sickle cell anemia and anesthesia
641.7.T5 Thalassemia
642 Hemophilia
642.5 Preleukemia
643 Leukemia
644 Hodgkin's disease
644.5 Hematopoietic system diseases
For cancer, see RC280.H47
645 Spleen diseases
645.5 Reticulo-endothelial system diseases
Bone marrow diseases
645.7 General works
645.73 Myelodysplastic syndromes
Myeloproliferative disorders
645.75 General works
645.76 Myelofibrosis
646 Lymphatic system diseases
Cf. RC581+, Immunologic diseases
646.2 Lymphoproliferative disorders
646.3 Lymph circulation disorders. Lymph stasis
646.5 Podoconiosis

Specialties of internal medicine
Diseases of the blood and
blood-forming organs.
Hematologic diseases -- Continued

647.A-Z Other diseases of the blood and blood-forming organs, A-Z
Cf. RJ271, Hemorrhagic diseases of the newborn
647.B5 Blood platelet disorders
647.B6 Blood protein disorders
647.C55 Coagulation disorders
647.C6 Cold agglutinin syndrome
647.D5 Disseminated intravascular coagulation
647.E7 Erythrocyte disorders
647.H44 Hemolytic-uremis syndrome
647.H9 Hypergammaglobulinemia
647.H95 Hyperviscosity syndrome
647.M4 Methemoglobinemia
647.P3 Parasitic diseases
647.P6 Polycythemia
647.P63 Polycythemia vera
647.P8 Purpura
647.V65 Von Willebrand's disease
647.5.A-Z Diseases of the exocrine glands
647.5.A1 General works
647.5.A2-Z Special, A-Z
647.5.S5 Sjogren's syndrome

Diseases of the endocrine glands. Clinical endocrinology
Cf. QP186+, Endocrinology
Cf. RB48.5, Clinical pathology
Cf. RD87.3.E53, Endocrine diseases and anesthesia
Cf. RD599+, Surgery
Cf. RG159+, Endocrine gynecology
Cf. RG580.E53, Endocrine diseases in pregnancy
Cf. RJ418+, Pediatrics
648.A1 Periodicals. Societies. Serials
648.A3-Z General works
649 General special
649.5 Clinical cases
650 Diseases of the hypothalamus
Diseases of the spleen, see RC645
Diseases of the thyroid and parathyroid glands
Cf. RE715.T48, Thyroid eye disease
655 General works
655.49 Pathology
655.5 Examination. Diagnosis
656.A-Z Goiter. Hyperthyroidism
656.A1 Periodicals. Societies. Serials
656.A2 Congresses
656.A3-Z General works
656.3 General special

Specialties of internal medicine
Diseases of the
endocrine glands. Clinical endocrinology
Diseases of the thyroid
and parathyroid glands -- Continued

657 Myxedema. Cretinism. Hypothyroidism
657.5.A-Z Other diseases, A-Z
657.5.G7 Graves' disease
657.5.T48 Thyroiditis

Diseases of the pituitary gland
Cf. RG871.S53, Sheehan's syndrome

658 General works
658.2 Examination. Diagnosis
658.3 Acromegaly
658.5 Diabetes insipidus
658.7 Pituitary dwarfism
659 Diseases of the adrenal (suprarenal) glands. Addison's disease

Diabetes mellitus and other disorders of the pancreatic internal secretion
Cf. RA645.D5, Public health aspects
Cf. RC422.D52, Diabetic neuropathies
Cf. RC700.D5, Diabetic angiopathies
Cf. RC918.D53, Diabetic nephropathies
Cf. RE661.D5, Diabetic retinopathy
Cf. RG580.D5, Diabetes in pregnancy
Cf. RJ420.D5, Pediatrics

660.A1 Periodicals. Societies. Serials
660.A15 Congresses
660.A2-Z General works
660.4 Popular works
660.5 Juvenile works
660.7 Hospitals, clinics, etc.
660.75 Diabetes in old age
661.A-Z Special therapies, A-Z
661.A1 Chemotherapy (General)
661.A33 Acarbose
661.A47 Alternative treatment
661.E94 Exercise therapy
661.G55 Glibenclamide
661.G56 Gliclazide
661.H4 Herbs
661.H63 Home care
661.I55 Immunotherapy
661.I6 Insulin
661.I63 Insulin pumps
661.S85 Sulphonamides
661.T6 Tolbutamide
662 Diet and dietary cookbooks for diabetics
662.18 Non-insulin-dependent diabetes
662.2 Hypoglycemia
662.4 Insulin resistance
663 Diseases of the thymus glands

Specialties of internal medicine
Diseases of the
endocrine glands. Clinical endocrinology -- Continued
Ovarian dysfunction, see RG444
Testicular dysfunction, see RC898+
664 Polyglandular dysfunction and other diseases of the endocrine glands
665 Congenital anomalies
Wounds and injuries, see RD599+
665.5 Diseases of the epithelium
Diseases of the circulatory (cardiovascular) system
Cf. RA645.C34, Public health
Cf. RA975.5.C3, Hospital services
Cf. RB150.S5, Shock
Cf. RC681+, Diseases of the heart
Cf. RD87.3.C37, Cardiovascular diseases and anesthesia
Cf. RD597+, Surgery
Cf. RJ421+, Pediatrics
666 Periodicals. Societies. Serials
666.2 Congresses
666.3 Dictionaries and encyclopedias
666.5 History
Biography
666.7 Collective
666.72.A-Z Individual, A-Z
667 General works
669 General special
669.15 Handbooks, manuals, etc.
669.2 Problems, exercises, examinations
669.7 Cardiovascular diseases in old age
669.9 Pathology
Examination. Diagnosis
670 General works
670.5.A-Z Special diagnostic methods, A-Z
670.5.H45 Hemodynamic monitoring
670.5.I56 Intravascular ultrasonography
670.5.M33 Magnetic resonance imaging
670.5.R32 Radioisotope scanning. Radionuclide imaging
670.5.R43 Radiolabeled blood platelets
Therapeutics
671 General works
671.5.A-Z Special therapies, A-Z
671.5.G44 Gene therapy
671.5.H45 Hemodilution
672 Popular works
673 Juvenile works
674 Cardiovascular disease nursing
675 Cardiovascular emergencies
Cf. RC684.C36, Cardiac intensive care
677 Cardiovascular toxicology
678 Cardiovascular infections

Specialties of internal medicine
Diseases of the circulatory (cardiovascular) system -- Continued
Diseases of the heart
Including the great vessels
Cf. RA975.5.C6, Coronary care units
Cf. RA1170.H4, Forensic cardiology
Cf. RC702, Diseases of the cardiopulmonary system
Cf. RD87.3.H43, Heart disease and anesthesia
Cf. RG580.H4, Diseases in pregnancy

681.A1 Periodicals
681.A2 Congresses
681.A25 Collected works (nonserial)
681.A3-Z General works
682 General special
682.9 Pathology. Pathogenesis
Examination. Diagnosis
683 General works
683.5.A-Z Special diagnostic methods, A-Z
683.5.A43 Ambulatory blood pressure monitoring
683.5.A45 Ambulatory electrocardiography
683.5.A5 Angiocardiography
683.5.A9 Auscultation
683.5.B3 Ballistocardiography
Biochemical diagnosis, see RC683.5.C5
683.5.B5 Biopsys
683.5.B63 Body surface mapping
683.5.C25 Cardiac catheterization
683.5.C3 Cardiography
683.5.C5 Chemical diagnosis
683.5.C54 Cineangiography
683.5.D36 Data processing
683.5.D54 Digital subtraction angiography
Echocardiography, see RC683.5.U5
683.5.E5 Electrocardiography
Electrocardiography, Ambulatory, see RC683.5.A45
683.5.E6 Electrokymography
683.5.E94 Exercise tests
683.5.H4 Heart function tests
683.5.I42 Imaging
683.5.I45 Impedance plethysmography
683.5.I48 Indicator dilution
683.5.I5 Intravenous catheterization
683.5.K5 Kinematocardiography
683.5.M35 Magnetic resonance imaging
683.5.N65 Noninvasive diagnosis
683.5.P5 Phonocardiography
683.5.P55 Physical diagnosis (General)
683.5.P65 Polarcardiography
683.5.P75 Psychological stress tests
683.5.P84 Pulmonary artery catheterization
683.5.R3 Radiography

Specialties of internal medicine
Diseases of the circulatory (cardiovascular) system
Diseases of the heart
Examination. Diagnosis
Special diagnostic methods, A-Z -- Continued
683.5.R32 Radioimmunoimaging
683.5.R33 Radioisotope scanning. Radionuclide imaging
683.5.S77 Stress echocardiography
683.5.T66 Tomography
683.5.T83 Transesophageal echocardiography
Treadmill exercise tests, see RC683.5.E94
683.5.U5 Ultrasonic cardiography. Echocardiography
683.5.V4 Vectorcardiography
Therapeutics
683.8 General works
684.A-Z Special therapies, A-Z
684.A34 Adrenergic alpha blockers
684.A35 Adrenergic beta blockers
684.A44 Aldosterone antagonists
684.A48 Alternative treatment
684.A53 Angiotensin converting enzyme inhibitors
684.A6 Anticoagulants
Artificial heart, see RD598.35.A78
Artificial pacemaker, see RC684.P3
Beta-blockers, see RC684.A35
684.B56 Bisoprolol
684.C34 Calcium antagonists
684.C36 Cardiac intensive care
684.C37 Carnitine
Cardioversion, see RC684.E4
684.C48 Chemotherapy
684.C7 Crataegus oxyacantha
Defibrillation, see RC684.E4
684.D5 Diet therapy
684.D52 Dihydropyridine
684.D55 Diuretics
684.E4 Electric countershock. Cardioversion. Defibrillation
Including defibrillators and implantable cardioverter-defibrillators
684.E75 Estrogen
684.E9 Exercise
684.F44 Fendiline
684.G34 Gallopamil
684.G37 Garlic
684.G5 Glycosides
684.H47 Herbs
684.H65 Hormone antagonists
Intensive care, Cardiac, see RC684.C36
684.I58 Intra-aortic balloon counterpulsation
684.M55 Milrinone
684.N56 Nitrates
684.P3 Pacemaker, Artificial

Specialties of internal medicine
Diseases of the circulatory (cardiovascular) system
Diseases of the heart
Therapeutics
Special therapies, A-Z -- Continued

684.P5 Phentolamine
684.P57 Physical therapy
684.P74 Prenylamine
684.P76 Prostaglandins
684.T47 Testosterone
684.V38 Vasodilators
685.A-Z Individual diseases of the heart, A-Z
Including manifestations of disease
Allorhythmia, see RC685.A65
685.A6 Angina pectoris
685.A65 Arrhythmia. Allorhythmia
Arteriosclerotic heart disease, see RC685.C6
685.A72 Atrial arrhythmias
Including atrial fibrillation and atrial flutter
685.B55 Block
685.C15 Calcification
685.C16 Carcinoid heart disease
685.C173 Cardiac arrest
685.C18 Cardiogenic shock
Cardiomyopathies, see RC685.M9
685.C53 Congestive heart failure
685.C55 Cor pulmonale
685.C58 Coronary artery stenosis
685.C6 Coronary heart disease
Including occlusion, sclerosis, thrombosis, etc.
Cf. RC685.N65, Nonatherosclerotic myocardial ischemia
Cf. RC685.S48, Silent myocardial ischemia
685.C65 Coronary vasospasm
685.D4 Degenerative heart disease
685.D55 Dilatation
685.E5 Endocarditis
685.H8 Hypertension
Cf. RC776.P87, Pulmonary hypertension
Cf. RC848.P6, Portal hypertension
Cf. RC918.R38, Renal hypertension
Cf. RC918.R45, Renovascular hypertension
Cf. RE661.H8, Hypertensive retinal disease
Cf. RG580.H9, Hypertension in pregnancy
Cf. RJ426.H9, Pediatrics
685.H9 Hypertrophy
685.H93 Hypotension
685.I6 Infarction
685.M9 Myocardiopathies
685.M92 Myocarditis

Specialties of internal medicine
Diseases of the circulatory (cardiovascular) system
Diseases of the heart
Individual diseases
of the heart, A-Z -- Continued
685.N4 Necrosis
685.N65 Nonatherosclerotic myocardial ischemia
Occlusion, see RC685.C6
685.O78 Orthostatic hypotension
685.P5 Pericarditis
Rheumatic heart disease, see RC182.R4
685.R9 Rupture
Sclerosis, see RC685.C6
685.S48 Silent myocardial ischemia
Stenosis, Coronary artery, see RC685.C58
685.T33 Tachycardia
Thrombosis, see RC685.C6
Tuberculosis of the heart, see RC312.5.H4
685.V2 Valvular disease
Including mitral, tricuspid, and pulmonary aortic
Vasospasm, Coronary, see RC685.C65
685.V43 Ventricular fibrillation
685.V46 Ventricular septal defects
685.V57 Virus diseases
685.W6 Wolff-Parkinson-White syndrome
687 Congenital anomalies
687.5 Metabolic disorders
688 Parasites
Wounds and injuries, see RD598+
Diseases of the blood vessels
Including the aorta, arteries, veins, etc.
Cf. RC388.5, Cerebrovascular disease
Cf. RD598.5+, Surgery
691 General works
691.4 Pathology
Examination. Diagnosis
691.5 General works
691.6.A-Z Special diagnostic methods, A-Z
691.6.A53 Angiography
691.6.B55 Blood flow measurement
691.6.C35 Capillaroscopy
691.6.D87 Duplex ultrasonography
691.6.N65 Noninvasive diagnosis
691.6.T65 Tomography
691.6.U47 Ultrasonic diagnosis
691.6.V45 Venous pressure measurement
692 Arteriosclerosis. Atherosclerosis
Cf. RC694.35, Atheroembolism
Cf. RJ426.A82, Pediatrics
693 Aneurysms
694 Peripheral vascular diseases
Arterial embolism and thrombosis

Specialties of internal medicine
Diseases of the circulatory (cardiovascular) system
Diseases of the blood vessels
Arterial embolism and thrombosis -- Continued

| | |
|---|---|
| 694.3 | General works |
| 694.35 | Atheroembolism |
| 694.5.A-Z | Other diseases of the arteries, A-Z |
| 694.5.A55 | Aortitis |
| | Arteritis, Giant cell, see RC694.5.G5 |
| 694.5.C34 | Calcification |
| 694.5.E53 | Endarteritis |
| 694.5.G5 | Giant cell arteritis |
| 694.5.I53 | Inflammation |
| 694.5.P47 | Periarteritis nodosa. Polyarteritis nodosa |
| | Polyarteritis nodosa, see RC694.5.P47 |
| 694.5.T45 | Thromboangiitis obliterans |
| | Diseases of the veins. Varicose veins |
| 695 | General works |
| 696 | Phlebitis and thrombophlebitis |
| 697 | Venous embolism and thrombosis |
| 700.A-Z | Other diseases of the circulatory system, A-Z |
| 700.A5 | Angiomatosis |
| 700.D5 | Diabetic angiopathies |
| 700.M53 | Microcirculation disorders |
| 700.R38 | Raynaud's disease |
| 700.V45 | Venous insufficiency |
| 701 | Congenital anomalies |
| | Wounds and injuries, trauma, see RD598+ |
| 702 | Diseases of the cardiopulmonary system |
| | Diseases of the respiratory system |
| | Cf. QM251+, Anatomy |
| | Cf. QP121+, Physiology |
| | Cf. RC589+, Respiratory allergy |
| | Cf. RD535.7+, Surgery |
| | Cf. RF1+, Diseases of the nose and throat |
| | Cf. RJ431+, Pediatrics |
| 705 | Collections. Collected works |
| 711 | Pathology |
| 720 | Inhalation toxicology. Pulmonary toxicology |
| 731 | General works |
| 732 | General special |
| 732.5 | Respiratory diseases in old age |
| | Examination. Diagnosis |
| 733 | General works |
| 734.A-Z | Special diagnostic methods, A-Z |
| 734.A94 | Auscultation |
| 734.B56 | Biopsy |
| 734.B68 | Bronchial catheterization |
| 734.B69 | Bronchoalveolar lavage |
| 734.B7 | Bronchoscopy |
| 734.B76 | Bronchospirometry |
| | Diagnostic imaging, see RC734.I43 |
| 734.E43 | Electron microscopy |

Specialties of internal medicine
Diseases of the respiratory system
Examination. Diagnosis
Special diagnostic methods, A-Z -- Continued
734.E87 Exercise tests
734.E9 Exfoliative cytology
734.I43 Imaging
734.M34 Magnetic resonance imaging
734.M4 Mediastinoscopy
734.P55 Plethysmography
734.P84 Pulmonary function tests
734.R3 Radiography
734.R35 Radioisotope scanning
734.S65 Spirometry
734.T64 Tomography
734.U43 Ultrasonics
735.A-Z Special therapies, A-Z
735.A57 Antibiotics
735.C43 Cefuroxime axetil
735.C47 Chemotherapy
735.E95 Exercise
735.H47 Herbs
735.H54 High-frequency ventilation
735.H65 Home care
735.I5 Inhalation therapy. Respiratory therapy
Cf. RA975.5.R47, Hospital services
Cf. RJ434, Pediatrics
Cf. RM161, Inhalatory medication
Intensive care, Respiratory, see RC735.R48
735.P58 Physical therapy
735.P66 Piperacillin
735.P86 Pulmonary surfactant
735.R48 Respiratory intensive care. Respiratory emergencies
Respiratory therapy, see RC735.I5
Surgery, see RD539
735.3 Rehabilitation
735.5 Respiratory disease nursing
736 Popular works
Apnea
737 General works
737.5 Sleep apnea syndrome
Asthma, see RC591
740 Respiratory infections
Cf. RC150+, Influenza
Cf. RC152.7, Legionnaires' disease
Cf. RC204, Whooping cough
Cf. RF361+, Common cold
741 Catarrh
742 Empyema
Hay fever, see RC590
746 Croup
751 Diseases of the pleura. Pleurisy

Specialties of internal medicine
Diseases of the respiratory system -- Continued
752 Spontaneous pneumothorax. Hydropneumothorax
754 Diseases of the mediastinum
Diseases of the lungs
Cf. RC306+, Tuberculosis
Cf. RC702, Diseases of the cardiopulmonary system
Cf. RD539, Surgery
756 General works
Pulmonary toxicology, see RC720
Examination and diagnosis, see RC733+
Pneumonia. Lobar pneumonia
Cf. RC150+, Influenza
771 General works
772.A-Z Other types of pneumonia, A-Z
772.A8 Aspiration pneumonia
772.B7 Bronchopneumonia
772.I56 Interstitial plasma cell pneumonia. Pneumocystis carinii pneumonia
Pneumocystis carinii pneumonia, see RC772.I56
772.V5 Viral pneumonia
Pneumoconiosis. Dust diseases of the lungs
773 General works
774 Silicosis
775.A-Z Other types of pneumoconiosis, A-Z
775.A8 Asbestosis
775.B9 Byssinosis
775.H94 Hypersensitivity pneumonitis
776.A-Z Other diseases of the lungs, A-Z
776.A3 Abscess
Adult respiratory distress syndrome, see RC776.R38
776.A6 Arteriovenous fistula
776.A7 Atelectasis
Cf. RJ436.A84, Pediatrics
776.B75 Bronchiolar diseases
776.C2 Calcification
Cancer, see RC280.L8
776.D9 Dyspnea
776.E5 Emphysema (Alveolar)
776.F33 Farmer's lung
776.F5 Fibrosis
776.F8 Fungous diseases
776.H44 Hemophilus diseases
776.H9 Hyperventilation
776.I45 Immunologic diseases
776.I56 Interstitial lung diseases
776.L95 Lymphangiomyomatosis
776.M8 Mycetoma
776.O3 Obstructive diseases
776.P33 Paragonimiasis
776.P35 Parasitic diseases
776.P8 Pulmonary edema

Specialties of internal medicine
Diseases of the respiratory system
Diseases of the lungs
Other diseases of the lungs, A-Z -- Continued

776.P85 Pulmonary embolism
776.P87 Pulmonary hypertension
776.R38 Respiratory distress syndrome, Adult
776.R4 Respiratory insufficiency
Sarcoidosis, see RC182.S14
776.V37 Vascular disorders
Wounds and injuries, foreign bodies, see RD536
778 Diseases of the bronchi. Bronchitis
779 Other diseases of the respiratory system
For diseases of the throat (General), see RF459.2+
For otorhinolaryngology, see RF1+
For septic sore throat, see RC182.S3
Diseases of the digestive system. Gastroenterology
Cf. QM301+, Anatomy
Cf. QP145+, Physiology
Cf. RA645.D54, Public health
Cf. RA975.5.G37, Hospital services
Cf. RJ446+, Pediatrics
799 Periodicals. Societies. Serials
801 General works
802 General special
802.4.A-Z By age group, class, etc., A-Z
802.4.A34 Aged. Geriatric gastroenterology
Children, see RJ446+
Geriatric gastroenterology, see RC802.4.A34
802.9 Pathology
Examination. Diagnosis
803 General works
804.A-Z Special diagnostic methods, A-Z
804.A5 Angiography
804.B5 Biopsy
804.C64 Colonoscopy
804.D52 Diagnostic imaging
804.D79 Duodenoscopy
804.E4 Electrogastrography
804.E44 Electron microscopy
804.E59 Endoscopic ultrasonography
804.E6 Endoscopy
804.E64 Enteroscopy
804.E84 Esophagoscopy
804.F55 Fluoroscopy
804.G26 Gastrointestinal functional tests
804.G28 Gastrophotography
804.G3 Gastroscopy
Imaging, Diagnostic, see RC804.D52
804.R27 Radioisotope scanning
804.R6 Roentgenographic examination. X-ray diagnosis
804.S47 Sigmoidoscopy
804.T65 Tomography

Specialties of internal medicine
Diseases of the digestive system. Gastroenterology
Examination. Diagnosis
Special diagnostic methods, A-Z -- Continued
804.U4 Ultrasonic diagnosis
X-ray diagnosis, see RC804.R6
805.A-Z Instruments, apparatus, and appliances used in diagnosis and treatment, A-Z
805.S8 Stomach pump
806 Popular works
807 Atlases
808 Clinical cases
809 Abdominal pain, colic, nausea, etc.
Cf. RC944, Abdominal diseases
810 Visceroptosis. Splanchnoptosis
811 Motility disorders
Diseases of the mouth, tongue, and salivary glands. Stomatology
Cf. RD662, Surgery of neoplasms
Cf. RK301+, Dental medicine
Cf. RK529+, Oral surgery
815 General works
815.2 Ingestion disorders. Deglutition disorders
Diseases of the salivary glands
815.5 General works
815.6 Parotitis
815.7 Diseases of the esophagus
Diseases of the stomach and duodenum
Class here works on the stomach and intestines combined
Cf. RD540+, Surgery
816 General works
817 General special
Pathology, see RC802.9
Examination and diagnosis, see RC803+
Gastroscopy, see RC804.G3
819.A-Z Special therapies, A-Z
819.D5 Diet
821 Peptic ulcer
822 Gastric ulcer
824 Duodenal ulcer
825 Gastrojejunal ulcer
827 Disorders of the functions of the stomach
Including dyspepsia, gastric indigestion, disorders of gastric secretion, etc.
Gastritis and duodenitis
830 General works
831 Gastritis
832 Duodenitis
Neoplasms and cancer, see RC280.S8
840.A-Z Other diseases, A-Z
840.A25 Achlorhydria
840.A56 Anisakiasis

Specialties of internal medicine
Diseases of the digestive system. Gastroenterology
Diseases of the stomach and duodenum
Other diseases, A-Z -- Continued

840.G3 Gastroenteritis
840.G4 Gastroptosis
840.H38 Helicobacter pylori infections
840.H44 Hemorrhage
840.I53 Infections (General)
840.M4 Merycism
840.T7 Tropical sprue

Wounds and injuries, foreign bodies, see RD540+

Diseases of the liver, gallbladder, bile ducts, and pancreas
Cf. RD87.3.L58, Liver diseases and anesthesia
Cf. RD546, Surgery

845 General works
846 General special
846.9 Pathology
847 Examination. Diagnosis
847.5.A-Z Special diagnostic methods, A-Z
847.5.B56 Biopsy
847.5.E53 Endoscopic retrograde cholangiopancreatography
847.5.I42 Imaging
848.A-Z Individual diseases of the liver, A-Z
848.A2 Abscess

Acute yellow atrophy, see RC848.N4

848.A42 Alcoholic liver diseases

Cancer, see RC280.L5

848.C4 Chronic active hepatitis
848.C5 Cirrhosis of the liver
Cf. RJ456.C55, Pediatrics
848.D45 Delta infection
848.F27 Failure
848.F29 Fascioliasis. Flukes
848.F3 Fatty liver
848.F53 Fibrosis

Flukes, see RC848.F29

848.H38 Helminthiasis
848.H4 Hepatic coma. Hepatic encephalopathy
848.H42 Hepatits

Hepatitis, Chronic Active, see RC848.C4
Hepatitis, Infectious, see RC848.I6

848.H425 Hepatitis, Non-A, non-B. Hepatitis C
848.H43 Hepatitis, Viral

Hepatitis A, see RC848.I6

848.H44 Hepatitis B

Hepatitis C, see RC848.H425
Hepatitis D, see RC848.D45

848.H45 Hepatitis E
848.H46 Hepatorenal syndrome
848.H48 Hepatotoxicology
Cf. RC848.T6, Toxic hepatitis

Specialties of internal medicine
Diseases of the digestive system. Gastroenterology
Diseases of the liver, gallbladder, bile ducts, and pancreas
Individual diseases of the liver, A-Z -- Continued

848.I6 Infectious hepatitis. Hepatitis A
Cf. RG580.H53, Pregnancy
848.N4 Necrosis. Acute yellow atophy
Non-A, non-B hepatitis, see RC848.H425
848.P6 Portal hypertension
848.T6 Toxic hepatitis
Viral hepatitis, see RC848.H43
Diseases of the gallbladder and bile ducts
849 General works
850 Gallstones. Cholelithiasis
851 Jaundice. Icterus
853.A-Z Other diseases, A-Z
853.A3 Abscess
853.C5 Cholecystitis
853.C53 Cholecystoses
854.A-Z Diseases of the biliary tract, A-Z
854.C45 Cholestasis
854.I53 Infections
Diseases of the pancreas
Cf. RC660+, Diabetes and other disorders of the pancreatic internal secretion
857 General works
857.4 Pathology
857.5 Examination. Diagnosis
858.A-Z Individual diseases, A-Z
Cancer, see RC280.P5
858.C95 Cystic fibrosis
Cf. RJ456.C9, Pediatrics
Hypoglycemia, see RC662.2
858.P35 Pancreatitis
Diseases of the intestines
Including the jejunum, ileum, colon, and cecum
860 General works
Pathology, see RC802.9
Examination and diagnosis, see RC803+
861 Constipation
862.A-Z Other diseases, A-Z
Bowel diseases, Inflammatory, see RC862.I53
862.C44 Celiac disease
862.C47 Clostridium diseases
862.C6 Colitis
862.C63 Colitis, Ulcerative
Colon, Irritable, see RC862.I77
862.D5 Diarrhea
862.D6 Diverticulitis
862.D62 Diverticulosis
862.E47 Enteric infections

Specialties of internal medicine
Diseases of the digestive system. Gastroenterology
Diseases of the intestines
Other diseases, A-Z -- Continued

862.E5 Enteritis
862.E52 Enteritis, Regional
Enteropathies, Protein-losing, see RC862.P76
862.E6 Enteroptosis
862.F55 Flatulence
862.I5 Ileitis
Ileitis, Regional, see RC862.E52
862.I53 Inflammatory bowel diseases
862.I77 Irritable colon
862.I8 Ischemia
862.I82 Ischemic colitis
862.M3 Malabsorption syndromes
862.M35 Megacolon
862.M4 Melena
Neoplasms, see RC280.I5
862.O2 Obstruction
862.P76 Protein-losing enteropathies
Regional enteritis, see RC862.E52
Regional ileitis, see RC862.E52
862.T9 Typhlitis
Ulcerative colitis, see RC862.C63
862.U5 Ulcers
862.V3 Vascular disorders
862.V64 Volvulus
862.W47 Whipple's disease
Appendicitis, see RD542
Diseases of the rectum and anus. Proctology
Cf. RD544, Surgery
Cf. RD672, Neoplasms
864 General works
864.4 Pathology
864.5 Examination. Diagnosis
865 Hemorrhoids
866.A-Z Other diseases, A-Z
866.A3 Abscess
866.C4 Cellulitis of the anus
866.D43 Defecation disorders
Including fecal incontinence
Fecal incontinence, see RC866.D43
Incontinence, Fecal, see RC866.D43
866.M3 Malformations
867 Diseases of the peritoneum
869 Other diseases of the digestive system (not A-Z)
Cf. RC140, Dysentery

Specialties of internal medicine -- Continued
Diseases of the genitourinary system. Urology
Cf. QM401+, Anatomy
Cf. QP211, Urine (Physiology)
Cf. QP251+, Reproduction (Physiology)
Cf. RD571+, Surgery
Cf. RD670, Neoplasms
Cf. RG484, Gynecological and obstetrical urology
Cf. RJ466+, Pediatrics

870 Periodicals. Societies. Serials
870.8 History
Biography
870.9 Collective
870.92.A-Z Individual, A-Z
871 General works
872 General special
872.9 Handbooks, manuals, etc.
873 Problems, exercises, examinations
873.2 Outlines, syllabi, etc.
873.5 Genitourinary manifestations of general diseases
873.9 Pathology
874 Examination. Diagnosis
874.5.A-Z Special therapies, A-Z
874.5.C43 Cefuroxime axetil
874.5.D5 Diathermy
874.5.H4 Herbs
874.7 Urological nursing. Nursing in urology
Diseases and functional disorders of the genital organs (General and male). Andrology
Cf. RA1224.2, Reproductive toxicology
Cf. RD571+, Surgery
Cf. RG1+, Gynecology
Cf. RJ476.5+, Pediatrics
875 General works
877 General special
881 Popular works
Congenital anomalies
881.5 General works
882 Klinefelter's syndrome
883 Hermaphroditism
883.5.A-Z Other congenital anomalies, A-Z
883.5.H94 Hypospadias
883.5.S47 Sex differentiation disorders
884 Climacteric disorders
Cf. RG186+, Menopause
Tuberculosis of the genital organs, see RC312.5.G4+
Neoplasms and cancer, see RC280.G4+
888 Male contraception
Cf. RD585.5, Vasectomy
889 Impotence and infertility
Cf. RC560.I45, Psychiatry
Cf. RG201+, Infertility in women

Specialties of internal medicine
Diseases of the genitourinary system. Urology
Diseases and functional disorders of the genital organs (General and male). Andrology -- Continued

889.2 Spermatazoa motility disorders
889.5 Oligospermia
890 Spermatorrhea
892 Diseases of the urethra. Stricture
894 Diseases of the prepuce. Phimosis
Cf. RD590, Surgery
896 Diseases of the penis
897 Diseases of the scrotum
Diseases of testis and spermatic cord. Hydrocele. Varicocele
898 General works
898.3 Orchitis
899 Diseases of the prostate
899.5.A-Z Other diseases of the genital organs, A-Z
Diseases of the urinary organs. Urologic diseases
Cf. RG484, Urogynecology
900 General works
900.5 General special
900.9 Pathology
901 Examination. Diagnosis
Instruments, apparatus, and appliances used in diagnosis and treatment
901.5 General works
901.7.A-Z Special, A-Z
901.7.A7 Artificial kidney
901.7.B6 Bougies
901.7.C2 Catheters
Continuous ambulatory peritoneal dialysis, see RC901.7.P48
901.7.E53 Endoscopes
901.7.H45 Hemodialysis
901.7.H47 Hemofiltration
901.7.P48 Peritoneal dialysis. Continuous ambulatory peritoneal dialysis
901.75 Urination disorders
901.8 Urinary tract infections
901.9 Neurourology. Urodynamics
Diseases of the kidneys
Cf. RJ476.K5, Pediatrics
902.A1 Periodicals. Societies. Serials
902.A2 Congresses
902.A3-Z General works
903 General special
903.9 Pathology
904 Examination. Diagnosis
904.5.A-Z Special diagnostic methods, A-Z
904.5.I42 Imaging
904.5.R32 Radionuclide imaging

Specialties of internal medicine
Diseases of the genitourinary system. Urology
Diseases of the urinary organs. Urologic diseases
Diseases of the kidneys -- Continued

905 Albuminuria, glycosuria, peptonuria, etc.
907 Nephritis. Bright's disease
912 Pyuria
915 Uremia
916 Urinary calculi
Including calculi of the kidney and ureter
Cf. RC921.V4, Vesical calculi
918.A-Z Other diseases, A-Z
918.A2 Abscess
Amyloid degeneration, see RC918.D3
918.B34 Balkan nephropathy
Cancer, see RC280.K5
Chronic renal failure, see RC918.R4
918.C95 Cysts
918.D3 Degeneration, Amyloid
918.D53 Diabetic nephropathies
Floating kidney, see RC918.M8
918.G55 Glomerulonephritis
918.H4 Hematuria
918.H8 Hydronephrosis
918.I35 IgA glomerulonephritis
918.I53 Infections
Interstitial nephritis, see RC918.N37
918.L86 Lupus nephritis
918.M8 Movable kidney. Floating kidney
Neoplasms, see RC280.K5
918.N37 Nephritis, Interstitial
Nephropathies, Diabetic, see RC918.D53
918.N4 Nephrosclerosis
918.N43 Nephrotic syndrome
918.N45 Nephrotoxicology. Nephrotoxicity
918.O9 Oxaluria
918.P55 Plasma cell diseases
918.P58 Polycystic kidney disease
918.P9 Pyelonephritis
918.R38 Renal hypertension
918.R4 Renal insufficiency. Chronic renal failure
918.R45 Renovascular hypertension
Tuberculosis, see RC312.5.K5
918.T73 Tubular disorders
918.U7 Urine retention

Diseases of the bladder
919 General works
920 Cystoscopy
921.A-Z Individual diseases or disorders of the bladder, A-Z
921.C9 Cystitis
Cf. RG485.C9, Gynecology
921.F4 Fistula

Specialties of internal medicine
Diseases of the genitourinary system. Urology
Diseases of the urinary organs. Urologic diseases
Diseases of the bladder
Individual diseases or disorders of the bladder, A-Z -- Continued
921.I5 Incontinence
Cf. RC569.5.E5, Enuresis
Cf. RG485.S7, Gynecology
921.N4 Neurogenic bladder
Stress incontinence, see RC921.I5
921.V4 Vesical calculi
Cf. RJ476.B4, Pediatrics
921.V43 Vesico-ureteral reflux
922 Diseases of the ureters
Cf. RB53, Urine analysis
923 Congenital anomalies
Wounds and injuries, foreign bodies, see RD575
Diseases of the connective tissues
924 General works
924.5.A-Z Individual diseases, A-Z
Ehlers-Danlos syndrome, see RC580.E35
924.5.L85 Lupus erythematosus, Systemic
Marfan syndrome, see RC580.M37
924.5.M37 Mast cell disease
924.5.M58 Mixed connective tissue disease
924.5.S34 Scleroderma, Systemic
Systemic lupus erythematosus, see RC924.5.L85
Systemic scleroderma, see RC924.5.S34
Diseases of the musculoskeletal system
Cf. RA645.M85, Public health
Cf. RC280.M83, Neoplasms
Cf. RJ480+, Pediatrics
For surgical treatment, see RD680+
925.A1 Periodicals. Societies. Serials
925.A2-Z General works
925.5 General special
925.53 Musculoskeletal disorders in old age
925.55 Neuromuscular manifestations of general diseases
925.6 Pathology
925.7 Examination. Diagnosis
926 Musculoskeletal emergencies
Cf. RD680+, Surgery
Rheumatism
Cf. RA645.R5, Public health aspects
Cf. RC933.A+, Arthritis
927 General works
927.3 Muscular rheumatism. Fibromyalgia
927.5.A-Z Other, A-Z
927.5.N65 Nonarticular rheumatism
927.5.P6 Polymyalgia rheumatica
Diseases of bones and joints

Specialties of internal medicine
Diseases of the musculoskeletal system
Diseases of bones and joints -- Continued
Diseases of bones
Cf. RD684, Surgical treatment
930 General works
930.4 Pathology
930.5 Examination. Diagnosis
931.A-Z Individual diseases, A-Z
Arthritis, Psoriatic, see RC931.P76
931.B65 Bone resorption
931.C3 Caries
Cf. RK331, Dentistry
931.C97 Cysts
931.F5 Fibrous dysplasia
931.H94 Hyperostosis corticalis generalisata
Hyperostosis frontalis interna, see RC936
931.I3 Idiopathic femoral necrosis
931.I53 Infections
931.L5 Lipomembranous polycystic osteodysplasia
931.M45 Metabolic disorders
931.M47 Metaplastic ossification
931.N43 Necrosis
931.O64 Osteitis
931.O65 Osteitis deformans
931.O67 Osteoarthritis
931.O68 Osteogenesis imperfecta
931.O7 Osteomyelitis
931.O72 Osteopetrosis
931.O73 Osteoporosis
Osteopsathyrosis, see RC931.O68
931.O8 Osteosclerosis
931.P38 Periarthritis
931.P4 Petrositis
931.P76 Psoriatic arthritis
931.R4 Renal osteodystrophy
Tuberculosis, see RC312.5.B6
Diseases of joints
Cf. RD686, Surgical treatment
932 General works
Arthritis. Rheumatoid arthritis
Cf. RA1170.C35, Medical jurisprudence
Cf. RC629.3, Arthritis urica
Cf. RC927+, Rheumatism
Cf. RC931.O67, Osteoarthritis
Cf. RC931.P38, Periarthritis
Cf. RC931.P76, Psoriatic arthritis
933.A1 Periodicals. Societies. Serials
933.A2 Congresses
933.A3-Z General works
935.A-Z Other diseases of the musculoskeletal system, A-Z
935.A8 Atrophy, Muscular
935.B8 Bursitis

Specialties of internal medicine
Diseases of the musculoskeletal system
Other diseases of the musculoskeletal system, A-Z -- Continued

935.C43 Charcot-Marie-Tooth disease
935.C47 Chondrocalcinosis
935.C48 Chondromalacia patellae
935.D8 Dystonia
Muscular atrophy, see RC935.A8
935.M7 Muscular dystrophy
935.M77 Myalgia
935.M8 Myasthenia gravis
935.M9 Myositis
935.M95 Myotonia
935.P5 Phlegmon
935.R45 Rhabdomyolysis
935.S3 Scalenus anticus syndrome
935.S64 Spasticity
935.S67 Spondyloarthropathies
935.T4 Tendinitis

Diseases of regions of the body
Class here general works only
For individual diseases, see the disease

936 Head and neck
939 Shoulder
941 Chest
Breast
942 General and male
Female, see RG491+
944 Abdomen
Cf. RC809, Abdominal pain
Back, see RD768+
946 Pelvis
Cf. RD549+, Surgery
Cf. RG482+, Gynecology
951 Extremities
Cf. RD551+, Surgery
Cf. RD563, Podiatry
Cf. RD775+, Orthopedics

Special situations and conditions

Special situations and conditions -- Continued
Geriatrics
Cf. BJ1691, Ethics
Cf. BV4580.A1+, Religious life
Cf. GV184, Recreation
Cf. HD6279+, Employment
Cf. HQ1060+, Gerontology (Social aspects)
Cf. HV1450+, Protection, assistance, relief
Cf. QP86, Senescence and old age
Cf. QP90, Rejuvenation
Cf. RA413.7.A4, Private medical care plans
Cf. RA564.8, Public health
Cf. RA777.6, Health and grooming
Cf. RC451.4.A+, Psychiatry
Cf. RC524, Senile psychosis
Cf. RC802.4.A34, Gastroenterology
Cf. RD145, Surgery in old age
Cf. RD732.3.A+, Orthopedics
Cf. RE48.2.A5, Ophthalmology
Cf. RF47.A35, Otorhinolaryngology
Cf. RK55.A3, Dentistry
Cf. RL73.A35, Dermatology
952.A1 Periodicals. Societies. Serials
952.A2 Congresses
952.A6-Z General works
952.5 General special
952.55 Handbooks, manuals, etc.
952.6 Problems, exercises, examinations
952.7 Clinical cases
952.9 Pathology
953 Examination. Diagnosis
953.2.A-Z Special diagnostic methods, A-Z
953.2.R33 Radiography
Therapeutics
953.5 General works
953.7 Chemotherapy. Geriatric pharmacology
953.8.A-Z Special therapies, A-Z
953.8.A76 Art therapy
Chemotherapy, see RC953.7
953.8.D36 Dance therapy
953.8.E93 Exercise therapy
953.8.H85 Humor
953.8.O22 Occupational therapy
953.8.P58 Physical therapy
953.8.R43 Recreational therapy
Wit and humor, see RC953.8.H85
954 Nursing
Hospital and nursing home care
Cf. RA997+, Nursing home facilities
954.3 General works
By region or country
United States
954.4 General works

Special situations and conditions
Geriatrics
Hospital and nursing home care
By region or country
United States -- Continued
954.5.A-Z By region or state, A-Z
954.6.A-Z Other regions or countries, A-Z
Arctic medicine. Antarctic medicine. Circumpolar medicine
Including hygiene
Cf. QP82.2.C6, Physiology
Cf. RC88.5, Cold injuries
955 Periodicals. Societies. Serials
955.2 Congresses
957 General works
957.3 General special
958.A-Z By region or country, A-Z
Tropical medicine
Including hygiene
Cf. QP82+, Influence of environment
Cf. RC87.1, Heat prostration
Cf. RC103.H4, Heat disorders
960 Periodicals. Societies. Serials
961 General works
961.5 General special
961.6 Handbooks, manuals, etc.
962.A-Z By region or country, A-Z
Industrial medicine
Cf. HD5115+, Absenteeism
Cf. HD7260+, Industrial hygiene and welfare work
Cf. RA1229+, Industrial toxicology (General)
Cf. RA1231.A+, Industrial toxicology by specific poisons
Cf. RC965.A+, Industrial toxicology by industry or occupation
Cf. RD97.5, Industrial injuries
Cf. TD895+, Industrial sanitation
963.A1 Periodicals. Societies. Serials
963.A2 Congresses
963.A3 Dictionaries and encyclopedias
963.A6-Z General works
963.3 General special
963.32 Handbooks, manuals, etc.
Biography
963.33 Collective
963.34.A-Z Individual, A-Z
963.4 Disability evaluation. Work capacity evaluation
Job stress. Work stress conditions
963.48 General works
963.5.A-Z Special conditions, A-Z
963.5.H4 Heat
Cf. QP82.2.H4, Physiology

Special situations and conditions
Industrial medicine
Job stress. Work stress conditions
Special conditions, A-Z -- Continued
963.5.L54 Light
963.5.N6 Noise
Cf. QP82.2.N6, Physiology
Cf. RF293.5, Otology
963.5.S54 Shift systems
963.5.V5 Vibration
Cf. QP82.2.V5, Physiology
963.6.A-Z By age group, class, etc., A-Z
963.6.A43 Aged
963.6.A78 Artists
963.6.W65 Women
Cf. RG580.O33, Occupational diseases in pregnancy
963.6.Y68 Youth
963.7.A-Z By region or country, A-Z
Occupational diseases
Cf. RG580.O33, Occupational diseases and hazards in pregnancy
For general toxicology in specific industries, see RC965.A+
For industrial hygiene, see HD7260+
For toxicology of industries limited to specific poisons, see RA1230+
For individual occupational diseases, see the disease, e. g. RC774, Silicosis
964 General works
965.A-Z By industry or occupation, A-Z
965.A5 Agriculture
965.A56 Aluminum industry
965.A6 Animal technicians
Including animal health technicians and laboratory animal technicians
965.A7 Asbestos industry
965.A8 Atomic power industry
965.A9 Automobile mechanics
965.B5 Beryllium industry
965.B75 Building cleaning
965.B8 Building materials industry
965.C34 Candy industry
965.C4 Cement and concrete industries
965.C43 Ceramic industries
Including the pottery industry
965.C44 Chemical industries
965.C444 Chimney sweeps
965.C45 Chromate industry
965.C57 Clay industries
965.C58 Clothing industry
965.C6 Coal gasification industry
965.C64 Cold storage industry

Special situations and conditions
Industrial medicine
Occupational diseases
By industry or occupation, A-Z -- Continued

965.C7 Compressed air work
Concrete industry, see RC965.C4
Construction, Underground, see RC965.U53
965.C75 Construction industry
965.C76 Copper industry
965.C77 Cotton industry
965.D3 Dairying
965.E4 Electric industries
965.E43 Electronic industries
965.E45 Electroplating industry
965.E48 Emergency medical technicians
965.E53 Energy industries
Entertainers, see RC965.P46
965.F39 Feed mills
965.F4 Fertilizer industry
Fiber glass industry, see RC965.G55
965.F48 Firemen
965.F5 Fisheries
965.F54 Flour mills
965.F58 Food industry
965.F59 Forestry
965.F6 Founding
965.G3 Gas industry
Gasification, see RC965.C6
965.G55 Glass fiber industry
965.H54 Highway transport workers
Laboratory animal technicians, see RC965.A6
965.L4 Leather industry
965.L5 Linoleum industry
Logging, see RC965.F59
965.L6 Longshoremen
Lumbering, see RC965.F59
965.M27 Machinery operators
965.M3 Machinery repair
965.M35 Man-made fibers industry
965.M36 Marine mechanics
965.M38 Meat industry
965.M39 Medical personnel
965.M4 Metal industries
Mining
965.M48 General works
965.M5 Coal mining
965.M64 Potash mining
965.M65 Manganese mining
965.N6 Nonferrous metal industries
965.O3 Office work
965.P3 Painting
965.P33 Palm oil industry
965.P35 Paper industry

Special situations and conditions
Industrial medicine
Occupational diseases
By industry or occupation, A-Z -- Continued
965.P4 Peat industry
965.P46 Performing arts. Entertainers
965.P48 Petroleum industries
965.P65 Plantation workers
965.P7 Plastics industries
965.P75 Police
Pottery industry, see RC965.C43
965.P8 Printing industry
965.P85 Pumice industry
965.R25 Radiation industry
965.R3 Railroads
965.R37 Rayon industry
Research animal technicians, see RC965.A6
965.R63 Road construction industry
965.R64 Robotics
965.R8 Rubber industry
965.S4 Shipbuilding industry
965.S45 Shoe industry
965.S5 Silica industry
965.S65 Solvents industry
965.S8 Steel industry
965.T3 Telephone workers
965.T4 Textile industry
965.T54 Theaters
Transportation industry, see RC1030+
965.U53 Underground construction
965.U7 Uranium industry
965.V53 Video display terminal operators
965.W4 Welding
965.W58 Wood-using industries
965.W6 Woodworking industries
965.Z5 Zinc industry
966 Industrial nursing
Industrial ophthalmology, see RE825
967 Industrial hygiene
Including morbidity studies in industry
Cf. HD7260+, Administrative and statistical aspects of industrial hygiene
Industrial psychology, see HF5548.7+
Psychological aspects of work and fatigue, see BF481, T59.72
967.5 Industrial psychiatry
Cf. RC552.O3, Occupational neuroses
Cf. RC969.P8, Psychiatric services
Medical departments
968 General works
969.A-Z Special services, A-Z
969.D4 Dental services
969.E54 Emergency medical services

Special situations and conditions
Industrial medicine
Medical departments
Special services, A-Z -- Continued
969.H43 Health promotion services
969.P8 Psychiatric services
Cf. RC967.5, Industrial psychiatry
Forensic aspects of occupational diseases and injuries, see RA1055.4
Military medicine
Cf. RD151+, Military surgery
Cf. UH201+, Military science
970 Periodicals. Societies. Serials
971 General works
Naval medicine
Including merchant marine
Cf. RD151+, Naval surgery
Cf. VG20+, Naval science
981 Periodicals. Societies. Serials
986 General works
Submarine medicine
Cf. QP82+, Influence of environment
Cf. RC88, Drowning
1000 Periodicals. Societies. Serials
1005 General works
1015 Underwater physiology
1020 Saturation diving
Transportation medicine
Cf. RA615+, Public health aspects of transportation
1030 Periodicals. Societies. Serials
1032 General works
1035.A-Z Special topics, A-Z
1035.I55 Inland water transportation
Automotive medicine
Cf. HE5613.5+, Traffic accidents
Cf. RD96.6, Crash injuries
Cf. TL152.3+, Automobile drivers
Cf. TL250, Human engineering
For medical examination of drivers, see TL152.35
1040 Periodicals. Societies. Serials
1042 General works
1045.A-Z Special topics, A-Z
1045.C35 Cardiovascular diseases
1045.C4 Chronic diseases
1045.D7 Drugs
Cf. HE5620.D65+, Drugged driving
1045.F37 Fatigue
1045.P78 Psychological aspects
1045.V5 Vision

Special situations and conditions -- Continued
Aviation medicine
Class here works on aviation and space medicine combined
Cf. TL555, Medical examinations for aviators
1050 Periodicals. Societies. Serials
1050.5 Congresses
1051 Dictionaries and encyclopedias
1052 History
1054.A-Z By region or country, A-Z
1058 Research. Experimentation
1062 General works
1063 General special
1067 Addresses, essays, lectures
Aviation physiology
1075 General works
1076.A-Z Special aspects, A-Z
1076.A26 Acceleration
1076.J48 Jet lag
1077 Aviation hygiene
Cf. RA615.2, Sanitary and public health aspects
1085 Aviation psychology
1090 Aviation psychiatry
1095 Aviation ophthalmology
1097 Aviation nursing
Space medicine
Cf. QH327+, Space biology (Animals and plants)
Cf. TL856, Medical examinations for astronauts
Cf. TL943, Planetary quarantine
1120 Periodicals. Societies. Serials
1121 Congresses
1123 Dictionaries and encyclopedias
1125 History
1128.A-Z By region or country, A-Z
1130 Research. Experimentation
1132 Bioinstrumentation
1135 General works
1137 General special
1145 Addresses, essays, lectures
Space physiology
1150 General works
1151.A-Z Special aspects, A-Z
1151.A26 Acceleration
1151.B54 Biological rhythms
1151.C37 Cardiovascular system
1151.C45 Central nervous system
1151.C46 Centrifugal force
1151.E83 Exercise
1151.G37 Gastrointestinal system
1151.I45 Immune system
1151.R33 Radiation
1151.R47 Respiration

Special situations and conditions
Space medicine
Space physiology
Special aspects, A-Z -- Continued
1151.T55 Time perception
1151.V57 Visual perception
1151.W44 Weightlessness
1152 Space hygiene
1160 Space psychology
Sports medicine
Cf. GV344, Safety measures
Cf. GV346, Safety measures
Cf. RC451.4.A83, Psychiatry
Cf. RD97, Sports injuries
Cf. RE827, Sports ophthalmology
For first aid for special sports, see RC88.9.A+
1200 Periodicals. Societies. Serials
1201 Congresses
1206 Dictionaries and encyclopedias
1210 General works
1211 Handbooks, manuals, etc.
1215 Addresses, essays, lectures
1218.A-Z By age group, class, etc., A-Z
1218.A33 Aged
1218.C45 Children
1218.H54 High school athletes
1218.M53 Middle aged persons
1218.W65 Women
Cf. RG207, Sports gynecology
1220.A-Z Medical and physiological aspects of special activities. By activity, A-Z
For first aid for special sports and activities, see RC88.9.A+
1220.A65 Aquatic sports
1220.B27 Ballet dancing
1220.B3 Baseball
1220.B33 Basketball
1220.B5 Boating
1220.B6 Boxing
1220.B8 Bullfighting
1220.C77 Cross-country skiing
1220.C8 Cycling
1220.D35 Dancing
Dancing, Ballet, see RC1220.B27
1220.D5 Diving
Cf. RC1000+, Underwater diving
1220.E53 Endurance sports
1220.F6 Football
1220.G64 Golf
1220.G95 Gymnastics
Hatha yoga, see RC1220.Y64
1220.H67 Horsemanship
1220.J38 Javelin throwing

Special situations and conditions
Sports medicine
Medical and physiological aspects of special activities. By activity, A-Z -- Continued

Jogging, see RC1220.R8
1220.J83 Judo
1220.K3 Karate
1220.M35 Marathon running
1220.M36 Martial arts
1220.M57 Motorsports
1220.M6 Mountaineering
1220.P37 Parachuting
1220.R24 Racket games
1220.R67 Rowing
1220.R75 Rugby
1220.R8 Running. Jogging
Running, Marathon, see RC1220.M35
1220.S47 Shooting
1220.S5 Skiing
Skiing, Cross-country, see RC1220.C77
1220.S53 Sled dog racing
1220.S57 Soccer
1220.S6 Speleology
1220.S76 Sumo
1220.S77 Surfing
1220.S8 Swimming
1220.T4 Tennis
1220.T73 Track and field
1220.T75 Trampolining
1220.T78 Triple jump
1220.W44 Weight lifting
1220.W55 Winter sports
1220.W73 Wrestling
1220.Y64 Yoga, Hatha
1225 Medical examination of athletes
1226 Massage
1230 Doping in sports
Physiology of sports
For individual sports, see RC1220.A+
1235 General works
1236.A-Z Special organs or systems, A-Z
1236.E38 Eye
1236.H43 Heart
1236.I55 Immune system
1236.L43 Leg
1236.N47 Nervous system
1238 Effect of environmental factors on athletic performance
1245 Effect of alcohol on athletic performance

Surgery
For psychic surgery, see RZ403.P75
1 Periodicals. Societies. Serials
Hospitals, clinics, etc , see RA960+
9 Yearbooks
9.2 Congresses
Directories of surgeons
10.A1 General
10.A3-Z By region or country, A-Z
Collected works (nonserial)
11 Several authors
14 Individual authors
16 Nomenclature. Terminology. Abbreviations
Cf. RB115, Pathology
17 Dictionaries and encyclopedias
17.3 Communication in surgery
History
19 General works
21 General special
22 Primitive
Cf. GN477.5+, Ethnology
23 Ancient
25 Medieval
27 Modern
27.3.A-Z By region or country, A-Z
Biography
For anesthetists, see RD80.6+
For neurosurgeons, see RD592.8+
For orthopedists, see RD727+
27.34 Collective
27.35.A-Z Individual, A-Z
Practice of surgery. Surgical economics
Including business methods and employment surveys
27.4 General works
By region or country
United States
27.42 General works
27.43.A-Z By region or state, A-Z
27.44.A-Z Other regions or countries, A-Z
27.5 Surgery as a profession
27.7 Surgical ethics
27.8 Unnecessary surgery
27.85 Surgical errors
Study and teaching
28.A1 General and United States
28.A3-Z Other regions or countries, A-Z
28.5.A-Z Laboratories, institutes, etc.
28.5.A1 General works
28.5.A5-Z Individual. By city, A-Z
Museums and exhibitions, see R871+
Research. Experimentation
29 General works
29.5.A-Z By laboratory animal, A-Z

Research. Experimentation
By laboratory animal, A-Z -- Continued
29.5.R33 Rabbits
29.5.S54 Sheep
29.5.S94 Swine
29.7 Computer applications. Data processing
Including computer simulation
General works
30 Through 1900
31 1901-
31.3 Popular works
31.5 General special
31.7 Psychological aspects
Operative surgery. Technique of surgical operations
32 General works
32.3 Assisting at operations. Operating room nursing, technicians, etc. Surgical technology
32.5 Preliminary preparation of the patient and operating room
32.7 Positioning in surgery and anesthesia
33 Ligature of arteries, etc.
33.3 Hemorrhage and hemostasis
Cf. RD33.57, Therapeutic embolization
Cf. RJ271, Newborn infants
Cf. RM171+, Blood transfusion
Computer simulation, see RD29.7
33.4 Cryosurgery
33.5 Electrosurgery. Galvanosurgery
33.53 Endoscopic surgery. Surgical endoscopy
Cf. RD73.L3, Laser endoscopy
Interventional radiology
33.55 General works
33.56 Magnetic resonance imaging
33.57 Therapeutic embolization
33.6 Microsurgery
Including experimental microsurgery
Cf. RD655, Mohs surgery
33.65 Reoperation
33.7 Ultrasonics in surgery
33.9 Other
34 Clinical cases
35 Examination. Diagnosis
For specific methods, see RC78+
37 Handbooks, manuals, etc.
37.2 Problems, exercises, examinations
37.3 Outlines, syllabi, etc.
39 Addresses, essays, lectures
41 Atlases. Pictorial works
Surgical illustration, see R836.A1+
Surgical anatomy, see QM531+
Surgical bacteriology, see QR46
Surgical nutrition, see RD52.N88, RD52.P37
Surgical pathology, see RD57

| | |
|---|---|
| 49 | Surgical therapeutics. Preoperative, intraoperative, and postoperative care |
| 50 | Preoperative care |
| 50.5 | Intraoperative care and monitoring |
| | For specific technique or aspects, see RD52.A+ |
| 51 | Postoperative care. Postoperative period. Recovery room |
| 51.3 | Post anesthesia nursing |
| 51.5 | Surgical intensive care |
| 52.A-Z | Special aspects, A-Z |
| 52.A58 | Anticoagulants |
| 52.B74 | Breathing exercises. Respiratory care |
| | Electrolyte therapy, see RD52.F59 |
| 52.E85 | Evoked potential monitoring |
| 52.F59 | Fluid therapy. Electrolyte therapy |
| 52.G59 | Glucocorticoid therapy |
| 52.M48 | Metabolic care |
| 52.N48 | Neurophysiologic monitoring |
| 52.N88 | Nutritional care. Surgical nutrition |
| 52.P37 | Parenteral feeding |
| 52.P59 | Physical therapy |
| | Cf. RD792+, Orthopedics |
| | Respiratory care, see RD52.B74 |
| 52.R47 | Respiratory gas monitoring |
| | Surgical nutrition, see RD52.N88 |
| 52.T73 | Transesophageal echocardiography |
| | Surgical care in special medical conditions, emergencies, and the at-risk patient |
| 54 | General works |
| 54.3.A-Z | Special conditions, A-Z |
| | AIDS patients, see RD54.3.H58 |
| 54.3.H58 | HIV patients. AIDS patients |
| 54.3.P34 | Pacemaker patients |
| 57 | Surgical pathology |
| 58 | Reparative processes after operations (Physiological) |
| 59 | Surgical shock. Traumatic shock |
| 63 | Operating rooms and theaters. Instruments, apparatus, and appliances |
| | Cf. R857.C6, Clean air systems |
| | Instruments, apparatus, and appliances |
| | Cf. RD78.8, Anesthesiology |
| | Cf. RD130, Prosthesis |
| | Cf. RD132, Artificial implants |
| | Cf. RD755+, Orthopedics |
| 71 | General works |
| 73.A-Z | Special, A-Z |
| 73.A3 | Adhesives |
| 73.A5 | Air-cushions |
| 73.B57 | Bone saws |
| 73.B6 | Bougies |
| 73.E8 | Extension windlass |
| 73.F52 | Fibrin tissue adhesive |
| 73.F7 | Forceps |

| | |
|---|---|
| | Instruments, apparatus, and appliances |
| | Special, A-Z -- Continued |
| 73.G5 | Gloves |
| 73.G67 | Gowns |
| 73.L3 | Lasers. Laser surgery |
| | Including laser endoscopy |
| 73.L5 | Ligatures |
| 73.N38 | Needle-holders |
| 73.N4 | Needles |
| 73.S7 | Speculum |
| 73.S75 | Staplers |
| 73.S78 | Surgical adjusters |
| 73.S8 | Suture materials |
| 73.S9 | Syringes |
| 73.T6 | Tourniquets |
| 73.T7 | Trochars |
| 73.T75 | Trusses |
| 76 | Catalogs. Trade directories |
| | Anesthesiology |
| | Cf. RA975.5.A5, Anesthesia services |
| | Cf. RD51.3, Post anesthesia nursing |
| | Cf. RD52.R47, Respiratory gas monitoring |
| | Cf. RD93.93, Traumatology |
| | Cf. RD139, Anesthesia in childhood |
| | Cf. RD145, Anesthesia in old age |
| | Cf. RD751, Orthopedics |
| | Cf. RE82+, Ophthalmology |
| | Cf. RF52, Otolaryngology |
| | Cf. RG732+, Obstetrics |
| | Cf. RK510+, Dentistry |
| 78.3 | Periodicals. Societies. Serials |
| 78.4 | Congresses |
| 78.5 | Dictionaries and encyclopedias |
| | Directories of anesthetists |
| 78.6 | General works |
| 78.62.A-Z | By region or country, A-Z |
| 78.8 | Instruments, apparatus, and appliances |
| | History |
| 79 | General works |
| 80.A-Z | Special, A-Z |
| 80.J3 | Claims of Jackson |
| 80.L9 | Claims of Long |
| 80.M9 | Claims of Morton |
| 80.W5 | Claims of Wells |
| | By region or country |
| 80.3 | United States |
| 80.5.A-Z | Other regions or countries, A-Z |
| | Biography |
| 80.6 | Collective |
| 80.62.A-Z | Individual, A-Z |
| 80.65 | Practice of anesthesiology |
| | Including business methods and employment surveys |
| 80.7 | Study and teaching |

| | |
|---|---|
| | Anesthesiology -- Continued |
| 80.9 | Research. Experimentation |
| 80.95 | Computer applications. Data processing |
| 81 | General works |
| 82 | General special |
| 82.2 | Handbooks, manuals, etc. |
| 82.3 | Problems, handbooks, examinations |
| 82.4 | Outlines, syllabi, etc. |
| 82.45 | Clinical cases |
| | Accidents and complications |
| | Cf. RA1270.A53, Toxicology |
| 82.5 | General works |
| 82.7.A-Z | Special complications, A-Z |
| 82.7.A48 | Anaphylaxis |
| 82.7.A6 | Apnea |
| 82.7.A7 | Arrhythmia |
| 82.7.D4 | Death |
| 82.7.D78 | Drug interactions |
| 82.7.E53 | Endocrine complications |
| 82.7.M3 | Malignant hyperthermia |
| 82.7.S53 | Side effects of anesthetic drugs |
| 83.5 | Neuromuscular blocking agents used in conjunction with anesthesia |
| 84 | Conduction anesthesia |
| | Including local anesthesia and nerve block |
| 85.A-Z | Special methods, A-Z |
| 85.A25 | Acupuncture anesthesia |
| 85.A43 | Alfentanil |
| | Block anesthesia, see RD84 |
| | Conduction anesthesia, see RD84 |
| 85.C64 | Conscious sedation |
| 85.E57 | Electric anesthesia |
| 85.E6 | Endotracheal anesthesia |
| 85.H9 | Hypnosis |
| 85.I48 | Inhalation anesthesia |
| 85.I496 | Intraosseous anesthesia |
| 85.I6 | Intravenous anesthesia |
| | Local anesthesia, see RD84 |
| | Nerve block, see RD84 |
| 85.N4 | Neuroleptanesthesia |
| 85.P3 | Paravertebral block |
| 85.P4 | Peridural anesthesia |
| 85.S7 | Spinal anesthesia |
| 85.5 | Anesthetics |
| 86.A-Z | Special anesthetics and adjuvants, A-Z |
| 86.B85 | Buprenorphine |
| 86.C5 | Chloroform |
| 86.C6 | Cocaine |
| 86.C8 | Curare |
| 86.D47 | Diazepam |
| 86.D5 | Ditilin |
| 86.E2 | Earths |
| 86.E47 | EMLA. Eutectic mixture of local anesthetics |

Anesthesiology
Anesthetics
Special anesthetics and adjuvants, A-Z -- Continued

86.E5 Enflurane
86.E8 Ether
86.E95 Etomidate
Eutectic mixture of local anesthetics, see RD86.E47
86.F3 Falicaine
86.F45 Fentanyl
86.H3 Halothane
86.H6 Hostacain
86.I84 Isoflurane
86.K4 Ketamine
86.L52 Lidocaine
86.M3 Magnesium
86.M67 Morphine
86.N25 Nalbuphine
86.N3 Naphthalene
Narcotics, see RD86.O64
86.N7 Nitrous oxide
Cf. RK512.N55, Dentistry
(86.N8) Novocaine
see RD86.P68
86.O64 Opioids. Narcotics
86.P35 Penthrane
86.P68 Procaine
86.P7 Propanidid
86.P73 Propitocaine
86.S65 Sodium oxybate
86.T7 Trichloroethylene
86.T75 Trimecaine
86.T76 Tromethamine
86.V42 Vecuronium bromide
(86.X8) Xylocaine
see RD86.L52

Anesthesia in special medical conditions, emergencies, and the at-risk patient

87 General works
87.3.A-Z Special conditions, A-Z
87.3.C37 Cardiovascular diseases
87.3.E53 Endocrine diseases
87.3.G45 Genetic disorders
87.3.H43 Heart diseases
87.3.L58 Liver diseases
87.3.L85 Lung diseases
87.3.N47 Nervous system diseases
87.3.O23 Obesity
87.3.P73 Pregnancy
Cf. RG732+, Anesthesia in obstetrics
Pulmonary diseases, see RD87.3.L85
87.3.R35 Rare diseases
87.3.S53 Sickle cell anemia

Anesthesiology
Anesthesia in special medical conditions, emergencies, and the at-risk patient
Special conditions, A-Z -- Continued
87.3.T7 Transplantation of organs, tissues, etc.
87.3.U76 Urologic diseases
Asepsis and antisepsis. Sterilization (Operative)
91 General works
91.5.A-Z General antiseptics, A-Z
Cf. RM400, Therapeutics
91.5.P6 Povidone-iodine
Emergency surgery. Wounds and injuries
Cf. RA645.T73, Public health
Cf. RA975.5.T83, Trauma centers
For medico-legal aspects of wounds and injuries, see RA1071+
For wounds and injuries of individual regions, organs, etc., see RD520+, RE831+, RF195, RF437, RF547
92 Periodicals. Societies. Serials
92.2 Congresses
93 General works
93.3 Atlases
93.5.A-Z By age group, class, etc., A-Z
93.5.A35 Aged
93.5.C4 Children
Cf. RA1122.5, Battered child syndrome
Newborn infants. Neonatology, see RJ325
Pregnant women, see RG580.W68
93.6.A-Z By ethnic group, A-Z
93.6.I53 Indians
93.7 Examination. Diagnosis
By region or country
93.8 United States
93.9.A-Z Other regions or countries, A-Z
93.93 Anesthesia and analgesia
93.95 Trauma nursing
94 Wound healing
95 Care of aseptic and infected wounds
Wounds by type or causative agent
Cf. RD156, War wounds
96 Operative wounds
(96.1) Stab wounds
see RD96.35
96.15 Nonpenetrating wounds. Blunt trauma
Penetrating wounds
96.18 General works
96.2 Wounds from animal and insect bites
96.3 Gunshot wounds
96.35 Stab wounds. Cutting wounds. Lacerations
Burns and scalds
96.4 General works
96.45 Chemical burns

Emergency surgery. Wounds and injuries
Wounds by type or causative agent
Burns and scalds -- Continued
96.5 Electrical burns
Cf. RC87.5, Electric shock
96.55 Radiation burns
96.58 Crush syndrome
Fractures, see RD101
96.6 Crash injuries
Cf. RD533.5, Whiplash injuries
96.7 Blast injuries
97 Sports injuries
97.5 Industrial injuries
97.6 Overuse injuries
97.8.A-Z Other injuries, A-Z
97.8.B43 Bed injuries
97.8.S53 Skateboard injuries
97.8.S74 Step stool injuries
Surgical complications
98 General works
98.2 Wound disruption. Delayed healing
98.3 Postoperative wound infections
98.4 Postoperative pain
Surgical nursing
Cf. RD32.3, Operating room nursing
Cf. RD51.3, Post anesthesia nursing
Cf. RD93.95, Trauma nursing
Cf. RD110.5, Ambulatory surgical nursing
Cf. RD596, Neurosurgical nursing
Cf. RD753, Orthopedic nursing
Cf. RE88, Ophthalmic nursing
Cf. RF52.5, Otolaryngological nursing
Cf. RG105, Gynecologic nursing
Cf. RG951, Obstetric nursing
For nursing of other types of surgery, by type of surgery, see RD520+
99.A1 Periodicals. Societies. Serials
99.A2 Congresses
99.A3-Z General works
99.24 Handbooks, manuals, etc.
99.25 Problems, exercises, examinations
99.3 Atlases. Pictorial works
99.32 Surgical nursing as a profession
99.35 Study and teaching
100 Transportation of the injured
Cf. UH500+, Military medical service
101 Fractures (General)
For fractures of individual bones or regions or the body, see RD521+
102 Examination. Diagnosis
103.A-Z Special therapies, A-Z
103.B65 Bone wiring
103.E4 Electric stimulation

Fractures (General)
Special therapies, A-Z -- Continued
103.E88 External skeletal fixation
103.F58 Fixation (General)
103.I5 Internal fixation
103.I53 Intramedullary fixation. Intramedullary rods
103.U47 Ultrasonic therapy
104.A-Z Special types of fractures, A-Z
104.A95 Avulsion fractures
104.S77 Stress fractures
106 Dislocations and sprains (General)
For individual dislocations and sprains, see RD520+
108 Foreign bodies
For foreign bodies in individual organs, see RD520+
Outpatient surgery. Ambulatory surgery
Cf. RD137.7, Ambulatory surgery in childhood
110 General works
110.5 Ambulatory surgical nursing
Minor surgery
111 General works
Bandaging. Dressings
113 General works
113.4.A-Z Special, A-Z
113.4.O22 Occlusive dressings
113.7 Splints
114 Plaster casts, etc.
Plastic surgery. Reparative surgery
Cf. RA623.5, Post-mortem plastic surgery
Cf. RE87, Ophthalmology
Cf. RF127, Otology
Cf. RG104.5, Gynecology
For works on reparative or general plastic surgery of particular regions of the body, see RD520+
118.A1 Periodicals. Societies. Serials
118.A2 Congresses
118.A3-Z General works
118.3 Clinical cases
118.5 Psychological aspects
118.7 Complications and unfavorable results
118.8 Endoscopic surgery
Cosmetic surgery
119 General works
119.5.A-Z Special, A-Z
119.5.A24 Abdomen
Blepharoplasty, see RD119.5.E94
119.5.B82 Body piercing
119.5.B83 Body shaping
119.5.C45 Chin. Genioplasty
119.5.E94 Eyelids. Blepharoplasty
119.5.F33 Face. Face lift
Genioplasty, see RD119.5.C45
119.5.L55 Liposuction. Liposculpture
Including ultrasound-assisted liposuction

| | |
|---|---|
| | Plastic surgery. Reparative surgery |
| | Cosmetic surgery |
| | Special, A-Z -- Continued |
| 119.5.N67 | Nose. Rhinoplasty |
| | Rhinoplasty, see RD119.5.N67 |
| | Suction lipectomy, see RD119.5.L55 |
| 119.5.T57 | Tissue expansion |
| | Ultrasound-assisted liposuction, see RD119.5.L55 |
| 120 | Use of plastics and paraffin prosthesis |
| 120.5 | Other materials |
| | Transplantation of organs, tissues, etc. |
| | Cf. QP89, Physiology |
| | Cf. RD87.3.T7, Anesthesia |
| 120.6 | History |
| 120.63.A-Z | By region or country, A-Z |
| 120.7 | General works |
| 120.75 | Popular works |
| 120.76 | Juvenile works |
| 120.77.A-Z | By age group, class, etc., A-Z |
| 120.77.C45 | Children |
| 120.78 | Complications of transplantation |
| 120.8 | Surgical flaps |
| 120.9 | Fetal tissues |
| | Skin |
| 121 | General works |
| 121.5 | Hair |
| | Bone |
| 123 | General works |
| 123.5 | Bone marrow |
| | Including Graft versus host disease |
| 124 | Nerve |
| 124.5 | Omentum |
| 125 | Muscles. Myoblasts |
| 126 | Organs |
| | For transplantation of particular organs, see RD539 |
| | Tissue banks. Organ banks |
| | Cf. RE89, Eye banks |
| | Cf. RM172, Blood banks |
| 127 | General works |
| 127.3 | Brain banks |
| 128 | Musculoskeletal banks. Bone banks |
| 128.5 | Skin banks |
| 129 | Techniques of preservation of organs, tissues, etc. |
| 129.5 | Donation of organs, tissues, etc. |
| | Including procurement and allocation |
| | History, see RD120.6+ |
| 129.8 | Nursing |

130 Prosthesis. Artificial organs
Cf. RD756+, Artificial limbs and braces
Cf. RD756.22, Artificial hands
Cf. RE986+, Artificial eyes and other prostheses
Cf. RK641+, Prosthetic dentistry
For prosthesis of other particular parts and organs, see RD520+
132 Artificial implants and implant materials
Cf. RD120, Plastic surgery
Cf. RD755.5+, Orthopedic implants
Cf. RE988, Intraocular
Cf. RF305, Cochlear implants
Cf. RK667.I45, Implant dentures
Surgery in childhood
Cf. RD590, Circumcision
Cf. RD732.3.C48, Orthopedics
Cf. RK529.5.C45, Oral surgery
137.A1 Periodicals. Societies. Serials
137.A2 Congresses
137.A3-Z General works
137.2 Popular works
137.3 Atlases. Pictorial works
137.5 Surgery in infancy. Neonatal surgery
Cf. RD732.3.I53, Orthopedia
137.7 Ambulatory surgery
139 Anesthesia in childhood
142 Surgery in adolescence
144 Surgery in pregnancy
145 Surgery in old age
Including anesthesia
Cf. RD732.3.A44, Orthopedics
Surgery in individual diseases, see RD520+
Military and naval surgery
151 General works
153 General special
156 War wounds
By region or country
Cf. UH201+, Military medical service
United States
200 General works
201 General special
202 Revolution, 1775-1783
203 War of 1812
204 Mexican War, 1846-1848
205 Civil War and period from 1865 to 1898
206 Spanish-American War, 1898
207 World War I, 1914-1918
209 World War II, 1939-1945
211 Other wars. By date
214.A-Z By region or state, A-Z
216 Canada
221 Mexico
Central America

| | |
|---|---|
| | Military and naval surgery |
| | By region or country |
| | Central America -- Continued |
| 224 | General works |
| 225.A-Z | By region or country, A-Z |
| | West Indies |
| 231 | General works |
| 232.A-Z | By island or group of islands, A-Z |
| | South America |
| 235 | General works |
| 236 | Argentina |
| 239 | Bolivia |
| 241 | Brazil |
| 244 | Chile |
| 247 | Colombia |
| 251 | Ecuador |
| 254 | Guianas |
| 257 | Paraguay |
| 261 | Peru |
| 264 | Uruguay |
| 267 | Venezuela |
| | Europe |
| 268 | General works |
| 269 | World War I, 1918-1918 |
| 270 | World War II, 1939-1945 |
| 271 | Other wars. By date |
| | Great Britain |
| 273 | General works |
| 274 | Napoleonic Wars, 1789-1815 |
| 275 | War of 1812 |
| 277 | Crimean War, 1853-1856 |
| 279 | Sepoy Mutiny, 1857-1858 |
| 281 | First Boer War, 1880-1881 |
| 283 | Egypt and Sudan campaigns, 1882-1900 |
| 285 | Second Boer War, 1899-1902 |
| 287 | World War I, 1914-1918 |
| 288 | World War II, 1394-1458 |
| 289 | Other wars. By date |
| 291 | Austria |
| 301 | Belgium |
| 311 | Denmark |
| | France |
| 321 | General works |
| 323 | Napoleonic Wars, 1789-1815 |
| 325 | Franco-German War, 1870-1871 |
| 327 | World War I, 1914-1918 |
| 329 | World War II, 1939-1945 |
| 330 | Other wars. By date |
| | Germany |
| 331 | General works |
| 335 | World War I, 1914-1918 |
| 337 | World War II, 1939-1945 |
| 339 | Other wars. By date |

Military and naval surgery
By region or country
Europe -- Continued
341 Greece
351 Netherlands
Italy
361 General works
367 Austrian Campaign, 1859
368 Austrian Campaign, 1866
369 World War II, 1939-1945
370 Other wars. By date
371 Norway
381 Portugal
391 Soviet Union
Spain
401 General works
405 Cuban Revolution, 1895-1898
406 Spanish-American War, 1898
408 Other wars. By date
411 Sweden
421 Switzerland
Turkey and the Balkan States
431 General works
435 Balkan War, 1912-1913
438 Other wars. By date
441.A-Z Other European regions or countries, A-Z
441.C9 Czechoslovakia
Asia
445 General works
451 China
460 Pakistan
461 India
462 Sri Lanka
463 Burma
Japan
465 General works
471 War with China, 1894-1895
473 Russo-Japanese War, 1904-1905
474 World War II, 1939-1945
475 Other wars. By date
476.A-Z Other Asian regions or countries, A-Z
476.K6 Korea
Turkey, see RD431+
Africa
481 General works
486 Egypt
489.A-Z Other African regions or countries, A-Z
493 Australia
493.5 New Zealand
498.A-Z Pacific islands, A-Z

Surgery by region, system, or organ
For cosmetic surgery by region of the body, see RD119.5.A+
For the locomotor system (General), see RD680+
For tumor and cancer surgery by region, system, or organ, see RD655
520 Skin and subcutaneous tissue
Cf. RD528, Scalp
Cf. RL120.L37, Laser surgery
Head and neck
For ear, nose, and throat surgery, see RF1+
For eye surgery, see RE80+
For oral surgery, see RK529+
521 General works
523 Face surgery
Cf. RD119.5.F33, Face lift
524 Lips
525 Palate
526 Jaws
526.5 Chin
527.A-Z Other, A-Z
527.E94 Eye sockets
527.P3 Parotid gland
527.S3 Salivary glands
528 Scalp
529 Skull
Cf. RD594+, Brain surgery
531 Neck
For the pharynx and tonsils, see RF484+
For the trachea, larynx, vocal cords, and epiglottis, see RF516+
Spine
Cf. RD592.5+, Neurosurgery
Cf. RD768+, Deformities of the spine
533 General works
533.5 Whiplash injuries
Chest. Thoracic surgery
Biography
535.7 Collective
535.8.A-Z Individual, A-Z
536 General works
Heart, see RD598+
539 Lungs
539.5 Esophagus
539.8 Breast
Including augmentation and reduction mammaplasty, breast implants
Abdomen. Gastrointestinal surgery
540 General works
540.2 Abdominal wall
540.3 Abdominal aorta
Stomach. Gastrectomy
Including gastroduodenal surgery

Surgery by region, system, or organ
Abdomen. Gastrointestinal surgery
Stomach. Gastrectomy -- Continued
540.5 General works
Peptic ulcer surgery
540.53 General works
540.57 Vagotomy
Intestines
540.6 General works
Small intestine
540.7 General works
Duodenum
Cf. RD540.5+, Gastroduodenal surgery
540.75 General works
Duodenal ulcer, see RD540.53+
Jejunum
540.8 General works
540.85 Jejunoileal bypass
540.9 Ileum. Ileostomy
Large intestine
541 General works
542 Appendectomy. Appendicitis
543.A-Z Other, A-Z
543.C4 Cecostomy
543.C57 Colectomy
543.C6 Colostomy
544 Lower sigmoid, rectum, and anal region
Including proctocolectomy
546 Liver, gallbladder, bile ducts, and pancreas
Cf. RD599.5.I84, Islands of Langerhans
547 Gallstones. Biliary calculi
547.5 Spleen
548 Peritoneum
Hernia, see RD621+
Pelvis. Hip
Cf. RD772, Congenital dislocation, etc.
Cf. RG104+, Gynecologic surgery
549 General works
549.5 Sacroiliac joint
550 Groin
Extremities
551 General works
553 Amputations and excisions
For amputation of particular extremities, see RD557+
For biography of amputees, see RD796.A2+
Upper extremities
557 General works
557.5 Shoulder. Shoulder joint
558 Elbow
559 Hand. Wrist
Lower extremities
560 General works

Surgery by region, system, or organ
Extremities
Lower extremities -- Continued
561 Knee. Knee ligaments
562 Ankle
563 Foot. Podiatry. Chiropody
Including care of feet
Genitourinary organs. Urological surgery
Including male genitourinary organs
For female genitourinary and generative organs, see RG104+
571 General works
572 Endourology. Endoscopic surgery of genitourinary organs
Cf. RC901.7.E53, Endoscopes
Cf. RC920, Cystoscopy
574 Urolithiasis. Urinary calculi
575 Kidneys
578 Ureters
Bladder
580 General works
581 Lithotomy. Lithotripsy
583 Urethra
Generative organs
584 General works
Sterilization (Birth control). Sterilization reversal
For sterilization of women, see RG138
585 General works
585.5 Vasectomy
Male generative organs
586 General works
587 Prostate
Penis
589 General works
590 Foreskin. Circumcision. Phimosis
591 Phalloplasty
592 Testes
Nervous system. Neurosurgery
592.5 Directories
Biography
592.8 Collective
592.9.A-Z Individual, A-Z
593 General works
593.5 Computer-assisted neurosurgery
Brain
Including the effects of surgery
594 General works
594.12 Intracerebral transplantation
594.15 Radiosurgery
594.2 Blood vessels. Neurovascular surgery
Including cerebrovascular surgery
594.3 Spinal cord

Surgery by region, system, or organ
Nervous system. Neurosurgery -- Continued
595 Nerves
595.5 Pain surgery. Surgical analgesia
596 Neurosurgical nursing
Cardiovascular system
597 General works
Heart
Including coronary arteries
598 General works
Cardiac implants and assist devices and techniques
598.3 General works
598.35.A-Z Special devices or techniques, A-Z
598.35.A53 Angioplasty
598.35.A77 Artificial circulation
598.35.A78 Artificial heart
Batista technique, see RD598.35.P27
598.35.C35 Cardiac catheterization
598.35.C37 Cardiomyoplasty
598.35.C39 Catheter ablation
598.35.C67 Coronary artery bypass
598.35.H42 Heart valve prosthesis
598.35.I53 Induced cardiac arrest
598.35.I55 Interventional radiology
598.35.L37 Laser surgery
Cf. RD598.35.T67, Transmyocardial laser revascularization
598.35.M42 Mechanical heart
598.35.M95 Myocardial revascularization
Cf. RD598.35.T67, Transmyocardial laser revascularization
Myocardioplasty, see RD598.35.C37
598.35.P27 Partial left ventriculectomy. Batista technique
598.35.P37 Percutaneous balloon valvuloplasty
598.35.R45 Reoperation
598.35.S73 Stents
598.35.T67 Transmyocardial laser revascularization
598.35.T7 Transplantation
Transplanted skeletal muscle for cardiac assist, see RD598.35.C37
Blood vessels. Vascular surgery
Including visceral vascular surgery
For vascular surgery by region of the body, see RD520+
598.5 General works
598.55 Vascular grafts. Blood vessel prosthesis
Including endothelial seeding
Arteries
Cf. RD598+, Coronary arteries
598.6 General works
598.65 Endarterectomy. Atherectomy
598.67 Interventional radiology

Surgery by region, system, or organ
Cardiovascular system
Blood vessels. Vascular surgery -- Continued
598.7 Veins
598.8 Lymphatic system
Cf. RD547.5, Spleen
Endocrine glands
599 General works
599.5.A-Z Special glands, A-Z
599.5.A37 Adrenal glands
599.5.I84 Islands of Langerhans
599.5.P37 Parathyroid gland
599.5.P58 Pituitary gland
599.5.T46 Thyroid gland
Surgical treatment of functional disorders
605 Metabolic disorders
Conditions which usually require surgery
For surgical pathology, see RD57
608 Exostosis
Hernia
621 General works
Mechanical applications
625 General works
626 Catalogs
628 Necrosis. Gangrene
Cf. RB133, Manifestations of disease
641 Suppuration. Abscesses
643 Fistulae. Fissures
645 Contractions
Cf. RD96.4+, Burns and scalds (Emergency surgery)
646 Calculi
Cf. RD547, Gallstones
Cf. RD574, Urinary calculi
647.A-Z Other, A-Z
647.A3 Adhesions
Neoplasms. Tumors. Oncology
Cf. RC254+, Nonsurgical treatment
651 General works
652 Intraoperative radiotherapy
653 Endocrine glands
654 Connective tissues
655 Skin
Including Mohs surgery
Cf. RD677, Dermoid cysts
Head and neck
Including parotid gland
For larynx, see RF516+
661 General works
661.5 Face
662 Mouth. Tongue. Palate
662.5 Skull. Skull base
663 Brain. Nervous system

Neoplasms. Tumors. Oncology -- Continued
Chest
667 General works
667.3 Esophagus
667.5 Breast
Abdomen
668 General works
668.3 Stomach
668.5 Intestines
Cf. RD672, Rectum
669 Liver, gallbladder, bile ducts, and pancreas
669.5 Pelvis
670 Genitourinary organs
For female genitourinary organs, see RG104.6
672 Rectum
673 Spine and spinal cord
674 Extremities
675 Bone tumors
Cystic tumors
676 General works
677 Dermoid cysts
678 Retention cysts
Diseases of the locomotor system (Surgical treatment)
Cf. RC925+, Nonsurgical treatment
Cf. RD761+, Deformities
For extremities, see RD551+
For the pelvis and hip, see RD549+
For the spine, see RD533+
680 General works
684 Bones
Cf. RD675, Bone tumors
686 Joint (General)
For joints of specific parts of the body, see RD521+
688 Muscles. Tendons. Bursae
Orthopedia. Orthopedic surgery
701 Periodicals. Societies. Serials
Hospitals
705 General works
By region or country
United States
705.5.A1 General works
705.5.A2-Z By region or state, A-Z
*Under each state:*
*.x General works*
*.x2A-Z Local, A-Z*
706.A2-Z Other regions or countries, A-Z
*Under each country:*
*.x General works*
*.x2A-Z Local, A-Z*
711 Yearbooks
715 Congresses
721 Collections
723 Dictionaries and encyclopedias

Orthopedia. Orthopedic surgery -- Continued

724 Directories

History

725 General works

726.A-Z By region or country, A-Z

Biography

727 Collective

728.A-Z Individual, A-Z

731 General works

732 General special

732.3.A-Z By age group, class, etc., A-Z

732.3.A44 Aged

732.3.C48 Children

732.3.I53 Infants

732.3.M44 Mentally handicapped

732.5 Handbooks, manuals, etc.

732.6 Problems, exercises, examinations

732.7 Outlines, syllabi, etc.

732.8 Popular works

733 Addresses, essays, lectures

733.2 Atlases. Pictorial works

733.8 Clinical cases

Examination. Diagnosis

734 General works

734.3 Orthopedic disability evaluation

734.5.A-Z Special diagnostic methods, A-Z

734.5.L33 Laboratory technique

734.5.M33 Magnetic resonance imaging

734.5.M64 Moiré topography

734.5.P58 Physical orthopedic tests

734.5.R33 Radiography

734.5.R34 Radioisotope scanning

736.A-Z Special therapies, A-Z

736.B56 Blood transfusion

736.E88 Exercise therapy

736.E9 Extracorporeal shock wave therapy

736.H9 Hydrotherapy

736.M25 Manipulation

Cf. RZ201+, Chiropractics

Cf. RZ301+, Osteopathy

736.M3 Massage

736.O3 Occupational therapy

736.P47 Physical therapy

736.P5 Play therapy

736.R3 Radiotherapy

Shock waves, see RD736.E9

736.T7 Traction

750 Orthopedic emergencies

751 Anesthesia in orthopedics

752 Computer-assisted orthopedic surgery

753 Orthopedic nursing

Orthopedic instruments, apparatus, and appliances

755 General works

Orthopedia. Orthopedic surgery
Orthopedic instruments,
apparatus, and appliances -- Continued
Implants and implant materials
Cf. RD103.I5, Internal fracture fixation
Cf. RD103.I53, Intramedullary rods
Cf. RD686, Artificial joints

| | |
|---|---|
| 755.5 | General works |
| 755.6 | Bone substitutes |
| 755.65 | Hydroxyapatite coating |
| 755.7 | Intervertebral disk prostheses |
| | Artificial limbs |
| 756 | General works |
| | Arms. Upper extremities |
| 756.2 | General works |
| 756.22 | Hands |
| | Legs. Lower extremities |
| 756.4 | General works |
| 756.42 | Foot |
| 757.A-Z | Other apparatus, A-Z |
| 757.B73 | Braces |
| 757.C5 | Chairs |
| 757.K53 | Knee pads |
| 757.R4 | Reading devices |
| 757.S45 | Shoes |
| 757.S5 | Slings |
| 757.S67 | Splints |
| 757.W3 | Walkers |
| 757.W4 | Wheelchairs |
| | Deformities and disorders |
| | Cf. QM690+, Teratology |
| | Cf. RD118+, Plastic surgery |
| 761 | General works |
| 762 | Posture disorders |
| 763 | Head and neck |
| 766 | Trunk |
| | Spine. Back |
| 768 | General works |
| 771.A-Z | Special, A-Z |
| 771.A5 | Ankylosing spondylitis |
| 771.B217 | Backache |
| | Curvature of the spine, see RD771.S3 |
| 771.I58 | Instability |
| 771.I6 | Intervertebral disk (Displacement, herniation and rupture) |
| 771.K94 | Kyphosis |
| 771.O86 | Ossification of posterior longitudinal ligament |
| 771.O88 | Osteophytosis |
| 771.S3 | Scoliosis. Curvature of the spine |
| 771.S64 | Spondylitis |
| | Cf. RD771.A5, Ankylosing spondylitis |
| | Spondylosis, see RD771.O88 |
| 771.S74 | Stenosis of the spinal canal |

Orthopedia. Orthopedic surgery
Deformities and disorders -- Continued
772 Hip. Congenital dislocation, etc.
Extremities
Cf. RD551+, Regional surgery
Cf. RD756+, Artificial limbs
775 General works
Upper extremities. Arm
776 General works
Hand
778 General works
778.5 Dupuytren's contracture
Lower extremities. Leg
779 General works
779.3 Leg length inequality
Foot
781 General works
783 Clubfoot
785 Flatfoot
Toes
786 General works
787 Hallux valgus and varus. Bunion
789 Hammertoe
Physical rehabilitation
Cf. HD7255.A2+, Rehabilitation of disabled workers
Cf. HV3018+, Occupations for physically handicapped
Cf. RM695+, Physical therapy
Cf. UB360+, Rehabilitation of disabled veterans
792 Periodicals. Societies. Serials
792.5 Congresses
794 Directories
History
795 General works
795.5.A-Z By region or country, A-Z
Biography
Including personal narratives of individual cases
796.A2 Collective
796.A3-Z Individual, A-Z
797 General works
798 General special
799 Handbooks, manuals, etc.
804 Addresses, essays, lectures
Study and teaching
807 General works
808 Audiovisual aids
809.A-Z By region or country, A-Z
811 Clinical cases

Ophthalmology
Cf. RA1062.5, Forensic ophthalmology
1 Periodicals. Societies. Serials
Hospitals, clinics, etc.
Including hospitals for eye and ear; eye, ear, nose and throat
Cf. HV1783+, Schools and asylums for the blind
3 General works
3.2.A-Z By region or country, A-Z
6 Yearbooks
11 Congresses
Collected works (nonserial)
14 Several authors
16 Individual authors
20 Nomenclature. Terminology. Abbreviations
21 Dictionaries and encyclopedias
22 Directories of eye, ear, nose, and throat specialists
Government documents on ophthalmology and optometry
United States
24.A3 General works
24.A4-Z By region or state, A-Z
25.A-Z Other regions or countries, A-Z
History
26 General works
27 Ancient
28 Medieval
29 Modern
30.A-Z By region or country, A-Z
Biography
31 Collective
36.A-Z Individual, A-Z
Diseases of the eye and ear, nose, or throat
Cf. QP458, Physiology
Cf. RF40+, Ear, nose, and larynx
General works
41 Through 1900
45 1901-
Diseases of the eye (General)
Cf. N71.8, Vision disorders and art
Cf. QM511, Anatomy
Cf. QP474+, Physiology
For special diseases of the eye, see RE121+
46 General works
48 General special
48.2.A-Z By age group, class, etc., A-Z
48.2.A5 Aged
48.2.C5 Children
48.2.Y6 Youth
48.9 Handbooks, manuals, etc.
49 Problems, exercises, examinations
50 Outlines, syllabi, etc.

Diseases of the eye (General) -- Continued
51 Popular works
Including hygiene and sight conservation
Cf. LB3431, School hygiene
52 Juvenile works
56 Study and teaching
Cf. RE956, Optometry and opticians
58 Research. Experimentation
61 Addresses, essays, lectures
Laboratories, institutes, etc.
62 General works
63.A-Z Individual. By city, A-Z
64 Museums. Exhibitions
65 Medical ophthalmology. The eye in relation to other diseases
Cf. RC73.5, Eye in diagnosis
66 Pathological anatomy
66.5 Cytopathology
67 Clinical physiology of the eye
Cf. QP474+, Physiology
68 Immunological aspects
69 Clinical cases
71 Atlases. Pictorial works
Practice of ophthalmology. Ophthalmic economics
Including business methods and employment surveys
72 General works
72.5 Ophthalmic assistants
Cf. RE88, Ophthalmic nursing
73 Instruments, apparatus, and appliances
Cf. RE75+, Examination and diagnosis
Cf. RE780, Prisms for correcting muscular divergence or convergence
Cf. RE840, Protective apparatus
Examination. Diagnosis
Cf. RE918+, Tests of color vision
Cf. RE927+, Tests for refraction
75 General works
76 General special
77 Laboratory technique
78 Ophthalmoscopy
79.A-Z Other special, A-Z
79.A5 Angiography
79.B5 Biomicroscopy (Slit-lamp microscopy)
79.C65 Contrast sensitivity testing
Diagnostic imaging, see RE79.I42
79.E38 Electronic data processing
79.E39 Electrooculography
79.E4 Electroretinography
79.F55 Fluorimetry
79.G6 Gonioscopy
79.H57 History taking
79.I42 Imaging
79.M33 Magnetic resonance imaging

Examination. Diagnosis
  Other special, A-Z -- Continued
79.O6 Ophthalmodynamometry
79.P4 Perimetry
79.P5 Phorometer
79.P54 Photography
79.R3 Radiography
79.R33 Radioisotopes
79.S28 Scanning laser ophthalmoscopy
  Slit-lamp microscopy, see RE79.B5
79.S83 Stereoscope
79.T6 Tonometry
79.U4 Ultrasonography
Therapeutics, see RE991+
Eye surgery
  Including preoperative, and postoperative care
  Cf. RE451, Surgical treatment of cataract
  Cf. RE771, Surgical treatment of strabismus
80 General works
  Anesthesia in ophthalmology
82 General works
83.A-Z Anesthetics, A-Z
83.P4 Phenacaine
85 Complications and sequelae
86 Laser surgery
87 Ophthalmic plastic surgery
  Cf. RD119.5.E94, Cosmetic surgery of the eyelids
  Cf. RE986+, Artificial eyes and other prostheses
88 Ophthalmic nursing
  Including eye, ear, nose, and throat combined
  For works limited to otorhinolaryngological nursing, see RF52.5
89 Eye banks
Vision disorders. Blindness
  Cf. HV1571+, Social pathology
  Cf. RE735, Binocular imbalances
  Cf. RE921, Color blindness
  Cf. RE925+, Refractive errors
91 General works
92 Amaurosis. Amblyopia
92.5 Amaurosis fugax
93 Hemeralopia (Day blindness). Nyctalopia (Night blindness)
94 Hemianopsia. Hemiopia
95 Monocular vision
96 Infections and inflammation of the eye. Ophthalmia
  Cf. RE320, Conjunctivitis
  Cf. RJ296, Diseases of newborn infants
  For individual diseases, see RE901.A+
Diseases of the eyelids
121 General works

Diseases of the eyelids -- Continued
Granulation, see RE320
141 Blepharitis
142 Blepharospasm
151 Ectropion and entropion
155.A-Z Other diseases of the eyelids, A-Z
155.A3 Abscess
155.B5 Blepharoptosis
155.E3 Eczema
155.H6 Hordeolum (Sty)
Sty, see RE155.H6
Diseases of the lacrimal glands and ducts
201 General works
212 Dacryocystitis
214 Obstruction of nasal, lacrimal, or lacrimonasal duct
216.A-Z Other diseases of the lacrimal glands and ducts, A-Z
216.A3 Abscess
216.D78 Dry eye syndromes
Diseases of the conjunctiva
Cf. RE96, Ophthalmia
310 General works
320 Conjunctivitis (other than trachoma)
Trachoma
321 General works
322.A-Z By region or country, A-Z
Other diseases of the conjunctiva, A-Z
326.A3 Abscess
326.E3 Edema
326.F6 Folliculosis
326.P7 Pterygium
326.T8 Tuberculosis
326.V3 Vascular diseases
328 Diseases of the sclera
Diseases of the anterior segment
334 General works
Diseases of the cornea
Including surgical treatment
336 General works
338 Keratitis
339 Keratoconus
340 Corneal ulcer
Diseases of the uvea (Iris, ciliary body, and choroid)
350 General works
Uveitis
351 General works
Iritis
352 General works
352.5 Iridocyclitis
353 Posterior uveitis. Choroiditis
355.A-Z Other diseases of the uveal tract, A-Z
355.C4 Choroidoretinitis
401 Diseases of the crystalline lens

Diseases of the crystalline lens -- Continued
451 Cataract
Including surgical treatment
461 Other diseases of the lens (not A-Z)
Diseases of the posterior segment
475 General works
501 Diseases of the vitreous body
545 Diseases of the fundus oculi
Diseases of the retina
551 General works
601 Retinitis
603 Detachment of the retina
651 Thrombosis
661.A-Z Other diseases of the retina, A-Z
661.D3 Degeneration
661.D5 Diabetic retinopathy
661.G45 Genetic disorders
661.H8 Hypertensive retinal disease
661.M3 Macular diseases
661.P75 Proliferative vitreoretinopathy
661.R45 Retinitis pigmentosa
Retrolental fibroplasia, see RJ313
661.V3 Vascular diseases
Diseases of the optic nerve, see RE727+
711 Diseases of the orbit
Diseases of the eyeball
714 General works
715.A-Z Special, A-Z
715.E9 Exophthalmos
715.T48 Thyroid eye disease
720 Blood vessels of the eye (Diseases and anomalies)
Cf. RE661.H8, Hypertensive retinal disease
Neuroophthalmology. Neurogenic disturbances of vision
725 General works
Diseases and abnormalities of the optic nerve
727 General works
728.A-Z Special, A-Z
Choked disc, see RE728.P35
728.O67 Optic disc abnormalities
728.O68 Optic neuritis
728.P35 Papilledema. Choked disc
Neuromuscular mechanism of the eye (Diseases and anomalies)
731 General works
735 Binocular imbalance
738 Diplopia. Double vision
748 Nystagmus
Including electronystagmography
760 Paralysis of the eye
771 Strabismus
Including surgical treatment
776 Heterophoria

Neuroophthalmology. Neurogenic disturbances of vision
Neuromuscular mechanism of the eye (Diseases and anomalies) -- Continued
780 Prisms for correcting muscular divergence or convergence
825 Industrial ophthalmology
827 Sports ophthalmology
Wounds and injuries
831 General works
835 Foreign bodies
837 Radiation injuries
840 Protective apparatus
Including eyeglasses, etc.
Cf. T55+, Safety measures and appliances (Technology)
871 Glaucoma
Neoplasms of the eye, see RC280.E9
901.A-Z Other diseases of the eye, A-Z
901.A4 Allergy
901.F8 Fungous diseases
901.H4 Herpes
901.H5 Histoplasmosis
901.L4 Leprosy
901.T67 Toxic diseases
901.T69 Toxoplasmosis
Tuberculosis, see RC312.5.E9
901.V55 Virus diseases
906 Congenital abnormalities
Neurogenic disturbances of vision, see RE725+
912 Psychogenic disturbances of vision
Color vision tests, charts, etc.
Cf. BF789.C7, Psychology of color
Cf. QP483, Physiology
Cf. TF620, Tests of vision in railroad personnel
918 General works
921 Color blindness
923 Night vision tests, etc.
Refraction and errors of refraction and accommodation
Cf. QP474+, Physiological optics
925 General works
926 General special
Tests for refraction
Class here works on the use of trial cases, etc.
927 General works
928 Skiascopy, retinoscopy, etc.
929 Test-types, pictographs, etc.
930 Ametropia
931 Aniseikonia
932 Astigmatism
935 Hypermetropia
938 Myopia

| | |
|---|---|
| | Refraction and errors of refraction and accommodation -- Continued |
| 938.5 | Presbyopia |
| 939 | Other (not A-Z) |
| | Optometry. Opticians. Eyeglasses |
| 939.2 | Periodicals. Societies. Serials |
| 939.7 | Dictionaries and encyclopedias |
| 940 | Directories |
| 941 | History |
| | By region or country |
| | United States |
| 942 | General works |
| 943.A-Z | By region or state, A-Z |
| 944.A-Z | Other regions or countries, A-Z |
| | Biography |
| 945 | Collective |
| 946.A-Z | Individual, A-Z |
| 951 | General works |
| 952 | General special |
| 952.5.A-Z | By age group, class, etc., A-Z |
| 952.5.C45 | Children |
| 952.5.H35 | Handicapped |
| 952.9 | Handbooks, manuals, etc. |
| 953 | Problems, exercises, examinations |
| 953.2 | Outlines, syllabi, etc. |
| 956 | Study and teaching |
| 959 | Optometry as a profession. Opticianry as a profession |
| | Practice of optometry. Optometric economics |
| | Including business methods and employment surveys |
| | For catalogs of supplies, see RE981 |
| 959.3 | General works |
| 959.5 | Optometric assistants |
| 960 | Behavioral optometry. Visual training |
| 961 | Optical theory, calculations, tables, etc. |
| 962 | Mechanical work of opticians |
| | Class here works on lenses and frames |
| 971 | Popular works |
| | Eyeglasses. Lenses |
| | Cf. GT2370, Clothing and dress |
| 976 | General works |
| 977.A-Z | Special, A-Z |
| 977.B5 | Bifocals |
| 977.C6 | Contact lenses |
| 977.I7 | Iseikonic lenses |
| 979 | Fitting of eyeglasses |
| 981 | Catalogs of optometrists' supplies and other trade publications |
| | Artificial eyes and other prostheses |
| 986 | General works |
| 988 | Intraocular lenses |
| | Ocular therapeutics |
| 991 | General works |
| 992.A-Z | Special therapies and drugs, A-Z |

Ocular therapeutics
Special therapies and drugs, A-Z -- Continued
992.A3 Adrenocortical hormones
992.A56 Anti-infective agents
992.A8 Atropine
992.B56 Biological response modifiers
Chemotherapy, see RE994
992.C7 Cryotherapy
992.D5 Diathermy
(992.H57) Holocaine
see RE992.P47
992.H58 Homatropine
992.H6 Hormone therapy
992.H88 Hyaluronic acid
992.H9 Hyaluronidase
992.I45 Immunosuppressive agents
992.I5 Iodine therapy
992.M4 Mercury
992.O7 Orthoptics
992.O9 Oxygen therapy
992.P47 Phenacaine
992.P5 Phototherapy
992.R3 Radiotherapy
992.S4 Serotherapy
992.S9 Sulphonamides
992.T7 Trace elements
992.V5 Vitamin therapy
992.V57 Vitreous substitutes
994 Materia medica and pharmacology. Mydriatics (General)
Including chemotherapy
For particular therapies and drugs, see RE992.A +

Otorhinolaryngology
Cf. QM251+, Anatomy of organs of respiration
Cf. QM505, Anatomy of the nose
Cf. QP460+, Physiology
Cf. RC705+, Diseases of the respiratory system
Cf. RE41+, Eye, ear, nose, and throat

1 Periodicals. Societies. Serials

Hospitals, clinics, etc.
Cf. RE3+, Hospitals for the eye, ear, nose and throat

5 General works

6.A-Z By region or country, A-Z

11 Yearbooks

16 Congresses

Collected works (nonserial)

20 Several authors

21 Individual authors

23 Dictionaries and encyclopedias

24 Nomenclature. Terminology. Abbreviations

History

25 General works

26.A-Z By region or country, A-Z

28 Directories

Laboratories, institutes, etc.

29 General works

30.A-Z Individual. By city, A-Z

Museums. Exhibitions

32 General works

33.A-Z By region or country, A-Z
*Under each country:*
*.x* *General works*
*.x2A-Z* *Special. By city, A-Z*

Biography

37 Collective

38.A-Z Individual, A-Z

General works

40 Through 1900

46 1901-

46.5 General special

47.A-Z By age group, class, etc., A-Z

47.A35 Aged

47.C4 Children

47.5 Pathology. Histopathology

Examination. Diagnosis
Cf. RF123+, Diseases of the ear
Cf. RF345, Diseases of the nose
Cf. RF476, Diseases of the throat
Cf. RF482, Diseases of the pharynx and tonsils
Cf. RF512+, Diseases of the larynx, vocal cords, etc.

48 General works

48.5.A-Z Special diagnostic methods, A-Z

Examination. Diagnosis
Special diagnostic methods, A-Z -- Continued
48.5.E53 Endoscopy. Rhinolaryngoscopy
Cf. RF514+, Laryngoscopy
48.5.R3 Radiography
Rhinolaryngoscopy, see RF48.5.E53
49.A-Z Specific diseases, A-Z
Class here diseases affecting all three organs: ear, nose, and throat
49.I53 Infectious diseases
50 Wounds and injuries
Surgery
51 General works
51.3 Complications and sequelae
51.5 Laser surgery
52 Anesthesia
52.5 Nursing
Therapeutics
53 General works
54.A-Z Special therapies, A-Z
54.D3 Diathermy
54.E5 Electrotherapy
54.H94 Hyperbaric oxgenation
54.M5 Mineral waters
54.R33 Radiotherapy
54.U48 Ultrasonic therapy
54.U5 Ultraviolet ray therapy
55 Materia medica and pharmacology
Including chemotherapy
56 Handbooks, manuals, etc.
57 Problems, exercises, examinations
58 Outlines, syllabi, etc.
59 Popular works
62 Study and teaching
63 Research. Experimentation
64 Otorhinolaryngology as a profession
69 Clinical cases
71 Addresses, essays, lectures
81 Atlases. Pictorial works
Practice of otolaryngology. Otolaryngologic economics
Including business methods and employment surveys
85 General works
By region or country
United States
85.5 General works
85.6.A-Z By region or state, A-Z
85.7.A-Z Other regions or countries, A-Z
87 Instruments, apparatus, and appliances
89 Otolaryngologic emergencies
Otology. Diseases of the ear
Including manifestations of diseases
Cf. QM507, Anatomy
Cf. QP460+, Physiology

| | |
|---|---|
| | Otology. Diseases of the ear -- Continued |
| | Periodicals, societies, serials, see RF1 |
| | Hospitals, clinics, etc , see RE3+, RF6.A+ |
| | Yearbooks, see RF11 |
| | History |
| 110 | General works |
| 111.A-Z | By region or country, A-Z |
| | General works |
| 120 | Through 1900 |
| 121 | 1901- |
| 122 | General special |
| 122.5.A-Z | By age group, class, etc., A-Z |
| 122.5.C4 | Children. Pediatric otology |
| | Cf. RF291.5.C45, Hearing disorders |
| 122.5.Y6 | Youth |
| | Cf. RF291.5.Y68, Hearing disorders |
| 122.7.A-Z | By race, ethnic group, etc., A-Z |
| 122.7.A88 | Australian aborigines |
| | Study and teaching, see RF62 |
| | Examination. Diagnosis |
| 123 | General works |
| 123.5.A-Z | Special diagnostic methods, A-Z |
| | Audiometry, see RF294+ |
| 123.5.I4 | Imaging |
| 124 | Therapeutics |
| | Surgery. Operative technique |
| 126 | General works |
| 127 | Plastic surgery of the ear. Otoplasty |
| | Nursing, see RF52.5 |
| 130 | Handbooks, manuals, etc. |
| 131 | Problems, exercises, examinations |
| 132 | Outlines, syllabi, etc. |
| 135 | Popular works |
| 137 | Clinical cases |
| 140 | Addresses, essays, lectures |
| 145 | Atlases. Pictorial works |
| | Methods of examination, otoscopy, see RF123+ |
| 155 | Complications. Reflex disturbances |
| | Diseases of the external ear and auricle |
| 175 | General works |
| 180 | Otitis externa |
| 185 | Impacted cerumen |
| 187 | Congenital abnormalities |
| 190 | Foreign bodies |
| 195 | Wounds and injuries |
| 200.A-Z | Other, A-Z |
| 200.E8 | Exostosis |
| 200.H4 | Hematoma auris |
| | Othematoma, see RF200.H4 |
| 210 | Diseases of the tympanic membrane |
| | Diseases of the middle ear |
| 220 | General works |
| | Otitis media |

Otology. Diseases of the ear
Diseases of the middle ear
Otitis media -- Continued
225 General works
225.5 Acute otitis media
225.7 Otitis media with effusion
228 Complications
229 Cholesteatoma
230 Diseases of the eustachian tubes
235 Diseases of the mastoid process
Including sinus complications
Diseases of the internal ear (Labyrinth)
260 General works
270 Otosclerosis
275 Ménière's disease
285.A-Z Other diseases of the ear, A-Z
285.B37 Barotrauma, Aural
Neoplasms, see RC280.E2
285.O83 Ototoxic effects
Audiology. Hearing disorders. Deafness
Cf. HV2350+, Deaf
286 Periodicals. Societies. Serials
286.5 Congresses
290 General works
291 General special
291.3 Problems, exercises, examinations
291.35 Popular works
291.37 Juvenile works
291.5.A-Z By age group, class, etc., A-Z
291.5.A35 Aged
Including presbycusis
291.5.C45 Children
Cf. LB3453, School hygiene
291.5.Y68 Youth
Congenital and hereditary deafness
292 General works
292.8 Usher's syndrome
293 Psychogenic and neurogenic deafness
293.4 Postlingual deafness
293.5 Noise-induced deafness. Acoustic trauma
293.7 Hyperacusis
293.8 Tinnitus
Clinical hearing tests. Audiometry
294 General works
294.5.A-Z Special tests and methods, A-Z
294.5.E43 Electrocochleography
294.5.E87 Evoked response audiometry
294.5.I5 Impedance audiometry
294.5.M37 Masking
294.5.O76 Otoacoustic emissions
294.5.S6 Speech audiometry
294.5.S64 Speech perception tests
294.5.S72 Staggered Spondaic Word Test

RF

Otology. Diseases of the ear
Audiology. Hearing
disorders. Deafness -- Continued
295 Surgical treatment
297 Other treatment
e.g. Training of hearing by phonograph
Instruments, apparatus and appliances
298 General works
Hearing aids
300 General works
303 CIC hearing aids
305 Implanted hearing aids. Cochlear implants
308 FM auditory training systems
310 Trade publications
320 Deaf-mutism
Rhinology. Diseases of the nose, accessory sinuses, and nasopharynx
Including manifestations of disease
Cf. QM505, Anatomy
Cf. QP458, Physiology
Cf. RE41+, Eye, ear, nose, and throat
Cf. RF40+, Ear, nose, and throat
Periodicals, societies, serials, see RF1
Hospitals, clinics, etc , see RE3+, RF6.A+
341 General works
342 General special
343 Nasal manifestations of general diseases
345 Examination. Diagnosis
Therapeutics
348 General works
349.A-Z Special therapies, A-Z
349.G2 Galvanocautery
350 Surgery
Cf. RD119.5.N67, Cosmetic surgery
354 Popular works
Nursing, see RF52.5
Rhinitis. Acute nasopharyngitis (Common cold)
361 General works
Catarrh, see RC741
Hay fever, see RC590
363 Nosebleed
365 Rhinoscleroma
Neoplasms, see RC280.N6
410 Hypertrophies. Atrophies
415 Deflected nasal septum
Diseases of the accessory sinuses
Including the antrum, and the frontal, sphenoidal, and ethmoidal sinuses
421 General works
425 Sinusitis
431.A-Z Other diseases of the nose, A-Z
431.O9 Ozena
435 Foreign bodies

Rhinology. Diseases of the nose, accessory sinuses, and nasopharynx -- Continued

437 Wounds and injuries

Laryngology. Diseases of the throat

Including the pharynx, larynx, vocal cords, trachea, etc.

Periodicals, societies, serials, see RF1

Hospitals, clinics, etc , see RE3+, RF6.A+

Yearbooks, see RF11

Study and teaching, see RF62

460 General works

465 Popular works

470 General special

476 Examination. Diagnosis

Cf. RC804.G3, Gastroscopy

Cf. RF514+, Laryngoscopy

Diseases of the pharynx and tonsils

481 General works

482 Examination. Diagnosis

483 Therapeutics

Surgery

484 General works

484.5 Tonsillectomy

485 Pharyngitis

Cf. RF361+, Nasopharyngitis

491 Tonsilitis

496 Hypertrophy of the tonsils and adenoids

497.A-Z Other diseases of the pharynx, A-Z

497.A27 Abscess

497.H96 Hypopharyngeal diverticula

497.V84 Velopharyngeal insufficiency

499.A-Z Other diseases of the tonsils, A-Z

499.A3 Abscess

Diseases of the larynx, vocal cords, epiglottis, and trachea

Including voice disorders

510 General works

511.A-Z By age group, class, etc., A-Z

Adolescents, see RF511.Y68

511.C45 Children

511.S55 Singers

511.Y68 Youth

511.5 Pathology

Examination. Diagnosis

512 General works

Laryngoscopy

514 General works

514.5 Laryngostroboscopy

Including videolaryngostroboscopy

Surgery

Including oncological surgery

516 General works

RF

Laryngology. Diseases of the throat
Diseases of the larynx,
vocal cords, epiglottis, and trachea
Surgery -- Continued
517 Laryngostomy. Intubation
Artificial larynx, see RF538
Foreign bodies, see RF545
Wounds and injuries, see RF547
520 Laryngitis and tracheitis
522 Neurological disorders of the larynx
Neoplasms, see RC280.T5
Diseases of the vocal cords
526 General works
Hygiene of the voice, see RF465
529 Diseases of the trachea
535.A-Z Other diseases of the larynx and trachea, A-Z
538 Artificial larynx
540 Rehabilitation. Retraining in the use of the voice and speech
Cf. RC423+, Speech disorders (Internal medicine)
545 Foreign bodies in air and food passages
547 Wounds and injuries of the throat

Gynecology and obstetrics
Cf. RJ478+, Pediatrics
1 Periodicals. Societies. Serials
Hospitals, clinics, etc.
For maternity hospital and hospital maternity services, see RG500+
12 General works
14.A-Z By region or country, A-Z
16.A-Z By city, A-Z
Laboratories, institutes, etc.
17 General works
18.A-Z Individual. By city, A-Z
Museums. Exhibitions
21 General works
21.2.A-Z By region or country, A-Z
*Under each country:*
*.x* *General works*
*.x2A-Z* *Special. By city, A-Z*
26 Yearbooks
31 Congresses
Directories of gynecologists
32 General works
33.A-Z By region or country, A-Z
Collected works (nonserial)
39 Several authors
41 Individual authors
45 Dictionaries and encyclopedias
47 Nomenclature. Terminology. Abbreviations
History
51 General works
53 Primitive
55 Oriental (China, India, etc.)
Ancient
57 General works
58 Near East
59 Greek and Roman
61 Medieval
63 Modern
67.A-Z By region or country, A-Z
Biography
71 Collective
76.A-Z Individual, A-Z
77 Pathology
Including surgical pathology
79 Atlases. Pictorial works
General works
Through 1900
81 Greek authors
83 Latin authors
Medieval
85 General works
87 Arabic authors
Modern

General works
Through 1900
Modern -- Continued
91 15th-16th centuries
93 17th-18th centuries
95 19th century
101 1901-
Popular works, see RG121
103 General special
103.4 Standards for gynecologic and obstetric care. Evaluation and quality control of gynecologic and obstetric care
103.5 Psychological and psychosomatic aspects
Cf. RG560, Pregnancy
103.7 Decision making
Operative gynecology. Gynecologic surgery
Including gynecologic pelvic surgery
Cf. RD549+, Pelvic surgery
Cf. RG108+, Surgical instruments
Cf. RG138, Sterilization
Cf. RG391, Hysterectomy
Cf. RG481, Ovariotomy
Cf. RG484, Urogynecologic surgery
104 General works
104.2 Complications
104.3 Vesicovaginal fistualae
104.5 Gynoplastics
104.6 Oncological surgery
104.7 Endoscopic surgery. Laparoscopic surgery
105 Gynecological nursing. Nurses' manuals
Cf. RG951, Maternity nursing. Obstetrical nursing
106 Clinical cases
Cf. RG12+, Hospitals and clinics
Statistics and surveys
106.3 General works
106.4.A-Z By region or country, A-Z
Examination. Diagnosis
107 General works
107.5.A-Z Special diagnostic methods, A-Z
107.5.C57 Colpomicroscopy
107.5.C6 Colposcopy
107.5.C8 Culdoscopy
107.5.C95 Cytodiagnosis
Cf. RG107.5.E9, Exfoliative cytology
107.5.E48 Endoscopic ultrasonography
107.5.E5 Endoscopy
107.5.E9 Exfoliative cytology (General)
Cf. RG107.5.P3, Pap test
107.5.H96 Hysterosalpingo-contrast sonography
107.5.H97 Hysterosalpingography
Hysteroscopy, see RG304.5.H97
107.5.L34 Laparoscopy

Examination. Diagnosis
Special diagnostic methods, A-Z -- Continued
107.5.M34 Magnetic resonance imaging
107.5.P3 Pap test
107.5.R3 Radiography
Surgical pathology, see RG77
107.5.T73 Transvaginal ultrasonography
107.5.U4 Ultrasonics
Including Doppler ultrasonography
107.5.V3 Vaginal smears
Instruments, apparatus and appliances
Including feminine hygiene supplies
Cf. RG137+, Contraceptives
Cf. RG545, Obstetrics
108 General works
109.A-Z Special, A-Z
109.C6 Colposcope
109.L37 Lasers
109.S25 Sanitary napkins
109.S6 Speculum
109.T36 Tampons
110 Handbooks, manuals, etc.
111 Problems, exercises, examinations
112 Outlines, syllabi, etc.
121 Popular works
122 Juvenile works
123 Addresses, essays, lectures
Therapeutics
125 General works
126 General special
127 Electrotherapy
128 Radiotherapy
129.A-Z Other drugs and therapies, A-Z
129.A25 Acupuncture
129.A32 Adrenergic beta agonists
129.A56 Antibiotics
129.D35 Danazol
129.H47 Herbs
129.H6 Hormone therapy
Cf. RG137.5, Oral contraceptives
129.L87 Luteinizing hormone releasing hormone
(129.N6) Novocaine
see RG129.P64
129.P45 Physical therapy
129.P57 Piperacillin
129.P64 Procaine
129.P66 Progestational hormones
129.P7 Prostaglandins
129.P75 Psychotherapy
131 Materia medica and pharmacology
Cf. RG528, Obstetrics
For particular drugs and therapies, see RG129.A+

RG

133 Conception
Cf. QP281, Physiology
Cf. QP285, Physiology
Cf. RC889, Impotence and sterility (General and male)
Cf. RG201+, Sterility in women
133.5 Reproductive technology
133.7 Ovulation induction
134 Artificial insemination
Cf. HQ761, Eugenics
135 Fertilization in vitro
Class here works on conception of "test tube babies"
Contraception. Birth control
Cf. HQ763+, Social aspects of birth control
Cf. RC888, Male contraception
Cf. RG734+, Induced abortion
136.A1 Periodicals. Societies. Serials
136.A2 Congresses
136.A3-Z General works
136.2 Popular works
136.3 Juvenile works
136.5 Natural methods. Rhythm method
136.8 Immunological methods
136.85 Antifertility vaccines
Contraceptives
137 General works
137.2 Vaginal contraceptives
Including barrier devices and spermicides
Intrauterine contraceptives
137.3 General works
137.35 Levonorgestrel intrauterine contraceptives
Contraceptive drugs
137.4 General works
137.45 Herbal contraceptives
137.5 Oral contraceptives
137.55 Injectable contraceptives
137.6.A-Z Special contraceptive drugs, A-Z
137.6.G47 Gestodene
137.6.G68 Gossypol
137.6.L78 Luteinizing hormone releasing hormone
137.6.L86 Lynestrenol
137.6.M43 Medroxyprogesterone
137.6.M53 Mifepristone
137.6.N67 Norethindrone
137.6.N68 Norgestrel
138 Sterilization of women
Cf. RG201+, Infertility in women
Study and teaching
Cf. RG12+, Hospitals, clinics, etc.
Cf. RG970+, Maternal care
Cf. RG973, Childbirth education
141 General works
142 General special

Study and teaching -- Continued
By region or country
United States
143.A1 General works
143.A3-Z By region or state, A-Z
Other American regions or countries, A-Z
144.A1 General works
144.A2-Z By region or country, A-Z
*Under each country:*
*.x General works*
*.x2A-Z Local. By province, department, etc., A-Z*
Europe
145.A1 General works
145.A2-Z By region or country, A-Z
Apply table at RG144.A2-Z
Asia
146.A1 General works
146.A2-Z By region or country, A-Z
Apply table at RG144.A2-Z
Africa
147.A1 General works
147.A2-Z By region or country, A-Z
Apply table at RG144.A2-Z
Australia
148.A1 General works
148.A2-Z By state or territory, A-Z
148.5 New Zealand
Pacific islands, A-Z
149.A1 General works
149.A2-Z By island or group of islands, A-Z
155 Research. Experimentation
158 Gynecologic emergencies
Cf. RG571+, Obstetrical emergencies
Functional and systemic disorders. Endocrine gynecology
Including manifestations of disorders
Cf. RG129.H6, Hormone therapy
Cf. RG444, Ovarian dysfunction
159 General works
Menstrual disorders
Cf. QP263, Physiology
161 General works
163 General special
165 Premenstrual syndrome
171 Amenorrhea
Cf. RJ478.5.A43, Primary amenorrhea
176 Menorrhagia
181 Dysmenorrhea
Menopause
186 General works
188 Perimenopause
190 Leucorrhea

Functional and systemic disorders. Endocrine gynecology -- Continued
Infertility in women
Cf. RC889, Impotence and infertility (General and male)
201 General works
202 Examination. Diagnosis
205.A-Z Specific conditions, A-Z
205.L87 Luteal phase defects
207 Sports gynecology
Hyperandrogenism
207.5 General works
208 Virilism
Abnormalities and malformations of the female genital organs
Cf. RG321+, Uterus
211 General works
Hermaphroditism, see RC883
218 Infectious diseases of the female genital organs
220 Toxic shock syndrome
Tuberculosis, see RC312.5.G5
Neoplasms, see RC280.G5
Oncological surgery, see RG104.6
Diseases of the female pelvis and pelvic supporting structures, see RG482+
Diseases of the vulva
Including Bartholin's glands, clitoris, hymen, labia majora, and labia minora
261 General works
262.A-Z Special, A-Z
266 Wounds and injuries
Surgery, see RG104+
Diseases of the vagina
268 General works
269.A-Z Special, A-Z
269.A3 Abscess
269.B32 Bacterial vaginitis
269.C35 Candidiasis, Vulvovaginal
Vulvovaginal candidiasis, see RG269.C35
272 Wounds and injuries
Surgery, see RG104+
Diseases of the uterus
Including manifestations of diseases
301 General works
302 General special
Examination. Diagnosis
304 General works
304.5.A-Z Special diagnostic methods, A-Z
Hysterosalpingo-contrast sonography, see RG107.5.H96
Hysterosalpingography, see RG107.5.H97
304.5.H97 Hysteroscopy
304.5.R33 Radiography
304.5.U48 Ultrasonics

Diseases of the uterus -- Continued
306 Therapeutics
Diseases of the cervix uteri
310 General works
312 Cervicitis
314 Erosion of the cervix
315 Incompetence
316 Diseases of the endometrium
Cf. RG483.E53, Endometriosis
Abnormalities and malformations
321 General works
331 Atrophy
341 Hypertrophy
345 Abnormal position and form
Displacement
Including prolapse
361 General works
363 Instruments, apparatus, and appliances for correcting displacement
365 Abscess
Neoplasms, see RC280.U8
386.A-Z Other diseases of the uterus, A-Z
386.R89 Rupture
Tuberculosis, see RC312.5.G5
386.U5 Ulcer
Surgery. Endoscopic surgery
Cf. RG104+, Uterine surgery
390 General works
391 Hysterectomy
411 Diseases of the uterine appendages. Pelvic inflammatory disease
Diseases of the oviduct (Fallopian tube)
421 General works
431 Salpingitis
433.A-Z Other diseases of the oviduct, A-Z
Diseases of the ovaries
Including the parovarium
Cf. QP261, Ovary and ovulation (Physiology)
441 General works
444 Ovarian dysfunction. Anovulation. Premature ovarian failure
446 Oophoritis
Neoplasms, see RC280.O8
Other diseases of the ovaries, A-Z
480.H46 Hemorrhage
480.S7 Stein-Leventhal syndrome
481 Surgery. Ovariotomy
Diseases of the female pelvis and pelvic supporting structures
Cf. RC946, Diseases of the pelvic region
482 General works
483.A-Z Special, A-Z
483.C57 Circumvaginal impairment syndrome

Diseases of the female
pelvis and pelvic supporting structures
Special, A-Z -- Continued
483.E53 Endometriosis
483.P44 Pelvic pain
483.V3 Varicocele
484 Urogynecology and obstetric urology. Urogynecologic surgery
Cf. RG577, Urinary diseases in pregnancy
485.A-Z Special conditions, A-Z
485.C9 Cystitis
485.C94 Cystocele
Hernia of the bladder, see RG485.C94
485.S7 Stress incontinence
Diseases of the breast
Cf. RC942+, General and male
Cf. RD539.8, Surgery
Cf. RG861+, Diseases of lactation
491 General works
492 General special
Examination. Diagnosis
493 General works
493.5.A-Z Special diagnostic methods, A-Z
493.5.B56 Biopsy. Needle biopsy
493.5.C97 Cytodiagnosis
493.5.D52 Diagnostic imaging
493.5.M33 Magnetic resonance imaging
Needle biopsy, see RG493.5.B56
493.5.R33 Radiography
493.5.U47 Ultrasonics
493.5.X47 Xeroradiography
496.A-Z Special diseases, A-Z
496.C34 Calcification. Calcinosis
Calcinosis, see RG496.C34
496.F53 Fibrocystic disease
Neoplasms, see RC280.B8
Tuberculosis, see RC312.5.B7
499 Other
Obstetrics
Cf. QP251+, Reproduction
Periodicals, societies, serials, see RG1
Yearbooks, see RG26
Congresses, see RG31
Hospitals, clinics, etc.
Including hospital maternity services and birthing centers
500 General works
501.A-Z By region or country, A-Z
Laboratories, institutes, etc.
502.A2 General works
502.A3-Z Individual. By city, A-Z
Museums. Exhibitions
503 General works

Obstetrics
  Museums. Exhibitions -- Continued
503.2.A-Z By region or country, A-Z
      Apply table at RG21.2.A-Z
  Study and teaching of obstetrics, see RG141+, RG970+
  Childbirth education, see RG973
  Directories of obstetricians
504 General works
505.A-Z By region or country, A-Z
  Collected works (nonserial)
507 Several authors
508 Individual authors
  Biography
509 Collective
510.A-Z Individual, A-Z
  History
511 General works
512 Primitive
513 Ancient
514 Medieval
515 Modern through 1800
516 19th-20th centuries
518.A-Z By region or country, A-Z
519 Anatomical descriptions
520 Atlases. Pictorial works
  General works
      For works before 1800, see RG81+
521 1800-1900
522 1901-1930
524 1931-
525 Popular works
      Including works on the hygiene of pregnancy and guides for expectant parents
      For works on childbirth education, see RG973
525.5 Juvenile works
526 General special
  Psychological and psychosomatic aspects, see RG103.5
  Examination. Diagnosis
      Cf. RG563+, Pregnancy
527 General works
527.5.A-Z Special diagnostic methods, A-Z
527.5.L3 Laboratory technique
527.5.P44 Pelvimetry
527.5.R33 Radiography
527.5.U48 Ultrasonics
        Including Doppler ultrasonography
528 Materia medica and pharmacology
      Cf. RG627.6.D79, Fetal disease
      Cf. RG734.4+, Abortifacients
529 Clinical cases

Obstetrics -- Continued
Statistics and surveys
Including maternal morbidity, mortality, etc.
Cf. HV697+, Protection, assistance, etc., of mothers, widows, etc.
Cf. RG631+, Fetal death. Perinatal mortality
530 General works
530.3.A-Z By region or country, A-Z
*Under each country:*
*.x General works*
*.x2 Local, A-Z*
531 Handbooks, manuals, etc.
532 Problems, exercises, examinations
533 Outlines, syllabi, etc.
541 Addresses, essays, lectures
545 Instruments, apparatus, and appliances
Cf. RG739, Use of forceps
547 Computer applications
Including electronic data processing
Pregnancy
551 General works
556 General special
556.5 Pregnancy in adolescence
Cf. LB3433, Schoolgirl pregnancy
Cf. RJ507.A34, Mental health aspects of adolescent pregnancy
556.6 Pregnancy in middle age
557 Immunology of pregnancy
558 Physiology of pregnancy
Cf. RG610+, Fetus
Cf. RG655, Labor
558.5 Endocrinology of pregnancy
558.7 Exercise in pregnancy
559 Nutritional aspects of pregnancy
Cf. RG580.M34, Malnutrition
Hygiene of pregnancy, see RG525
560 Psychology of pregnancy
Cf. RG560, Mental illness in pregnancy
Cf. RG658, Childbirth
Cf. RG851, Puerperal psychoses
Examination. Diagnosis
563 General works
564.A-Z Specific diagnostic tests, A-Z
566 Determination of sex during pregnancy
Cf. QP251+, Physiology of sex
567 Multiple pregnancy
Cf. RG696+, Multiple birth

Obstetrics
Pregnancy -- Continued
Obstetrical emergencies. Diseases and conditions in pregnancy
Including complications due to pregnancy
Cf. RG626+, Fetal diseases
Cf. RG631+, Fetal death
Cf. RG648, Spontaneous abortion
Cf. RG701+, Complicated labor
571 General works
572 General special
573 Accidental complications due to diseases
Toxemia of pregnancy
Cf. RG580.H9, Hypertension in pregnancy
575 General works
575.5 Preeclampsia
576 Convulsions. Eclampsia
Cf. RG831, Puerperal convulsions
577 Urinary diseases in pregnancy
For specific diseases, see RG580.A+
578 Infectious diseases (General) during pregnancy
For specific diseases, see RG580.A+
579 Vomiting. Nausea. Morning sickness
580.A-Z Other diseases and conditions in pregnancy, A-Z
580.A28 Abuse
580.A44 AIDS (Disease)
580.A46 Alcoholism
580.A47 Allergy
580.A5 Anemia
580.A6 Appendicitis
580.B56 Blood coagulation disorders
Blood diseases, see RG580.H47
580.C3 Cancer
580.C32 Cardiopulmonary system
580.C33 Cardiovascular diseases
580.C6 Collagen diseases
580.C64 Connective tissue diseases
580.D5 Diabetes
580.D76 Drug abuse
580.E53 Endocrine diseases
580.E64 Epilepsy
580.G38 Gastrointestinal diseases
580.G45 Genetic disorders
580.H4 Heart diseases
580.H47 Hematologic diseases
580.H5 Hemorrhage
580.H53 Hepatitis, Infectious. Hepatitis A
580.H9 Hypertension
580.H93 Hyperthyroidism
580.H95 Hypotension
Icterus, see RG580.J3
580.I55 Immunologic diseases
Infectious hepatitis, see RG580.H53

Obstetrics
Pregnancy
Obstetrical emergencies.
Diseases and conditions in pregnancy
Other diseases and conditions
in pregnancy, A-Z -- Continued

580.J3 Jaundice. Icterus
580.K5 Kidney diseases
580.L58 Liver diseases
580.M34 Malnutrition
580.N47 Nervous system diseases
580.O33 Occupational diseases and hazards
580.P35 Parasitic diseases
580.P48 Physical handicaps
580.S54 Skin diseases
580.S73 Stress (Psychological and physiological)
580.S75 Substance abuse
Cf. RG580.A46, Alcoholism
Cf. RG580.D76, Drug abuse
Cf. RJ520.P74, Prenatal substance abuse (Pediatrics)
Surgery, see RD144
Surgical diseases, see RD144
580.S95 Syphilis
580.T45 Thromboembolism
580.T47 Thyroid gland diseases
580.T8 Tuberculosis
580.V5 Virus and diseases
580.W68 Wounds and injuries
586 Extrauterine pregnancy. Ectopic pregnancy
588 Mental disease connected with pregnancy and childbirth
Cf. RG850+, Postpartum psychiatric disorders
591 Diseases and abnormalities of the ovum, chorion, amnion, placenta, and umbilical cord. Molar pregnancy
The embryo and fetus. Perinatology
Class here works on the fetus after the third month
Cf. QM601+, Human embryology
Cf. RG781, Embryotomy
Cf. RG784, Fetal surgery
Cf. RJ251+, Neonatology
600 General works
605 Anatomy of the fetus
Physiology of the fetus
Cf. QP277, Embryo
610 General works
613 Growth and development
Cf. RG629.G76, Growth retardation
613.5 Gestational age
613.7 Immunology
614 Body fluids
615 Metabolism and nutrition
616 Endocrinology

Obstetrics
The embryo and fetus. Perinatology
Physiology of the fetus -- Continued
618 Cardiovascular system. Circulation
619 Hematology
620 Respiratory system. Respiration
621 Musculoskeletal system. Movements
622 Behavior
Diseases and abnormalities
Cf. QM690+, Teratology
626 General works
627 General special
627.2.A-Z By region or country, A-Z
Apply table at RG530.3.A-Z
Etiology. Theories of causation
627.5 General works
627.6.A-Z Special factors, A-Z
627.6.B44 Benzodiazepines
627.6.C45 Chemicals
627.6.D79 Drug effects. Perinatal pharmacology
627.6.M34 Malnutrition
627.6.N37 Narcotics
Perinatal pharmacology, see RG627.6.D79
627.6.R33 Radiation effects
Smoking, see RG627.6.T6
627.6.T6 Tobacco. Smoking
Examination. Diagnosis
628 General works
628.3.A-Z Special diagnostic methods, A-Z
628.3.A48 Amniocentesis
Including analysis of amniotic fluid
628.3.A5 Amnioscopy
628.3.B55 Blood analysis
628.3.C48 Chorionic villus sampling
628.3.E34 Echocardiography
628.3.F45 Fetal cells from maternal blood
628.3.F47 Fetoscopy
628.3.H42 Heart rate monitoring
Including electrocardiography and phonocardiography
628.3.P74 Preimplantation genetic diagnosis
628.3.U58 Ultrasonics
629.A-Z Special diseases and abnormalities, A-Z
629.A55 Anoxia
629.B33 Bacterial diseases
629.B73 Brain diseases. Brain damage
629.C4 Chondrodystrophy
Communicable diseases, see RG629.I53
629.C65 Congenital toxoplasmosis
629.D68 Down syndrome
629.E4 Ellis-van Creveld syndrome
629.E78 Erythroblastosis fetalis
Cf. RJ270, Newborn infants

Obstetrics
The embryo and fetus. Perinatology
Diseases and abnormalities
Special diseases
and abnormalities, A-Z -- Continued
629.F45 Fetal alcohol syndrome
629.G75 Growth disorders (General)
629.G76 Growth retardation
629.H45 Hemoglobinopathy
629.I53 Infectious diseases
629.N48 Neural tube defects
629.S49 Sexually transmitted diseases
629.S53 Skeletal abnormalities
629.S55 Skin diseases
629.V57 Virus diseases
Fetal death. Stillbirth. Perinatal mortality
For works limited to neonatal mortality, see RJ59+
631 General works
632.A-Z By region or country, A-Z
Apply table at RG530.3.A-Z
633 Retention of fetus. Lithopedion
Cf. RG650, Missed labor
635 Maternal impressions. Supposed effect of imagination on fetus
Cf. RG588, Mental disease during pregnancy
Cf. RJ91, Prenatal culture
648 Spontaneous abortion. Miscarriage
Cf. HQ767+, Social aspects
Cf. RA1067, Criminal abortion
Cf. RG734+, Induced abortion
649 Premature labor
Cf. RG736, Induction of labor
Cf. RJ250+, Premature infants (Care and treatment)
650 Missed labor. Protracted pregnancy
Cf. RG633, Retention of fetus. Lithopedion
Labor. Parturition
651 General works
652 General special
Asepsis and antisepsis, see RG730
655 Physiology
658 Psychology
Natural childbirth
Including psychological preparation for painless labor, psychoprophylactics, etc.
661 General works
661.5 Childbirth at home
662 Active childbirth
663 Underwater childbirth
664 Third state of labor
666 Clinical cases
Presentations. Positions
671 General works

Obstetrics
Labor. Parturition
Presentations. Positions -- Continued
676 Cephalic: Vertex, face, and brow
686 Breech and lower extremities
693 Other
Multiple birth (Twins, etc.)
Cf. RG567, Multiple pregnancy
696 General works
698.A-Z By region or country, A-Z
Apply table at RG530.3.A-Z
Complicated labor. Dystocia
Cf. RG671+, Presentations
701 General works
703 General special
705 Abnormal labor due to anomalies of expellant forces
Including spasms and hour-glass contraction
707 Abnormal labor due to mechanical obstacles
Including narrowness of pelvis and rigidity of the cervix
709 Abnormal labor due to disproportion of the fetus
Cf. RG671+, Presentations
710 Convulsions
711 Hemorrhage
713 Rupture and laceration of the genital tract and perineum
715 Complications from the placenta
Including retention, and placenta previa
719 Complications from the umbilical cord
Including prolapse, etc.
721 Other complications
Obstetric operations. Operative obstetrics
725 General works
727 General special
730 Asepsis and antisepsis
Anesthesia and analgesia
Cf. RD87.3.P73, Anesthesia in pregnancy
732 General works
733.A-Z Special anesthetics, A-Z
Induction of abortion
Cf. HQ767+, Social aspects
Cf. RA1067, Criminal abortion
Cf. RG648, Spontaneous abortion
734 General works
Abortifacients
734.4 General works
734.5.A-Z Special, A-Z
734.5.G45 Gemeprost
736 Induction of labor
Cf. RG649, Premature labor
739 Use of forceps
741 Extraction and version

Obstetrics
Obstetric operations.
Operative obstetrics -- Continued
761 Cesarean section
781 Embryotomy. Craniotomy
784 Fetal surgery
791 Other operations
Puerperal state
801 General works
811 Puerperal infection
Including puerperal septicemia (Puerperal fever), etc.
821 Hemorrhage
825 Thrombosis
831 Puerperal convulsions (Eclampsia)
Postpartum psychiatric disorders
850 General works
851 Puerperal psychoses
852 Postpartum depression
Diseases of lactation
Cf. RG491+, Diseases of the breast
861 General works
866 Breast pumps, etc.
871.A-Z Other diseases of the puerperal state, A-Z
871.G5 Glycosuria
871.S53 Sheehan's syndrome
Maternal care. Prenatal care services
Cf. HV697+, Maternal and infant welfare
For the care and treatment of premature and newborn infants, see RJ250+
940 General works
945 Preconception care
Midwifery. Midwives. Doulas
950.A1 Periodicals. Societies. Serials
950.A2-Z General works
951 Maternity nursing. Obstetrical nursing
Cf. RG105, Gynecological nursing
By region or country
United States
960 General works
961.A-Z By region or state, A-Z
962.A-Z By city, A-Z
962.5.A-Z Other special, A-Z
962.5.I6 American Indians
Other American regions or countries
963.A1 General works
963.A2-Z By region or country, A-Z
Apply table at RG144.A2-Z
Europe
964.A1 General works
964.A2-Z By region or country, A-Z
Apply table at RG144.A2-Z
Asia

Obstetrics
Maternal care. Prenatal care services
By region or country
Asia -- Continued
965.A1 General works
965.A2-Z By region or country, A-Z
Apply table at RG144.A2-Z
Africa
966.A1 General works
966.A2-Z By region or country, A-Z
Apply table at RG144.A2-Z
Australia
967.A1 General works
967.A2-Z By state or territory, A-Z
967.5 New Zealand
Pacific islands
968.A1 General works
968.A2-Z By island or group of islands, A-Z
Apply table at RG144.A2-Z
969 Arctic regions. Greenland
Study and teaching
970 General works
971 General special
973 Childbirth education. Expectant parents' classes
By region or country
United States
975 General works
980.A-Z By region or state, A-Z
981.A-Z By city, A-Z
Other American regions or countries
983.A1 General works
983.A2-Z By region or country, A-Z
Apply table at RG144.A2-Z
Europe
985.A1 General works
985.A2-Z By region or country, A-Z
Apply table at RG144.A2-Z
Asia
986.A1 General works
986.A2-Z By region or country, A-Z
Apply table at RG144.A2-Z
Africa
987.A1 General works
987.A2-Z By region or country, A-Z
Apply table at RG144.A2-Z
Australia
988.A1 General works
988.A2-Z By state or territory, A-Z
988.5 New Zealand
Pacific islands
989.A1 General works
989.A2-Z By island or group of islands, A-Z
Apply table at RG144.A2-Z

Obstetrics
Maternal care. Prenatal care services
Study and teaching
By region or country -- Continued
991 Arctic regions. Greenland

Pediatrics
Including clinical pediatrics and the physiology and hygiene of children
Class here works on infants through two years; children through 15 years; adolescents through 21 years
Cf. QM24.5, Anatomy of children

1 Periodicals. Societies. Serials
16 Yearbooks
21 Congresses
Collected works (nonserial)
23 Several authors
25 Individual authors
25.5 Classification
26 Dictionaries and encyclopedias
Communication in pediatrics
26.3 General works
Information centers
26.4 General works
26.5.A-Z By region or country, A-Z
Hospitals, clinics, trauma centers, etc.
Cf. RA995+, Ambulance service for children
Cf. RC427, Speech clinics
Cf. RJ101+, Child health services
Cf. RJ242, Hospital care of children
27 General works
By region or country
United States
27.2 General works
27.3.A-Z By region or state, A-Z
27.5.A-Z Other regions or countries, A-Z
28.A-Z Individual. By city, A-Z
29 Directories
Laboratories, institutes, etc.
31 General works
32.A-Z Individual. By city, A-Z
Laboratory technique, see RJ51.L3
Museums. Exhibitions
33 General works
33.2.A-Z By region or country, A-Z
*Under each country:*
*.x General works*
*.x2A-Z Special. By city, A-Z*
Practice of pediatrics. Pediatric economics
Including business methods and employment surveys
33.5 General works
By region or country
United States
33.6 General works
33.7.A-Z By region or state, A-Z
33.8.A-Z Other regions or countries, A-Z
Instruments, apparatus, and appliances
34 General works
34.5.A-Z Special, A-Z

RJ

Instruments, apparatus, and appliances
Special, A-Z -- Continued
34.5.I52 Incubators
History
36 General works
37 General special
38 Ancient
39 Medieval
40 Modern
42.A-Z By region or country, A-Z
Biography
43.A1 Collective
43.A3-Z Individual, A-Z
General works
44 Through 1900
45 1901-
47 General special
Genetic aspects
47.3 General works
47.4 Sex chromosome abnormalities
Psychological and psychosomatic aspects
47.5 General works
47.53 Child and adolescent health behavior
47.7 Social aspects
48 Handbooks, manuals, etc.
48.2 Problems, exercises, examinations
48.3 Outlines, syllabi, etc.
Popular works, see RJ61
48.5 Atlases. Pictorial works
Pathology
49 General works
49.4 Clinical biochemistry
Immunopathology, see RJ385+
Examination. Diagnosis
50 General works
50.5 Juvenile works
51.A-Z Special diagnostic methods, A-Z
51.C87 Cutaneous manifestations
Cf. RJ511+, Pediatric dermatology
51.C88 Cytodiagnosis
51.D48 Developmental screening tests
51.D5 Diagnostic imaging
51.D53 Differential diagnosis
Electrocardiography, see RJ423.5.E43
Electroencephalography, see RJ488.5.E44
51.E53 Endoscopy
51.E95 Exercise tests
51.F9 Function tests
Imaging, Diagnostic, see RJ51.D5
51.L3 Laboratory technique
51.M33 Magnetic resonance imaging
Pulmonary function tests, see RJ433.5.P8
51.R3 Radiography

Examinations. Diagnosis
Special diagnostic methods, A-Z -- Continued
51.R33 Radioisotopes
51.T65 Tomography
51.T73 Transdisciplinary Play-Based Assessment
51.U45 Ultrasonics
Therapeutics
52 General works
53.A-Z Special therapies, A-Z
53.A27 Acupuncture. Acupressure
53.A5 Antibiotic therapy
53.A68 Aquatic exercises
53.A76 Aromatherapy
53.B56 Blood transfusion
53.D53 Diet therapy
Including cookery for sick children
For specific groups of sick children, see the disease
53.E58 Enteral feeding
53.E95 Exercise therapy
53.F5 Fluid therapy
53.H47 Herbs
53.H9 Hydrotherapy
53.M35 Massage
53.O25 Occupational therapy
53.P37 Parenteral therapy and feeding
53.P5 Physical therapy
Cf. LB3458, Practice in schools
53.P85 Puppet therapy
53.R43 Recreational therapy
53.R46 Reflexology
Respiratory therapy, see RJ434
53.S7 Steroid hormones
53.S74 Stimulants
53.T7 Transdisciplinary Play-Based Intervention
53.V57 Vitamin therapy
Including specific vitamins
58 Clinical cases
Infant and neonatal morbidity and mortality
Including statistics and surveys
Cf. HB1323.I4, Demography
Cf. RG626+, Diseases of the fetus and birth defects
Cf. RG631+, Perinatal mortality
Cf. RJ254+, Diseases of newborn infants (Clinical aspects)
Cf. RJ320.S93, Sudden infant death syndrome
59 General works

Infant and neonatal morbidity and mortality -- Continued

60.A-Z By region or country, A-Z

*Under each country:*

.x *General works*

.x2 *Local, A-Z*

61 Popular works

Juvenile works, see R130.5

71 Addresses, essays, lectures

78 Pediatrics as a profession

Study and teaching

80 General works

82 Audiovisual aids

84.A-Z By region or country, A-Z

85 Research. Experimentation

91 Supposed prenatal influence. Prenatal culture. Stirpiculture

Cf. HQ750+, Eugenics

Cf. QH431, Human genetics

Cf. QP251+, Reproduction

Cf. RG635, Maternal impressions

Child health. Child health services. Preventive health services for children

Including adolescent health services

Cf. HQ768+, Management of children

Cf. HV701+, Child welfare

Cf. LB3401+, School hygiene

Cf. RA1122.5, Battered child syndrome

Cf. RJ61, Popular works

Cf. RJ499+, Child psychiatry. Child mental health services

101 General works

By class, etc.

101.3 Gay and lesbian teenagers

101.5 Refugee children

101.7 Juvenile works

By region or country

United States

102 General works

102.5.A-Z By region or state, A-Z

103.A-Z Other regions or countries, A-Z

104 Health risk assessment

106 Pediatric epidemiology

Mental health, see RJ499+

Mental health, see BF721+

Physiology of children and infants

Cf. RG600+, Fetal physiology

125 General works

128 Metabolism

Physiology of children and infants -- Continued
Growth and development
Cf. BF721+, Child psychology
Cf. GN63, Physical anthropology
Cf. RJ51.D48, Developmental screening tests
Cf. RJ482.G76, Growth disorders
131 General works
132 Growth testing. Age determination
133 Motor development. Exercise
Cf. BF723.M6, Child psychology
Cf. RJ53.E95, Exercise therapy
Cf. RJ496.M68, Movement disorders
134 Infant growth and development
Cf. RJ250.3, Premature infants
135 Arrested development. Failure to thrive syndrome
Cf. GN69.3, Dwarfs, midgets, etc.
Cf. RJ420.P58, Pituitary dwarfism
Cf. RJ506.I55, Infantilism
137 Growth and development of handicapped children
138 Medical rehabilitation of handicapped children
Physiology of adolescents
Cf. BF724, Psychology
Cf. HQ35, Sex instruction
Cf. HQ768+, Child rearing
140 General works
141 Growth and development
143 Boys
Girls
144 General works
145 Menarche
Nutrition and feeding of children
Cf. RJ53.D53, Diet therapy
Cf. RJ53.E58, Enteral feeding
Cf. RJ53.P37, Parenteral feeding
Cf. RJ390, Diseases of metabolism and nutrition
206 General works
216 Nutrition of infants
Including artificial feeding
231 Trade publications
233 Nutrition of handicapped children and adolescents
235 Nutrition of adolescents
240 Immunization of children (General)
For immunization against specific diseases, see RA644.A+
242 Hospital care of children
243 Hospital care of adolescents
Nursing of children. Pediatric nursing
245 General works
247 School nursing
249 Terminal care. Dying children

Premature infants
Including care and treatment
Cf. RG649, Premature labor
Cf. RJ281, Low birth weight
For specific diseases, see RJ256
250 General works
250.3 Growth and development of premature infants
Newborn infants. Neonatology
Cf. RD137.5, Surgery
For mortality, see RJ59+
251 General works
252 Physiology
Care and therapeutics
253 General works
Intensive care. Neonatal emergencies
253.5 General works
253.7.A-Z Special therapies, A-Z
253.7.C45 Chemotherapy
Diseases and abnormalities
Including diseases of early infancy
For statistics and surveys, see RJ59+
254 General works
255 General special
Examination. Diagnosis
255.5 General works
255.6.A-Z Special diagnostic methods, A-Z
255.6.D52 Diagnostic imaging
255.6.D55 DNA analysis
255.6.H4 Health risk assessment
255.6.R34 Radiography
255.6.T7 Transillumination
Therapeutics, see RJ253+
256 Asphyxia
266 Atelectasis
Brain diseases, see RJ290.5
266.8 Cholestasis. Biliary atresia
267 Colic
267.5 Dehydration
267.8 Diaphragmatic hernia
268 Edema
268.3 Enterocolitis, Neonatal necrotizing
268.6 Fluid imbalances
268.8 Gastrointestinal diseases
269 Heart diseases. Heart abnormalities
Hematologic diseases
269.5 General works
270 Hemolytic disease. Erythroblastosis
Cf. RG629.E78, Fetus
271 Hemorrhagic diseases
272 Hepatitis
274 Hyaline membrane disease. Respiratory distress syndrome
274.7 Hypothyroidism

Newborn infants
Diseases and abnormalities -- Continued
275 Infectious diseases
276 Jaundice. Icterus
Cf. RJ266.8, Cholestasis
278 Kidney diseases
281 Low birth weight
Cf. RJ250+, Premature infants
286 Metabolic disorders
Nervous system diseases. Nervous system abnormalities
290 General works
290.5 Brain diseases
296 Ophthalmia. Conjunctivitis
299 Pain
301 Paralysis
Neoplasms, see RC281.C4
312 Respiratory diseases. Respiratory insufficiency
313 Retrolental fibroplasia
316 Umbilical diseases
For hemorrhages, see RJ271
320.A-Z Other diseases, A-Z
320.A26 Acute abdomen
320.B75 Bronchopulmonary dysplasia
320.D9 Dysostosis
320.H94 Hypoglycemia
320.M2 Mastitis
320.S45 Septicemia
320.S93 Sudden infant death syndrome
320.T4 Tetanus
325 Injuries of newborn infants. Birth injuries
365 Pain in children
Diseases of children
Cf. RA1225, Toxicology
Cf. RC281.C4, Oncology
Cf. RC1218.C45, Sports medicine
Cf. RE48.2.C5, Ophthalmology
Cf. RF47.C4, Otolaryngology
Cf. RF122.5.C4, Otology
Cf. RJ254+, Diseases of newborn infants
Cf. RK55.C5, Dentistry
Cf. RX501+, Homeopathy
Cf. RZ390+, Osteopathy
370 Critical diseases. Emergencies. Intensive care
Cf. RD93.5.C4, Wounds and injuries
375 Abused children
Cf. RA1122.5, Battered child syndrome (Forensic medicine)
Cf. RJ507.A29, Child psychiatry
Chronic diseases
380 General works
381 Chronic fatigue syndrome
383 Environmentally induced diseases

| | |
|---|---|
| | Diseases of children -- Continued |
| 384 | Radiation injuries |
| | Immunologic diseases |
| | Including immunopathology |
| 385 | General works |
| | Allergy |
| | Cf. RJ436.A8, Asthma |
| 386 | General works |
| 386.3 | Hay fever |
| 386.5 | Food allergy |
| 387.A-Z | Other diseases, A-Z |
| | Acquired immune deficiency syndrome, see RJ387.A25 |
| 387.A25 | AIDS |
| 387.A8 | Ataxia telangiectasia |
| 387.C48 | Chronic granulomatous disease |
| 387.D42 | Deficiency syndromes |
| | Granulomatous disease, Chronic, see RJ387.C48 |
| 390 | Diseases and disorders of metabolism and nutrition |
| 396 | Rickets |
| 399.A-Z | Other, A-Z |
| | Allergy, see RJ386+ |
| 399.A45 | Amino acid metabolism disorders |
| 399.A6 | Anorexia |
| 399.C25 | Calcium metabolism disorders |
| 399.C3 | Carbohydrate metabolism disorders |
| 399.C6 | Corpulence |
| | Food allergy, see RJ386.5 |
| 399.H94 | Hypercholesteremia |
| 399.H96 | Hyperlipidemia |
| 399.I53 | Infant formula intolerance |
| 399.I75 | Iron deficiency diseases |
| | Cf. RJ416.I75, Iron deficiency anemia |
| 399.K9 | Kwashiorkor. Marasmus |
| 399.L33 | Lactose intolerance |
| 399.L47 | Lesch-Nyhan syndrome |
| 399.L68 | Lowe's syndrome |
| 399.L95 | Lysosomal storage diseases |
| 399.M26 | Malnutrition |
| | Marasmus, see RJ399.K9 |
| 399.M83 | Mucopolysaccharidosis |
| 399.N8 | Nutrition disorders |
| | Obesity, see RJ399.C6 |
| 399.P5 | Phenylketonuria |
| 399.P52 | Phosphorus metabolism disorders |
| | Pica, see RJ506.P53 |
| 399.P6 | Protein metabolism disorders |
| 399.S3 | Scurvy |
| 399.T36 | Tay-Sachs disease |
| 399.T4 | Tetany |
| 399.T7 | Trace element deficiency diseases |
| 399.V57 | Vitamin A deficiency |
| 399.W35 | Water-electrolyte imbalances |
| | Infectious and parasitic diseases |

Diseases of children
Infectious and parasitic diseases -- Continued
401 General works
406.A-Z By disease, A-Z
406.A73 Ascariasis
406.B32 Bacterial diseases
406.L37 Larva migrans, Visceral
406.L4 Leprosy
406.M83 Mucocutaneous lymph node syndrome
Neurologic infections, see RJ496.I53
406.N68 Nosocomial infections
406.R4 Rheumatic fever
Cf. RJ426.R54, Rheumatic heart disease
Sexually transmitted diseases, see RC200.7.C45
Tuberculosis, see RC312.6.C4
Venereal diseases, see RC200.7.C45
Visceral larva migrans, see RJ406.L37
Diseases of the hemic and lymphatic systems. Hematologic diseases. Pediatric hematology
411 General works
416.A-Z By disease, A-Z
416.A25 Acute myelocytic leukemia
416.A6 Anemia
Anemia, Iron deficiency, see RJ416.I75
Anemia, Sickle cell, see RJ416.S53
416.C63 Coagulation disorders
416.H43 Hemoglobinopathy
416.H45 Hemophilia
416.H46 Hemorrhagic diseases
416.H63 Hodgkin's diseases
416.I75 Iron deficiency anemia
416.L4 Leukemia
416.S53 Sickle cell anemia
416.T42 Thalassemia
416.T45 Thrombocytopenia
416.T47 Thrombopenic purpura
Diseases of the endocrine system. Pediatric endocrinology. Pediatric neuroendocrinology
418 General works
420.A-Z By disease, A-Z
420.A27 Adrenal gland diseases
420.A3 Adrenogenital syndrome
420.D5 Diabetes
420.G65 Goiter
420.H88 Hypothalamo-hypophyseal system diseases
420.H9 Hypothyroidism
Laron dwarfism, see RJ420.P58
420.P58 Pituitary dwarfism
Including Laron dwarfism
420.P73 Precocious puberty
Diseases of the cardiovascular system
421 General works
Examination. Diagnosis

| | |
|---|---|
| | Diseases of children |
| | Diseases of the cardiovascular system |
| | Examination. Diagnosis -- Continued |
| 423 | General works |
| 423.5.A-Z | Special diagnostic methods, A-Z |
| 423.5.A52 | Angiocardiography |
| 423.5.A53 | Angiography |
| 423.5.C36 | Cardiac catheterization |
| 423.5.D54 | Digital subtraction angiography |
| | Echocardiography, see RJ423.5.U46 |
| 423.5.E43 | Electrocardiography |
| 423.5.P47 | Phonocardiography |
| 423.5.R33 | Radiography |
| 423.5.U46 | Ultrasonic cardiography. Echocardiography |
| | Therapeutics |
| 424 | General works |
| 424.5.A-Z | Special therapies, A-Z |
| 424.5.C37 | Cardiac pacing |
| 424.5.C47 | Chemotherapy |
| | Pacing, Cardiac, see RJ424.5.C37 |
| 426.A-Z | By disease, A-Z |
| 426.A7 | Arrhythmia |
| 426.A82 | Atherosclerosis |
| 426.C64 | Congenital heart disease |
| 426.C67 | Coronary heart disease |
| 426.D52 | Diabetic angiopathies |
| 426.H9 | Hypertension |
| 426.H94 | Hypotension |
| 426.P84 | Pulmonary atresia |
| 426.R54 | Rheumatic heart disease |
| 426.T73 | Transposition of great vessels |
| 426.V3 | Valvular disease |
| 426.V4 | Ventricular septal defect |
| | Diseases of the chest and the respiratory system |
| 431 | General works |
| | Examination. Diagnosis |
| 433 | General works |
| 433.5.A-Z | Special diagnostic methods, A-Z |
| 433.5.D5 | Diagnostic imaging |
| | Imaging, Diagnostic, see RJ433.5.D5 |
| 433.5.P8 | Pulmonary function tests |
| 433.5.R25 | Radiography |
| 433.5.S6 | Spirometry |
| 434 | Therapeutics. Respiratory therapy |
| 436.A-Z | By disease, A-Z |
| 436.A8 | Asthma |
| 436.A84 | Atelectasis |
| 436.B67 | Bronchial diseases |
| 436.B7 | Bronchiectasis |
| 436.B73 | Bronchitis |
| 436.C8 | Croup |
| 436.E4 | Emphysema |
| 436.I5 | Influenza |

Diseases of children
Diseases of the chest and the respiratory system
By disease, A-Z -- Continued
436.I56 Interstitial lung diseases
436.P47 Phonocardiography
436.P6 Pneumonia
436.R33 Radiography
436.R47 Respiratory insufficiency
436.U46 Ultrasonic cardiography
Diseases of the digestive system. Pediatric gastroenterology
446 General works
Examination. Diagnosis
448 General works
449.A-Z Special diagnostic methods, A-Z
449.R32 Radiography
449.U45 Ultrasonics
456.A-Z By disease, A-Z
456.A26 Abdominal pain
456.A3 Acute abdomen
456.A6 Appendicitis
456.C44 Celiac disease
Cholera infantum, see RJ456.D5
456.C52 Cholestasis
Cf. RJ266.8, Newborn infants
456.C55 Cirrhosis of the liver
456.C7 Colic
456.C74 Colitis, Ulcerative
456.C76 Constipation
456.C9 Cystic fibrosis
456.D5 Diarrhea. Infantile diarrhea
456.D9 Dysentery
456.D94 Dyspepsia
(456.E48) Encopresis
see RJ506.E5
456.E5 Enteritis
456.E83 Esophageal atresia
456.E84 Esophageal diseases
456.F43 Fecal incontinence
456.F5 Fibrosis of the liver
456.G3 Gastritis
456.G33 Gastroesophageal reflux
456.G5 Glycogenosis
456.H46 Hepatitis, Viral
456.I45 Ileus
456.I5 Intussusception
456.L5 Liver diseases (General)
456.M3 Malabsorption syndromes
456.M4 Megacolon
456.M68 Motility disorders
456.O2 Obstruction
456.P4 Peritonitis
456.P9 Pyloric spasm

Diseases of children
Diseases of the digestive system. Pediatric gastroenterology
By disease, A-Z -- Continued
456.R4 Rectal diseases
456.S57 Small intestine diseases
456.S6 Stomach diseases
Ulcerative colitis, see RJ456.C74
Diseases of the mouth, tongue, and salivary glands. Pediatric oral medicine
Cf. RK55.C5, Pediatric dentistry
460 General works
463.A-Z By disease, A-Z
Aphthae, see RJ463.T4
Deglutition, see RJ463.I54
463.I54 Ingestion disorders. Deglutition disorders
Oidium, see RJ463.T4
463.T4 Thrush
Diseases of the genitourinary system. Pediatric urology
466 General works
Examination. Diagnosis
468 General works
469.A-Z Special diagnostic methods, A-Z
469.I4 Imaging
469.K53 Kidney function tests
469.R33 Radiography
Therapeutics
470 General works
470.5.A-Z Special therapies, A-Z
470.5.P47 Peritoneal dialysis
Including continuous ambulatory peritoneal dialysis and continuous cycling peritoneal dialysis
476.A-Z By urinary disease, A-Z
476.B4 Bladder calculi
476.E6 Enuresis
476.G5 Glomerulonephritis
476.H44 Hematuria
476.H84 Hydronephrosis
476.I6 Incontinence
476.K5 Kidney diseases
476.N45 Nephrotic syndrome
476.R46 Renal insufficiency
476.U74 Urinary obstruction
476.U76 Urinary tract infections
476.V4 Vesico-ureteral reflux
Diseases and functional disorders of the genital organs
476.5 General works
Diseases of the male genital organs
477 General works
477.5.A-Z By disease, A-Z

Diseases of children
Diseases of the genitourinary system. Pediatric urology
Diseases and functional disorders of the genital organs
Diseases of the male genital organs
By disease, A-Z -- Continued
477.5.C74 Cryptorchism
477.5.K55 Klinefelter's syndrome
Diseases of the female genital organs. Pediatric gynecology
Cf. RG556.6, Obstetrics
Cf. RJ145, Menarche
478 General works
478.5.A-Z By disease, A-Z
478.5.A43 Amenorrhea, Primary
Primary amenorrhea, see RJ478.5.A43
Diseases of the musculoskeletal system
Cf. RD732.3.C48, Orthopedics
480 General works
482.A-Z By disease, A-Z
482.A25 Achondroplasia
482.A77 Arthritis, Rheumatoid
Arthritis deformans, see RJ482.A77
482.A83 Atrophy, Muscular
Blount's disease, see RJ482.O8
482.B65 Bone diseases
482.C35 Cartilage diseases
482.C65 Connective tissue diseases
482.C73 Craniosynostoses
482.D78 Duchenne muscular dystrophy
482.D9 Dystrophy, Muscular
482.E42 Elbow diseases
482.G76 Growth disorders
Cf. RJ135, Arrested development
Cf. RJ399.C6, Obesity
Cf. RJ420.P58, Pituitary dwarfism
482.H55 Hip diseases
Legg-Calvé-Perthes disease, see RJ482.O8
482.M8 Muscle diseases
Cf. RJ496.N49, Neuromuscular diseases
Muscular atrophy, see RJ482.A83
Muscular dystrophy, see RJ482.D9
482.O8 Osteochondrosis
Including Blount's disease, Legg-Calvé-Perthes disease, and Scheuermann's disease
482.O82 Osteogenesis imperfecta
482.O84 Osteoporosis
482.R48 Rheumatism. Pediatric rheumatology
Rheumatoid arthritis, see RJ482.A77
Scheuermann's disease, see RJ482.O8
482.S3 Scoliosis
482.S64 Spinal diseases

Diseases of children
Diseases of the musculoskeletal system
By disease, A-Z -- Continued
482.T6 Torticollis
Diseases of the nervous system. Pediatric neurology
Cf. RJ418+, Pediatric neuroendocrinology
486 General works
Biological child psychiatry. Pediatric neuropsychiatry. Pediatric neuropsychology
486.5 General works
486.6 Neuropsychological tests
Examination. Diagnosis
488 General works
488.5.A-Z Special diagnostic methods, A-Z
488.5.A54 Angiography
488.5.E44 Electroencephalography
488.5.E93 Evoked potentials
488.5.M33 Magnetic resonance imaging
488.5.P54 Pneumoencephalography
Potentials, Evoked, see RJ488.5.E93
488.5.R33 Radiography
488.5.R4 Reflex testing
488.5.T65 Tomography
488.5.U47 Ultrasonic encephalography
492 Brain pathology
496.A-Z By disease, A-Z
496.A25 Acalculia
496.A32 Adrenoleukodystrophy
496.A4 Agraphia
496.A5 Alexia. Dyslexia
496.A53 Alternating hemiplegia of childhood
496.A6 Aphasia
496.A63 Apraxia
Articulation disorders, see RJ496.S7
496.A8 Ataxia
(496.A86) Attention deficit disorders
see RJ506.H9
496.B7 Brain damage
Including minimal brain dysfunction
Cf. RJ496.L4, Learning disabilities
496.C4 Cerebral palsy
496.C42 Cerebral sclerosis, Diffuse
496.C45 Cerebrovascular disease
Childhood disintegrative disorder, see RJ506.C5
496.C67 Communicative disorders
496.C7 Convulsions
Including febrile convulsions
Deafness, see RF291.5.C45
496.D5 Diastematomyelia
Diffuse cerebral sclerosis, see RJ496.C42
496.D9 Dysautonomia
Dysgraphia, see RJ496.A4
Dyslexia, see RJ496.A5

Diseases of children
Diseases of the nervous system
By disease, A-Z -- Continued

496.E5 Encephalitis
496.E6 Epilepsy
Epilepsy, Infantile myoclonic, see RJ496.S58
Febrile convulsions, see RJ496.C7
496.G34 Gait disorders
(496.G55) Gilles de la Tourette's syndrome
see RJ496.T68
496.H3 Headache
496.H4 Hematoma
496.H65 Holoprosencephaly
496.H9 Hydrocephalus
Infantile paralysis, see RJ496.P2
Infantile spasms, see RJ496.S58
496.I53 Infections and infectious diseases
496.I6 Insomnia
496.L35 Language disorders
Cf. RJ496.S7, Speech disorders
496.L4 Learning disabilities
Cf. LC4704+, Education
For psychopathological aspects, see RJ506.L4
496.L44 Lennox-Gastaut syndrome
Little's disease, see RJ496.C4
496.M45 Meningitis
496.M54 Migraine
Minimal brain dysfunction, see RJ496.B7
496.M68 Movement disorders
Including extrapyramidal disorders
Cf. RJ482.M8, Muscles diseases
Cf. RJ506.P68, Psychomotor disorders
496.M84 Multiple sclerosis
496.M93 Myelin sheath pathology
Myelomeningocele, see RJ496.S74
496.N49 Neuromuscular diseases
Paralysis, Cerebral, see RJ496.C4
Paralysis, Infantile, see RJ496.P2
Paralysis, Spastic, see RJ496.S6
496.P2 Poliomyelitis
496.P64 Polyradiculoneuritis
496.S58 Spasms, Infantile
496.S6 Spastic paralysis
496.S7 Speech disorders
Including infantile articulation disorders
Cf. RJ496.L35, Language disorders
496.S74 Spina bifida
Including myelomeningocele
496.S8 Stuttering
496.T5 Tic disorders
496.T68 Tourette syndrome
496.T8 Tuberous sclerosis

Diseases of children -- Continued
Mental disorders of children and adolescents. Child psychiatry. Child mental health services
Cf. HV891+, Welfare work with mentally handicapped children
Cf. LB1091, Educational psychology
Cf. LC4165+, Education of mentally ill children
Cf. LC4600.2+, Education of mentally handicapped children
Cf. RC451.4.S7, Student mental health

| | |
|---|---|
| 499.A1 | Periodicals. Societies. Serials |
| 499.A2-Z | General works |
| 499.3 | Handbooks, manuals, etc. |
| 499.32 | Problems, exercises, examinations |
| 499.34 | Popular works |
| 500 | Study and teaching |
| 500.2 | Research |
| 500.5 | Classification |
| | By region or country |
| | United States |
| 501.A2 | General works |
| 501.A3-Z | By region or state, A-Z |
| 502.A-Z | Other regions or countries, A-Z |
| 502.3 | Child psychiatric nursing. Adolescent psychiatric nursing |
| 502.4 | Home-based services |
| 502.5 | Infant psychiatry. Infant analysis |
| 503 | Adolescent psychiatry. Adolescent psychotherapy. Adolescent analysis |
| | For specific therapies and disorders, see RJ505.A+ |
| 503.3 | Clinical psychology |
| 503.45 | Mental health consultation |
| | Examination. Assessment. Diagnosis |
| 503.5 | General works |
| 503.6 | Interviewing in child psychiatry |
| | Including adolescent psychiatry |
| 503.7.A-Z | Specific diagnostic tests and procedures, A-Z |
| 503.7.A33 | Adjustment Scales for Children and Adolescents |
| 503.7.A36 | Adolescent Psychopathology Scale |
| 503.7.B44 | Behavior Disorders Identification Scale |
| 503.7.C48 | Child Behavior Checklist |
| 503.7.C66 | Cooper-Farran Behavioral Rating Scales |
| 503.7.E56 | Emotional or Behavior Disorder Scale |
| 503.7.H68 | House-tree-person technique |
| 503.7.M54 | Millon Adolescent Clinical Inventory |
| 503.7.M56 | Minnesota Multiphasic Personality Inventory for Adolescents |
| 503.7.P37 | Parent Behavior Checklist |
| 503.7.P47 | Personality assessment |
| 503.7.P55 | Play assessment |
| 503.7.P73 | Preschool and Kindergarten Behavior Scales |
| 503.7.P76 | Projective techniques |
| 503.7.S32 | Scale for Assessing Emotional Disturbance |

| | |
|---|---|
| | Diseases of children |
| | Mental disorders of children and adolescents. Child psychiatry. Child mental health services |
| | Examination. Assessment. Diagnosis |
| | Specific diagnostic tests and procedures, A-Z -- Continued |
| 503.7.T45 | Thematic Apperception Test |
| (503.7.T73) | Transdisciplinary Play-Based Assessment see RJ51.T73 |
| 503.7.Y68 | Youth Self-Report |
| | Child psychotherapy |
| 504 | General works |
| 504.15 | Juvenile works |
| 504.2 | Child analysis |
| 504.3 | Brief psychotherapy |
| 504.4 | Crisis intervention |
| 504.5 | Residential treatment. Psychiatric hospital care |
| 504.53 | Psychiatric day treatment |
| 504.55 | Therapeutic foster care |
| 504.7 | Chemotherapy. Psychopharmacology |
| 504.8 | Electroconvulsive therapy |
| 505.A-Z | Specific therapies and special aspects of therapy, A-Z |
| 505.A7 | Art therapy |
| 505.A75 | Assertiveness training |
| 505.A9 | Autogenic training |
| 505.B4 | Behavior therapy. Behavior modification |
| 505.B5 | Bibliotherapy |
| 505.C55 | Client-centered psychotherapy |
| 505.C63 | Cognitive therapy. Cognitive-behavior therapy |
| 505.C64 | Composition (Language arts). Writing. Written communication |
| 505.C65 | Constructivism (Education) |
| 505.C68 | Countertransference |
| 505.D3 | Dance therapy |
| 505.D48 | Developmental therapy |
| 505.D73 | Dream therapy. Dreams<br>Including dreams as indicators of developmental functioning or dysfunctioning |
| 505.E25 | Ecological intervention |
| 505.E83 | Exercise therapy |
| 505.E87 | Experiential psychotherapy |
| 505.E9 | Eye movement desensitization and reprocessing |
| 505.F34 | Fantasy. Imagery |
| 505.G47 | Gestalt therapy |
| 505.G7 | Group therapy |
| 505.H86 | Hypnotherapy |
| | Imagery, see RJ505.F34 |
| 505.M48 | Metaphor |
| 505.M54 | Milieu therapy |
| 505.M68 | Movement therapy |
| | Music therapy, see ML3920 |

Diseases of children
Mental disorders of children and adolescents. Child psychiatry. Child mental health services
Child psychotherapy
Specific therapies and special aspects of therapy, A-Z -- Continued

505.P33 Pair therapy
505.P37 Parent-child interaction therapy
505.P38 Parent participation
505.P46 Personal construct therapy
505.P47 Pet therapy
505.P6 Play therapy
Including group play therapy
505.P89 Psychodrama
505.P92 Psychodynamic psychotherapy
505.R33 Rational-emotive psychotherapy
505.R36 Recreation
505.R4 Relaxation
505.R45 Resistance
505.S44 Self-management
505.S64 Solution-focused therapy
505.S66 Sports therapy
505.S75 Storytelling
505.T47 Termination of therapy or analysis
505.T53 Therapeutic community
505.T69 Touch
505.T73 Transference
505.T84 Twelve-step programs
Writing. Written communication, see RJ505.C64
506.A-Z Specific disorders, A-Z
506.A33 Adjustment disorders
Affective disorders, see RJ506.D4
506.A35 Aggressiveness
506.A4 Alcoholism
Anorexia nervosa, see RC552.A5
506.A58 Anxiety
Attachment disorder, see RJ507.A77
Attention-deficit hyperactivity disorder, see RJ506.H9
506.A9 Autism. Infantile autism
506.B44 Behavior disorders
506.B65 Borderline personality disorder
Bulimia, see RC552.B84
506.C48 Child molesting
506.C5 Childhood disintegrative disorder
506.C63 Cognition disorders
506.C65 Conduct disorders
506.D4 Depression, Mental. Affective disorders
506.D47 Developmental disabilities
506.D55 Dissociative disorders
506.D68 Down syndrome

Diseases of children
Mental disorders of children and adolescents. Child psychiatry. Child mental health services
Specific disorders, A-Z -- Continued

506.D78 Drug abuse. Substance abuse
Including abuse of individual drugs, e.g. heroin
506.D83 Dual diagnosis
506.E18 Eating disorders
Elective mutism, see RJ506.M87
506.E5 Encopresis
Enuresis, see RJ476.E6
506.F34 Fantasy. Imagery
Fear, see RJ506.P38
506.F73 Fragile X syndrome
506.F85 Fugue
506.G35 Gender identity disorders
506.H34 Hallucinations
Heroin habit, see RJ506.D78
506.H65 Homicide. Homicidal behavior
506.H9 Hyperactivity. Attention-deficit hyperactivity disorder
506.H94 Hysteria
Infantile autism, see RJ506.A9
506.I55 Infantilism
506.J88 Juvenile delinquency
506.L4 Learning disabilities
Cf. LC4704+, Education
For neurological aspects, see RJ496.L4
506.L68 Low self-esteem
Mental depression, see RJ506.D4
506.M4 Mental retardation
Minimal brain dysfunction, see RJ496.B7
Mongolism, see RJ506.D68
506.M84 Multiple personality
Mutilation, Self, see RJ506.S44
506.M87 Mutism, Elective
506.N37 Narcissism
Narcotic habit, see RJ506.D78
506.N48 Neuroses
506.O25 Obsessive-compulsive neurosis
506.O66 Oppositional defiant disorder
506.P27 Parental alienation syndrome
506.P32 Personality disorders
506.P38 Phobias. Fear
Cf. BF723.F4, Child psychology
506.P53 Pica
506.P55 Post-traumatic stress disorder
506.P63 Problem children. Problem youth
506.P66 Psychic trauma
506.P68 Psychomotor disorders
506.P69 Psychoses
506.P72 Psychosexual disorders

Diseases of children
Mental disorders of children and adolescents. Child psychiatry. Child mental health services
Specific disorders, A-Z -- Continued

506.P95 Pyromania
506.R47 Rett syndrome
506.R57 Risk-taking
506.S3 Schizophrenia
506.S33 School phobia
506.S39 Self-destructive behavior
506.S44 Self-mutilation
506.S46 Separation anxiety
506.S47 Sex addiction
506.S48 Sex offenses
506.S55 Sleep disorders
Somatization disorder, see RJ506.S66
506.S66 Somatoform disorders. Somatization disorder
Substance abuse, see RJ506.D78
506.S9 Suicidal behavior
506.T75 Trisomy
506.V56 Violence
506.W44 Williams syndrome
507.A-Z Specific causative factors, situations, abilities, etc., A-Z
507.A29 Abused children. Abused teenagers
Cf. RJ375, Medical care of abused children
Abused teenagers, see RJ507.A29
507.A34 Adolescent pregnancy
507.A36 Adopted children
507.A42 Alcoholic parents
507.A77 Attachment behavior. Attachment disorder
507.D48 Developmentally disabled children
507.D57 Disasters. Child disaster victims
507.D59 Divorced parents
Cf. RJ506.P27, Parental alienation syndrome
507.E56 Emotional deprivation
507.E57 Employed mothers
507.F33 Family relationships (General)
507.F35 Family violence
507.F47 Feral children
507.G55 Gifted children
507.H35 Handicapped children
507.H64 Homeless children
507.L53 Life change events
Marital relations of parents, see RJ507.P35
507.M44 Mentally ill parents
507.M54 Minority children
507.N37 Narcotic addicted parents
507.P35 Parent and child. Parental influences (General)
Including parents' marital relations
Cf. RJ506.P27, Parental alienation syndrome
507.P37 Parental deprivation

Diseases of children
Mental disorders of children and adolescents. Child psychiatry. Child mental health services
Specific causative factors, situations, abilities, etc., A-Z -- Continued
Physical stimulation, see RJ507.S44
507.P64 Political persecution
Including children of political prisoners
Pregnancy, Adolescent, see RJ507.A34
507.P84 Psychotherapists' children
507.R44 Refugee children
507.S43 Self
507.S44 Sensory stimulation
507.S46 Separation-individuation
507.S49 Sexually abused children
507.S53 Sibling abuse. Victims of sibling abuse
507.S55 Single parents
507.S77 Stress
507.T45 Temperament
507.U96 Uxoricide
Victims of sibling abuse, see RJ507.S53
Violence, Family, see RJ507.F35
Diseases of the skin
Cf. RJ51.C87, Cutaneous manifestations
511 General works
516.A-Z By disease, A-Z
516.E35 Eczema
520.A-Z Other diseases, A-Z
520.C64 Collagen diseases
Cf. RJ406.R4, Rheumatic fever
Cf. RJ482.A77, Rheumatoid arthritis
Cf. RJ482.R48, Rheumatism
520.D45 Dehydration
520.F47 Fever
520.H94 Hypoglycemia
520.I28 Iatrogenic diseases
520.P6 Portal hypertension
520.P7 Prader-Willi syndrome
520.P74 Prenatal substance abuse
Cf. RG580.S75, Substance abuse in pregnancy
Cf. RG629.F45, Fetal alcohol syndrome
520.R4 Reticuloendotheliosis
520.R43 Reye's syndrome
Rheumatic fever, see RJ406.R4
Substance abuse, Prenatal, see RJ520.P74
520.S83 Sudden death
520.T87 Turner's syndrome
550 Diseases of adolescence
Including manifestations of diseases
For adolescent health services, see RJ101+
For specific diseases, therapies, etc., see RJ370+

RJ

Materia medica and pharmacology
Cf. RJ52+, Therapeutics
560 General works
570 Trade publications

Dentistry
Cf. RA1062, Forensic dentistry and dental jurisprudence
1 Periodicals. Societies. Serials
Hospitals, clinics, etc.
3 General works
3.2 Mobile dental clinics
3.5.A-Z By region or country, A-Z
Museums and exhibitions, see RK68+
Boards of dental examination and registration
4 General works
By region or country
United States
5.A1-A5 General works
5.A6-Z By region or state, A-Z
Canada. British North America
6.A1-A5 General works
6.A6-Z By region or state, A-Z
Mexico
7.A1-A5 General works
7.A6-Z By region or state, A-Z
8.A-Z Central America, A-Z
*Under each country:*
*.x* *General works*
*.x2* *Local, A-Z*
9.A-Z West Indies, A-Z
Apply table at RK8.A-Z
10.A-Z South America, A-Z
Apply table at RK8.A-Z
11.A-Z Europe, A-Z
Apply table at RK8.A-Z
12.A-Z Asia, A-Z
Apply table at RK8.A-Z
13.A-Z Africa, A-Z
Apply table at RK8.A-Z
14 Australia
14.5 New Zealand
15.A-Z Pacific islands, A-Z
Apply table at RK8.A-Z
16 Yearbooks
21 Congresses
Collected works (nonserial)
24 Several authors
25 Individual authors
27 Dictionaries and encyclopedias
28 Nomenclature. Terminology. Abbreviations
Communication in dentistry
28.3 General works
28.7 Dental literature
History
29 General works
30 General special
31 Ancient

History -- Continued
32 Medieval
33 Modern
34.A-Z By region or country, A-Z
Apply table at RK8.A-Z
37 Directories
Laboratories, institutes, etc.
38 General works
39.A-Z Individual. By city, A-Z
Biography
41 Collective
43.A-Z Individual, A-Z
General works
50 Through 1900
51 1901-
51.5 General special
51.7 Hospital dental service
Public health aspects. State dentistry. Dental care
Including statistics and surveys
Cf. LB3455, Schoolchildren's teeth
52 General works
By region or country
United States
52.2 General works
52.3.A-Z By region or state, A-Z
52.4.A-Z Other regions or countries, A-Z
52.45 Statistical theory, methods, etc.
52.5 Social aspects
52.7 Dental ethics
52.8 Standards for dental care. Evaluation and quality control of dental care
53 Psychological aspects
54 Aesthetic aspects
55.A-Z By age group, class, etc., A-Z
55.A3 Aged. Geriatric dentistry
Cf. RK651.5.A44, Prosthodontics
AIDS patients, see RK55.H58
55.C45 Cerebral palsied
55.C5 Children. Pedodontics
Cf. RK306.C5, Oral and dental medicine
Cf. RK529.5.C45, Oral surgery
Cf. RK651.5.C55, Prosthodontics
Chronically ill, see RK55.S53
Geriatric dentistry, see RK55.A3
55.H28 Handicapped
Cf. RK55.M4, Mentally handicapped
Cf. RK521.8.H35, Orthodontics
55.H3 Handicapped children
Cf. RK55.M43, Mentally handicapped children
55.H45 Hemophiliacs
55.H58 HIV patients. AIDS patients
55.I5 Inmates of institutions
55.M4 Mentally handicapped

| | |
|---|---|
| | By age group, class, etc., A-Z -- Continued |
| 55.M43 | Mentally handicapped children |
| | Pedodontics, see RK55.C5 |
| 55.S53 | Sick. Chronically ill |
| 55.Y68 | Youth |
| 55.3.A-Z | By race, ethnic group, etc., A-Z |
| | Afro-Americans, see RK55.3.B52 |
| 55.3.B52 | Blacks. Afro-Americans |
| 55.3.I54 | Indians |
| 56 | Handbooks, manuals, etc. |
| 57 | Problems, exercises, examinations |
| 57.5 | Outlines, syllabi, etc. |
| | Practice of dentistry. Dental economics |
| | Including business methods and employment surveys |
| | Cf. HG9387.7+, Dental insurance |
| 58 | General works |
| | By region or country |
| | United States |
| 58.5 | General works |
| 58.6.A-Z | By region or state, A-Z |
| 58.7 | Other regions or countries, A-Z |
| | Types of dental practice |
| 59 | General works |
| 59.3.A-Z | Special types, A-Z |
| 59.3.D45 | Dental health maintenance organizations |
| 59.3.G75 | Group practice |
| 59.3.S65 | Specialty practice. Specialization |
| 59.5 | Dental records |
| | Dentistry as a profession. Dental hygiene as a profession |
| 60 | General works |
| 60.3 | Women in dentistry. Women dentists |
| | Minorities in dentistry |
| 60.4 | General works |
| 60.45 | Blacks in dentistry. Black dentists |
| 60.5 | Dental hygienists. Dental assistants. Dental nurses |
| | Preventive dentistry |
| | Including dental prophylaxis and oral hygiene |
| 60.7 | General works |
| 60.75.A-Z | Special techniques of preventive dentistry, A-Z |
| 60.75.S27 | Scaling |
| 60.8 | Dental health education |
| | Cf. LB3455, School hygiene |
| 61 | Popular works. Care and hygiene for nonprofessionals |
| 63 | Juvenile works |
| 66 | Addresses, essays, lectures |
| | Museums. Exhibitions |
| 68 | General works |

| | |
|---|---|
| | Museums. Exhibitions -- Continued |
| 69.A-Z | By region or country, A-Z |
| | *Under each country:* |
| | *.x* *General works* |
| | *.x2* *Special. By city, A-Z* |
| | Study and teaching |
| 71 | General works |
| 76 | General special |
| 78 | Graduate dental education. Fellowships, internships, etc. |
| 78.5 | Continuing dental education |
| 79 | Dental auxiliary education |
| 80 | Research. Experimentation |
| | By region or country |
| | North America |
| 86 | General works |
| | United States |
| 91 | General works |
| 96.A-Z | By region or state, A-Z |
| 97.A-Z | Individual institutions. By name, A-Z |
| 98 | Canada (Table R6) |
| 100 | Mexico (Table R6) |
| | Central America |
| 102 | General works |
| 103.A-Z | By region or country, A-Z |
| | West Indies |
| 105 | General works |
| 106.A-Z | By island, A-Z |
| | South America |
| 111 | General works |
| 113.A-Z | By region or country, A-Z |
| | Apply table at RK8.A-Z |
| | Europe |
| 114 | General works |
| | Great Britain |
| 116 | General works |
| 119 | England (Table R6) |
| 123 | Scotland (Table R6) |
| 124 | Wales (Table R6) |
| 127 | Northern Ireland (Table R6) |
| 128 | Ireland (Table R6) |
| 134 | Austria (Table R6) |
| 137 | Belgium (Table R6) |
| 141 | Denmark (Table R6) |
| 144 | France (Table R6) |
| 147 | Germany (Table R6) |
| | Including West Germany |
| 148 | East Germany (Table R6) |
| 151 | Greece (Table R6) |
| 154 | Netherlands (Table R6) |
| 157 | Italy (Table R6) |
| 161 | Norway (Table R6) |
| 164 | Portugal (Table R6) |

Study and teaching
By region or country
Europe -- Continued
167 Soviet Union (Table R6)
171 Spain (Table R6)
174 Sweden (Table R6)
177 Switzerland (Table R6)
184.A-Z Other European regions or countries, A-Z
Apply table at RK8.A-Z
184.C9 Czechoslovakia
*Subarrangement:*
*.x General works*
*.x2A-Z Local, A-Z*
Asia
186 General works
187 China (Table R6)
191 India (Table R6)
192 Sri Lanka (Table R6)
193 Burma (Table R6)
193.5 Pakistan (Table R6)
194 Japan (Table R6)
197 Iran (Table R6)
207.A-Z Other Asian regions or countries, A-Z
Apply table at RK8.A-Z
207.T87 Turkey
Apply table at RK184.C9
Africa
214 General works
217 Egypt (Table R6)
221.A-Z Other African regions or countries, A-Z
Apply table at RK8.A-Z
227 Australia (Table R6)
227.5 New Zealand (Table R6)
231.A-Z Pacific islands, A-Z
Apply table at RK8.A-Z
240 Computer applications. Data processing
Instruments, apparatus, and appliances, see RK681+
280 Oral and dental anatomy and physiology
Class here clinical works
Cf. QM306, Mouth anatomy
Cf. QM311, Teeth anatomy
Cf. QP88.6, Teeth physiology
Cf. QP146+, Mouth physiology
281 Nutritional aspects of tooth development and disease
Oral and dental hygiene and prophylaxis, see RK60.7+
287 Atlases. Pictorial works
290 Oral and dental chemistry
Cf. RK653, Dental metallurgy
Oral and dental medicine. Pathology. Diseases
Including relation of oral and dental infection to systemic diseases
Cf. QR47, Dental microbiology
Cf. RC815+, Diseases of the mouth



RK

Oral and dental medicine.
Pathology. Diseases -- Continued

301 General works
305 General special
306.A-Z By age group, class, etc., A-Z
306.C5 Children
307 Oral and dental pathology
Cf. RK287, Atlases. Pictorial works
Examination. Diagnosis
Including differential diagnosis
Cf. RK522, Orthodontic diagnosis
308 General works
Diagnostic imaging
308.5 General works
Dental radiography
309 General works
309.5 Panoramic radiography
310.A-Z Other diagnostic methods, A-Z
310.C44 Cephalometry
310.E5 Electrodiagnosis
Imaging, see RK308.5+
310.L25 Laboratory technique
310.L3 Laser interferometry
Therapeutics
Cf. RK501+, Operative dentistry
Cf. RK527+, Orthodontic therapies and appliances
Cf. RK701+, Materia medica, pharmacology, and chemotherapy
318 General works
320.A-Z Special therapies or techniques, A-Z
320.A2 Acupuncture
320.A47 Alternative treatment
320.B55 Bleaching
320.E5 Electrotherapy
320.E53 Enamel microabrasion
320.I5 Iontophoresis
320.P4 Phototherapy
320.U4 Ultrasonic therapy
320.U5 Ultraviolet therapy
322 Toothache and related orofacial pain
325 Oral sepsis
328 Dental deposits
Including dental calculus, dental plaque, and materia alba
331 Dental caries
Diseases of the enamel and dentine
340 General works
341 Endemic dental fluorosis. Mottled enamel
Diseases of the dental pulp, root, and periapical tissue. Endodontics
351 General works
354 Pulpitis

| | |
|---|---|
| | Oral and dental medicine. Pathology. Diseases |
| | Diseases of the dental pulp, root, and periapical tissue. Endodontics -- Continued |
| 356 | Pulp necrosis |
| | Diseases of the supporting structures of teeth. Periodontics |
| | Cf. RK668, Periodontal prosthesis and splints |
| 361.A1 | Periodicals. Societies. Serials |
| 361.A2 | Congresses |
| 361.A3-Z | General works |
| 371 | Alveolar abscesses |
| 375.A-Z | Other abscesses, A-Z |
| 381 | Pyorrhea |
| | Diseases of the gums |
| 401 | General works |
| 410 | Gingivitis |
| 440 | Diseases of the alveolar process |
| 450.A-Z | Other diseases, A-Z |
| 450.P4 | Periodontitis |
| 470 | Diseases and dysfunctions of the temporomandibular joint |
| 480 | Disorders of mastication |
| | Wounds and injuries |
| 490 | General works |
| 493.A-Z | By age group, class, etc., A-Z |
| 493.C55 | Children |
| | Malformations and deformities, see RK520+ |
| | Operative dentistry. Restorative dentistry |
| | For crowns, see RK666 |
| 501 | General works |
| 501.5 | General special |
| | Operative dentistry for children, see RK55.C5 |
| 503 | Preoperative technique |
| | Including patient positioning |
| | Asepsis and antisepsis |
| 506 | General works |
| 508.A-Z | Special antiseptics, A-Z |
| 508.C47 | Chlorhexidine |
| | Anesthesia in dentistry |
| 510 | General works |
| 512.A-Z | Special anesthetics or methods of anesthesia, A-Z |
| 512.H95 | Hypnotism |
| 512.N55 | Nitrous oxide |
| 512.S44 | Sedatives |
| 513 | Complications |
| 515 | Cavity preparation and treatment |
| | Fillings. Inlays |
| 517 | General works |
| 519.A-Z | Types of fillings. By material, A-Z |
| 519.A4 | Amalgam |
| 519.G6 | Gold |
| 519.P55 | Plastics |

| | |
|---|---|
| | Operative dentistry. Restorative dentistry |
| | Fillings. Inlays |
| | Types of fillings. By material, A-Z -- Continued |
| 519.P65 | Porcelain |
| 519.R44 | Resins |
| 519.T55 | Tin |
| | Orthodontics |
| 520 | Periodicals. Societies. Serials |
| 520.3 | Congresses |
| 520.6 | Directories |
| 520.8 | History |
| 521 | General works |
| 521.8.A-Z | By age group, class, etc., A-Z |
| 521.8.H35 | Handicapped |
| 521.9 | Practice of orthodontics |
| | Including business methods and employment surveys |
| 522 | Examination. Diagnosis |
| 523 | Disorders of occlusion. Malocclusion |
| 525 | Disorders of dentition |
| | Including impacted teeth, unerupted teeth, etc. |
| | Therapies and appliances |
| 527 | General works |
| 527.4 | Complications |
| 527.5 | Early treatment. Interceptive orthodontics |
| 528.A-Z | Special methods and appliances, A-Z |
| 528.B43 | Begg appliance |
| 528.E93 | Exercise. Myofunctional therapy |
| 528.E98 | Extraoral traction appliances |
| 528.M37 | Maxillary expansion |
| 528.M4 | Mechanical appliances |
| | Myofunctional therapy, see RK528.E93 |
| 528.O6 | Oral dynamics |
| 528.R45 | Removable appliances |
| 528.U5 | Universal appliances |
| | Oral surgery |
| | Cf. RD523, Face surgery |
| | Cf. RD526, Jaw surgery |
| | Cf. RK667.I45, Implant dentures |
| 529 | General works |
| 529.5.A-Z | By age group, class, etc., A-Z |
| 529.5.C45 | Children |
| 530 | Electrosurgery |
| 530.5 | Laser surgery |
| | Extraction of teeth. Exodontics |
| 531 | General works |
| 531.5 | Third molars |
| 533 | Transplantation and reimplantation of teeth |
| 535.A-Z | Other surgical procedures, A-Z |
| 535.A64 | Apicoectomy |
| 535.F53 | Flaps |
| | Prosthetic dentistry. Prosthodontics |
| 641 | History |
| 651 | General works |

| | |
|---|---|
| | Prosthetic dentistry. Prosthodontics -- Continued |
| 651.5.A-Z | By age group, class, etc., A-Z |
| 651.5.A44 | Aged |
| 651.5.C35 | Cancer patients |
| 651.5.C55 | Children |
| 652 | Dental technology. Laboratory technique |
| | Dental materials |
| | Cf. RA1270.D46, Toxicology |
| 652.5 | General works |
| | Dental adhesives and cements. Bonding |
| 652.7 | General works |
| 652.8.A-Z | Special adhesives and cements, A-Z |
| 652.8.G55 | Glass ionomer cements |
| 653 | Dental metallurgy |
| | Cf. RK290, Oral and dental chemistry |
| 653.5 | Dental ceramic metals |
| 655 | Dental ceramics. Dental porcelain |
| 655.3 | Fibrous composites in dentistry |
| 655.5 | Polymers in dentistry |
| | Dentures. Complete dentures |
| 656 | General works |
| 658 | Dental impressions and casts. Waxing |
| 660 | Preparation of vulcanite and cellullid bases |
| 663 | Preparation of other bases |
| | Including gold, silver, cadmium, etc. |
| | Partial dentures |
| 664 | General works |
| 665 | Removable partial dentures and their attachments |
| 666 | Crown and bridgework |
| 667.A-Z | Special topics, A-Z |
| 667.I45 | Implant dentures |
| 667.P5 | Pins |
| 667.T57 | Tissue-integrated prostheses |
| 668 | Periodontal prosthesis. Periodontal splints |
| | Instruments, apparatus, and appliances |
| | Cf. RK309+, Dental roentgenology |
| | Cf. RK527+, Orthodontic appliances |
| 681 | General works |
| 685.A-Z | Special, A-Z |
| 685.A75 | Articulators |
| 685.L37 | Lasers |
| | Cf. RK310.L3, Laser interferometry |
| | Cf. RK530.5, Laser surgery |
| 686 | Catalogs |
| | Materia medica and pharmacology |
| | Including chemotherapy |
| 701 | General works |
| 715.A-Z | Individual drugs and other agents, A-Z |
| 715.A58 | Antibiotics |

RK

| | |
|---|---|
| | Dermatology |
| 1 | Periodicals. Societies. Serials |
| | Hospitals, clinics, etc. |
| 20 | General works |
| 21.A-Z | By region or country, A-Z |
| 26 | Yearbooks |
| 31 | Congresses |
| | Collected works (nonserial) |
| 36 | Several authors |
| 37 | Individual authors |
| 39 | Nomenclature. Terminology. Abbreviations |
| 41 | Dictionaries and encyclopedias |
| 43 | Directories |
| 46 | History |
| | Biography |
| 46.2 | Collective |
| 46.3.A-Z | Individual, A-Z |
| | Museums. Exhibitions |
| 46.9 | General works |
| 47.A-Z | By region or country, A-Z |
| | *Under each country:* |
| | *.x* *General works* |
| | *.x2A-Z* *Special. By city, A-Z* |
| | Laboratories, institutes, etc. |
| 48 | General works |
| 49.A-Z | Individual. By city, A-Z |
| 55 | Instruments, apparatus, and appliances |
| | General works |
| 61 | Through 1900 |
| 71 | 1901- |
| 72 | General special |
| 73.A-Z | By age group, class, etc., A-Z |
| 73.A35 | Aged |
| | Children, see RJ511+ |
| 73.W65 | Women |
| | Ethnic groups |
| 73.3 | General works |
| 73.4.A-Z | Individual, A-Z |
| 74 | Handbooks, manuals, etc. |
| 74.2 | Problems, exercises, examinations |
| 74.3 | Outlines, syllabi, etc. |
| 75 | Addresses, essays, lectures |
| 77 | Study and teaching |
| 79 | Research. Experimentation |
| 81 | Atlases. Pictorial works |
| 85 | Popular works |
| 86 | Juvenile works |
| | Care and hygiene |
| | Cf. TT950+, Beauty care, manicuring, etc. |
| 87 | General works |
| 89 | Suntanning |
| | Cf. RM843, Therapy |
| | Hair |

Care and hygiene
Hair -- Continued
91 General works
92 Hair removal
94 Nails
Cf. TT958.3, Professional nail care
95 Pathological anatomy
Cf. QM481+, Normal anatomy
Cf. QM561, Histology
96 Clinical physiology and pathology
Cf. QP88+, Normal physiology
Cf. QP451, Touch
97 Immunological aspects. Immunodermatology
98 Clinical cases
100 Skin manifestations of systemic disease
Cf. RC73.7, Diagnosis
Examination. Diagnosis
105 General works
106.A-Z Special methods, A-Z
106.B5 Biopsy
106.E44 Electron microscopy
106.R34 Radiography
106.T48 Thermography
106.U48 Ultrasonic imaging
110 Therapeutics
113 Radiotherapy
Electrotherapy
Including electrolysis
115 General works
115.5 Hair removal by electrolysis
120.A-Z Other therapies, A-Z
120.C45 Chemotherapy
Cf. RL801, Materia medica and pharmacology
120.C55 Climatotherapy
120.C6 Cold. Cryotherapy
Cryotherapy, see RL120.C6
120.C9 Cytotoxic drugs
Cf. RC280.S5, Skin tumors
120.G58 Glucocorticoids
120.H6 Hormone therapy
120.L37 Lasers
120.P46 Photochemotherapy
120.P48 Phototherapy
120.R48 Retinoids
120.V5 Vitamin therapy
Surgery of the skin, see RD520+
125 Dermatological nursing
Diseases of the sebaceous glands
130 General works
131 Acne
Diseases of the sweat glands
Cf. QP220+, Secretions of the skin
141 General works

Diseases of the sweat glands -- Continued
143 Heat rash. Prickly heat
Diseases of the hair, scalp, and hair follicles
151 General works
Alopecia. Baldness
Cf. RD121.5, Hair transplantation
155 General works
155.5 Alopecia areata
159 Other
Diseases of the nails
165 General works
Nail manifestations of systemic diseases
Cf. RC73.6, Diagnosis
169 General works
170 Onychomycosis
Hyperemias, inflammations, and infections of the skin
Cf. RL765+, Dermatomycoses
201 General works
221 Boils and carbuncles. Furuncles
225 Cellulitis
Dermatitis
231 General works
241 Occupational dermatitis due to drugs, radiation, etc.
Diseases associated with hypersensitivity. Allergic diseases of the skin
242 General works
243 Atopic dermatitis
244 Contact dermatitis
247 Photosensitivity disorders. Photodermatitis
249 Urticaria
251 Eczema
271 Erythema
Herpes, see RC147.H6
283 Impetigo
291 Lichen planus
301 Pemphigus
311 Petyriasis
321 Psoriasis
Cf. RC931.P76, Psoriatic arthritis
331 Other
391 Atrophies
Hypertrophies
401 General works
411 Corns and callosities
Cf. RD563, Podiatry
431 Hypertrichosis
435 Keratosis. Ichthyosis
451 Scleroderma
Cf. RC924.5.S34, Systemic scleroderma
471 Verrucae. Warts
489 Other
Lupus and tuberculosis of the skin, see RC312.5.S5

Neoplasms of the skin, see RC280.S5
675 Chronic ulcer of the skin. Bedsores
Diseases due to psychosomatic and nerve disorders. Dermatoneuroses
701 General works
711 Anesthesia
721 Dermatalgia. Pruritis and related conditions
751 Other
Diseases due to parasites
760 General works
764.A-Z Diseases due to animal parasites, A-Z
764.C8 Cutaneous leishmaniasis
764.P4 Pediculosis. Phthiriasis
Phthiriasis, see RL764.P4
764.S28 Scabies
764.S8 Straw itch
Tick fever, see RC182.R6
Diseases due to vegetable parasites. Dermatomycoses
765 General works
Actinomycosis, see RC120
Blastomycosis, see RC123.B6
770 Favus
775 Pinta disease
780 Tinia. Ringworm
785 Other
790 Pigmentations. Albinism
793 Congenital disorders of the skin. Nevi. Moles
799 Other dermatoses (not A-Z)
801 Materia medica and pharmacology
Cf. RL110, Therapeutics
Cf. RL120.C45, Chemotherapy
Cf. RM303+, Drugs acting on the skin
803 Dermatotoxicology

Therapeutics. Pharmacology
For therapeutics for individual diseases, see the disease in RC-RL
1 Periodicals. Societies. Serials
16 Yearbooks
21 Congresses
Collected works (nonserial)
30 Several authors
31 Individual authors
36 Dictionaries and encyclopedias
38 Nomenclature. Terminology. Abbreviations
39 Directories
History
41 General works
42 General special
43 Ancient
44 Medieval
45 Modern
47.A-Z By region or country, A-Z
Biography
61 General works
62.A-Z Individual, A-Z
General works
Through 1500, see R126+
81 16th century
84 17th-18th centuries
88 19th century
101 20th century
Cf. RM121+, Therapeutics (General)
Cf. RM300+, Pharmacology (General)
103 General special
104 Handbooks, manuals, etc.
105 Problems, exercises, examinations
106 Outlines, syllabi, etc.
107 Addresses, essays, lectures
Study and teaching
108 General works
108.5.A-Z By region or country, A-Z
111 Experimental therapeutics
Cf. RM301.25, Experimental pharmacology
Therapeutics
Cf. RS78, Pharmacy
Cf. RS153, Materia medica
121 General works
121.5 Handbooks, manuals, etc.
122 Outlines, syllabi, etc.
122.5 Popular works
For popular works on drugs and their actions, see RM301.15
123 Laboratory manuals
125 Nurses' manuals
126 Problems, exercises, examinations
127 Commercial manuals

138 Drug prescribing
Including dosage
Cf. RS55.2, Generic drug substitution
139 Prescription writing
Including dosage
143 Incompatibilities in prescriptions
145 Dose books
Misuse of therapeutic drugs. Medication errors
For studies on drug abuse, see RC563+
For individual diseases, see the disease, e.g., RC271.C5, Cancer
146 General works
146.5 Physician-prescribed medication
146.7 Self-medication
Administration of drugs and other therapeutic agents
For therapy for specific diseases, see the disease
147 General works
149 Parenteral medicine. Parenteral therapy
Cf. RM224, Parenteral feeding
151 External medication. Transdermal medication
Cf. RM801+, Balneotherapy
Cf. RM884, Iontophoresis
160 Intranasal medication. Transnasal medication
161 Inhalatory medication. Respiratory therapy
Cf. RA975.5.R47, Hospital services
Cf. RC735.I5, Inhalation therapy in respiratory diseases
Cf. RJ434, Pediatrics
162 Oral medication
163 Rectal medication. Enemas
169 Hypodermic, intradermal, and intramuscular medication
Infusion. Transfusion
170 General works
170.5 Infusion pumps
Blood transfusion
Cf. RB45, Examination of the blood
Cf. RJ53.B56, Pediatrics
171 General works
171.3 Blood transfusion committees
171.4 Blood products
Cf. TP248.65.B56, Biotechnology
171.45 Plasma products
171.5 Blood coagulation factors
171.7 Blood substitutes. Plasma substitutes
172 Blood banks
172.5 Bloodmobiles
172.7 Autologous blood transfusion
173 Hemapheresis
173.3.A-Z Special, A-Z
173.3.P55 Plasmapheresis
174 Hemoperfusion
Plasma transfusion
175 General works

Administration of drugs and other therapeutic agents
Infusion. Transfusion
Plasma transfusion -- Continued
176 Plasma banks
177 Platelet transfusion
178 Infusion of glucose, saline solution, amino acids, etc.
180 Peritoneal transfusion
Other therapeutic procedures
182 Bloodletting. Leeching. Venipuncture
184 Cupping. Acupuncture. Artificial hyperemia. Mustard plasters
Cf. RM723.A27, Acupressure
184.5 Acupuncture points
186 Pneumatic aspiration
188 Spinal puncture. Cisternal puncture. Ventricular puncture
190 Pericardial puncture
Diet therapy. Clinical nutrition
Cf. RJ53.D53, Pediatrics
Cf. UH487+, Military medical services
For diet therapy for individual diseases or diseases of organs or regions, see the disease
214 Periodicals. Societies. Serials
214.3 Communication in diet therapy
214.5 History
Biography
214.6 Collective
214.62.A-Z Individual, A-Z
General works
215 Through 1900
216 1901-
217 General special
217.2 Handbooks, manuals, etc.
217.5 Outlines, syllabi, etc.
218 Study and teaching
218.5 Practice of dietetics. Dietetic economics
Including business methods and employment surveys
218.7 Nutrition counseling
Dietary cookbooks
Including hygienic cookbooks, cookery, and dietaries for the sick
219 General works
(221) Cookbooks for special groups
See the disease in RC or RJ, e.g., RC684.D5, Cardiacs; RC821, Peptic ulcer patients
Diets to control weight
222 General works
222.2 Reducing weight
Cf. RC552.O25, Psychiatric aspects of obesity
Cf. RC628+, Clinical aspects of obesity
222.3 Gaining weight
Methods of feeding

Diet therapy. Clinical nutrition
Methods of feeding -- Continued

222.5 General works
223 Rectal feeding
Cf. RM163, Rectal medication
224 Parenteral feeding
225 Enteral feeding. Tube feeding
Fasting
226 General works
226.5 General special
228.A-Z Cases, A-Z
229 Elemental diet
Animal diet
230 Meat
Including raw meat and meat juices
Cf. TX371+, Animal foods
231 Seafood
232 Egg-free diet
Milk diet
233 General works
234 Sour milk. Buttermilk
234.5 Milk-free diet
235 Macrobiotic diet
235.5 Orthomolecular therapy
236 Vegetable diet
Including raw vegetables and vegetable juices
Cf. TX391+, Vegetable foods and vegetarianism
237 Fruit diet
Including raw fruit and fruit juices
Raw foods
Cf. TX391+, Vegetable foods
237.5 General works
Raw juice diet, see RM255+
Raw meat diet, see RM230
Raw vegetable diet, see RM236
237.55 Natural food diet
237.56 High-calcium diet
237.58 Complex-carbohydrate diet
237.59 High-carbohydrate diet
237.6 High-fiber diet
237.63 High-potassium diet
237.65 High-protein diet
Low-calorie diet, see RM222.2
237.7 Low-fat diet
Cf. RM222.2, Reducing diets
237.73 Low-carbohydrate diet
Cf. RM222.2, Reducing diets
237.75 Low-cholesterol diet
237.77 Monosodium glutamate-free diet
237.8 Salt-free diet
237.85 Sugar-free diet
237.86 Gluten-free diet
237.87 Wheat-free diet

Diet therapy. Clinical nutrition -- Continued

237.9 Other diets

Liquid diet. Beverages

General works

238 Through 1900

239 1901-

Tea. Coffee. Chocolate. Cocoa

240 General works

241 Chocolate. Cocoa

246 Coffee

251 Tea

Cf. RM257.M3, Mate

Water

252 General works

253 Hot water

Juice diet

255 General works

Meat juice diet, see RM230

Vegetable juice diet, see RM236

Fruit juice diet, see RM237

256 Wine

257.A-Z Other beverages, A-Z

257.A42 Alcoholic beverages

257.B4 Beer

Herbal teas, see RM666.H33

257.K4 Kephir

257.K8 Kumiss

257.M3 Mate

Milk, see RM233+

258 Other food preparations

Including commercial preparations

Dietary supplements

For individual dietary supplements, see RM666.A+

258.5 General works

259 Vitamin therapy

For individual vitamins, see RM666.A+

Chemotherapy

For antibacterial agents, see RM409

For individual drugs, see RM666.A+

For chemotherapy for individual diseases, see RC

260 Periodicals. Societies. Serials

260.2 Congresses

History

261 General works

261.3.A-Z By region or country, A-Z

262 General works

263 General special

Antibiotic therapy. Antibiotics
For dentistry, see RK715.A58
For gynecology and obstetrics, see RG129.A56
For individual drugs, see RM666.A+
For pediatrics, see RJ53.A5
For pharmaceutical microbiology, see QR46.5
For specific antibiotics and groups of antibiotics, see RM666.A+
For antibiotic therapy for individual diseases, see RC
265 Periodicals. Societies. Serials
265.2 Congresses
267 General works
Immunotherapy. Serotherapy
Cf. QR180+, Immunology
Cf. RA638, Preventive immunization
For immunotherapy or serotherapy of individual diseases, see the disease, e.g. RC271.I45, Cancer; RE992.S4, Eye diseases
270 Periodicals. Societies. Serials
271 Laboratories, institutes, etc.
History
272 General works
273.A-Z By region or country, A-Z
275 General works
276 General special
278 Antitoxins
279 Immune sera. Convalescent sera
280 Protein therapy
281 Vaccinotherapy. Vaccines
282.A-Z Other, A-Z
282.A5 Antilymphocytic serum
282.C95 Cytokines
282.G3 Gamma globulin
282.I44 Immunoglobulins
282.I47 Interleukin 1
282.M65 Monoclonal antibodies
Cf. QR186.85, Immunology
282.O6 Opsonins
282.P5 Phytohemagglutinins
282.T7 Transfer factor
Cf. QR185.8.T67, Immunology
Endocrinotherapy. Organotherapy
For endocrinotherapy in individual diseases, see RC
283 Periodicals. Societies. Serials
History
284 General works
285.A-Z By region or country, A-Z
286 General works
287 General special
Drugs of endocrine origin
Cf. RG129.H6, Gynecology
288 General works

RM

Endocrinotherapy. Organotherapy
Drugs of endocrine origin -- Continued

289 Thyroid
290 Parathyroid
Anterior pituitary hormones
291 General works
291.2.A-Z Individual hormones, A-Z
ACTH, see RM291.2.C65
291.2.C65 Corticotropin
291.2.F65 Follicle-stimulating hormone
FSH, see RM291.2.F65
291.2.G6 Gonadotropin
291.2.S6 Somatropin
291.2.T4 Thyrotropin
Posterior pituitary hormones
291.5 General works
291.7.A-Z Individual hormones, A-Z
291.7.O9 Oxytocin
291.7.V3 Vasopressin
Adrenal hormones
292 General works
Adrenocortical hormones
292.2 General works
Glucocorticoids
292.3 General works
292.4.A-Z Individual, A-Z
292.4.C6 Corticosterone
292.4.C67 Cortisone
292.4.H9 Hydrocortisone
292.4.P7 Prednisone
Mineralocorticoids
292.5 General works
292.6.A-Z Individual, A-Z
292.6.A4 Aldosterone
Adrenal medulla hormones
292.7 General works
292.8.A-Z Individual, A-Z
292.8.A3 Adrenaline
292.8.N6 Norepinephrine
292.9 Glucagon
293 Insulin
294 Sex hormones
295 Female
296 Male
296.5.A-Z Individual, A-Z
296.5.D45 Dehydroepiandrosterone
296.5.T47 Testosterone
297.A-Z Other, A-Z
297.M44 Melatonin
297.P4 Peptide hormones
297.S74 Steroid hormones
298.A-Z Extracts and secretions of other organs, A-Z
298.C64 Colostrum

Endocrinotherapy. Organotherapy
Extracts and secretions
of other organs, A-Z -- Continued
298.L9 Lymph
298.P5 Placenta
298.T5 Thymus
298.U7 Urine
Drugs and their actions
Cf. RA1160, Forensic pharmacology
Cf. RA1238, Drug toxicology
Cf. RC953.7, Geriatric pharmacology
Cf. RG627.6.D79, Drug effects on the fetus
Cf. RJ560+, Pediatric pharmacology
For individual drugs, see RM666.A+
300 General works
301 General special
301.12 Handbooks, manuals, etc.
301.13 Problems, exercises, examinations
301.14 Outlines, syllabi, etc.
301.15 Popular works
301.17 Juvenile works
301.25 Research. Experimental pharmacology. Drug development
301.27 Clinical trials
301.28 Clinical pharmacology
301.3.A-Z Special factors in drug response, A-Z
301.3.C47 Chronopharmacology
301.3.G45 Genetics. Pharmacogenetics
Pharmacogenetics, see RM301.3.G45
301.3.S48 Sex
301.35 Developmental pharmacology
301.4 Biopharmaceutics
301.41 Drug receptors
301.42 Structure-activity relationship
301.45 Therapeutic equivalency
Cf. RS55.2, Generic drug substitution
301.5 Pharmacokinetics
Drug metabolism
301.55 General works
301.56 Activation
301.57 Prodrugs
301.6 Bioavailability
301.63 Drug targeting
Bioequivalency, see RM301.45
301.65 Molecular pharmacology
301.7 Quantum pharmacology
301.8 Dose-response relationship of drugs
301.9 Drug monitoring
302 Drug interactions
Cf. QP624.75.D77, DNA-drug interactions
For drug interactions in anesthesia, see RD82.7.D78
302.2 Drug antagonism
302.3 Drug synergism

Drugs and their actions
Drug interactions -- Continued
302.4 Drug-nutrient interactions
302.5 Drug side effects (General)
302.6 Drug withdrawal symptoms
302.7 Drug discrimination
Drugs acting on the skin
303 General works
305 Irritants
306 Epispastics. Vesicants. Moxa
307 Protectives. Emollients
309 Other
e.g. Demulcents
312 Drugs acting on the skeletal muscles
Cf. RD83.5, Neuromuscular blocking agents in anesthesia
Drugs acting on the nervous system. Neuropsychopharmacology
Cf. RC483+, Psychotherapy
315 General works
316 Drugs of abuse. Designer drugs
319 Anodynes. Analgesics
321 Antipyretics. Febrifuges
Cf. RM405, Anti-inflammatory agents
322 Antispasmodics
Autonomic drugs
323 General works
323.3 Parasympatholytic agents
323.4 Parasympathomimetic agents
323.5 Sympatholytic agents
323.6 Sympathomimetic agents
324.8 Hallucinogens
325 Hypnotics. Sedatives
Cf. RK512.S44, Dental anesthetics
328 Narcotics
Cf. RA1242.N3, Toxicology
330 Depressants
Cf. RD78.3+, Anesthesiology
331 Placebos
Stimulants. Antidepressants
332 General works
332.3 Appetite depressants
333 Tranquilizing drugs
333.5 Anti-psychotic drugs
334 Nootropic agents
335 Drugs acting on the blood cells and bloodforming organs
340 Drugs affecting blood coagulation
Drugs acting on the cardiovascular system
345 General works
347 Depressants
349 Stimulants
Including cardiac glycosides

Drugs and their actions -- Continued
Drugs acting on the digestive system
355 General works
356 Anthelmintics. Vermifuges
357 Cathartics. Purgatives
359 Emetics
361 Digestants
365 Gastric antacids
367 Drugs acting on the liver
Drugs acting on the immune system. Immunopharmacology
Cf. RM270+, Immunotherapy
370 General works
371 Antiallergic agents
373 Immunosuppressive agents
Drugs acting on the urinary organs
375 General works
377 Diuretics and antidiuretics
Drugs acting on the reproductive organs
Cf. RG137.4+, Contraceptive drugs
Cf. RG137.5, Oral contraceptives
Cf. RG734.4+, Abortifacients
Cf. RM294, Sex hormones
380 General works
382 Emmenagogues
384 Oxytocics
386 Other
Including aphrodisiacs and anaphrodisiacs
Drugs acting on the respiratory system. Pulmonary pharmacology
388 General works
388.5 Bronchodilators
388.7 Mucoactive drugs
Drugs affecting secretions
390 General works
392 Astringents
400 Antiseptics and disinfectants
Cf. RA761+, Public health and hygiene
405 Anti-inflammatory agents. Antiphlogistics
Cf. RM321, Antipyretics
405.5 Nonsteroidal anti-inflammatory agents
409 Antibacterial agents
410 Antifungal agents
Antineoplastic agents, see RC271.C5
411 Antiviral agents
412 Antiparasitic agents
Cf. RM356, Anthelmintics
666.A-Z Individual drugs and other agents, A-Z
666.A12 Abecarnil
ACTH, see RM291.2.C65
666.A13 Acacia
666.A15 Acarbose
666.A18 Acemetacin
666.A19 Acetaminophen



RM

Drugs and their actions
Individual drugs and other agents, A-Z -- Continued

666.A23 Acetophenetidin
666.A26 Aconite
666.A27 Actinomycin
Activated carbon, see RM666.C34
Adrenal hormones, see RM292+
666.A275 Adenine arabinoside
666.A278 Adenosylmethionine
Adrenal medulla hormones, see RM292.7+
Adrenalin, see RM292.8.A3
Adrenocortical hormones, see RM292.2+
Adriamycin, see RM666.D68
666.A33 Albuterol
Aldosterone, see RM292.6.A4
666.A4 Alkaloids
666.A412 Almond
666.A414 Aloe
666.A42 Alum
666.A423 Amantadine
666.A425 Amidines
666.A426 Amiloride
666.A45 Amino acids
Amino acids, Excitatory, see RM666.E87
666.A456 Aminoglycosides
666.A465 Aminopyridines
666.A48 Amitriptyline
666.A485 Amlodipine
666.A49 Amoxicillin
666.A493 Amphetamine
666.A495 Anise
Anterior pituitary hormones, see RM291+
666.A5 Antihistamines
Antilymphocytic serum, see RM282.A5
666.A55 Antimony
666.A555 Antioxidants
666.A56 Antipyrine
666.A564 Antisense nucleic acids
666.A57 Antlers
666.A617 Apomorphine
666.A62 Apple
666.A65 Arnica
666.A68 Aromatic plants. Aromatherapy
Including essences and essential oils
666.A7 Arsenic and arsenic compounds
Arsenobenzol, see RM666.A77
666.A77 Arsphenamine. Arsenobenzol. Salvarsan "606"
666.A78 Arylindandiones
666.A79 Ascorbic acid. Vitamin C
666.A815 Asparagus
666.A82 Aspirin
666.A823 Astemizole
666.A83 Atabrine

Drugs and their actions
Individual drugs and other agents, A-Z -- Continued

666.A9 Aureomycin
666.A93 Azapropazone
666.A95 Aztreonam
666.B2 Bacitracin
666.B213 Bael (Tree)
666.B22 Bamboo
666.B23 Bamethan
666.B24 Banyan tree
666.B3 Barbiturates
666.B34 Barley. Green barley. Dried green barley juice
666.B375 Bee pollen
666.B378 Bee products
666.B38 Bee venom
666.B4 Belladonna
666.B416 Bentonite
666.B42 Benzodiazepines
666.B425 Benzopyran
666.B45 Bermuda grass
666.B46 Beta lactam antibiotics
666.B467 Bifonazole
666.B47 Biguanide
666.B48 Bioflavonoids. Vitamin P
666.B54 Bitumen
666.B57 Black cumin
666.B68 Bradykinin
666.B74 Brevicolline
666.B82 Bromocriptine
666.B84 Bumetanide
666.B87 Buspirone
666.C13 Cabbage
666.C24 Calcium
666.C243 Calcium antagonists
Camomiles, see RM666.C3797
666.C25 Camphor
666.C266 Cannabis. Marijuana
666.C27 Cantharides
Capsaicin, see RM666.H57
666.C29 Carbenoxolone
Carbolic acid, see RM666.P5
666.C34 Carbon, Activated
Cardiac glycosides, see RM349
666.C364 Carfecillin
666.C365 Carisoprodol
666.C367 Carnitine. Vitamin BT
666.C3675 Carprofen
666.C368 Carrots
666.C37 Cascara
666.C375 Castor oil
666.C377 Catapresan
666.C378 Catecholamines
666.C37817 Cefoperazone

Drugs and their actions
Individual drugs and other agents, A-Z -- Continued

666.C37819 Cefotaxime
666.C3782 Cefotetan
666.C3783 Cefuroxime
666.C3785 Celandine
666.C3786 Celery
666.C3788 Centrophenoxine
666.C379 Cephalosporins
666.C3794 Cephradine
666.C3797 Chamomiles
Including German chamomile and Roman chamomile
666.C38 Chaulmugra oil
666.C39 Chitin. Chitosan
Chloramphenicol, see RM666.C516
666.C42 Chlorella
666.C516 Chloromycetin. Chloramphenicol
666.C5215 Chloroquine
666.C522 Chlorothiazide
666.C524 Chocolate
Cider vinegar, see RM666.V55
666.C529 Cimetidine
666.C53 Cinchona. Quinine
666.C5415 Cinnarizine
666.C5418 Ciprofloxacin
666.C542 Citrullus colocynthis
666.C545 Clay
Cf. RM822.M9, Mud baths
666.C547 Clindamycin
666.C548 Clofibrate
666.C55 Clonazepam
666.C56 Clonidine
666.C564 Clopenthixol
666.C566 Co-trifamole
666.C567 Co-trimoxazole
666.C59 Coca
666.C6 Cod liver oil
666.C63 Codeine
Coenzyme Q, see RM666.U24
666.C68 Collagenase
666.C69 Comfrey
666.C72 Coriander
Corticosterone, see RM292.4.C6
Corticotropin, see RM291.2.C65
Cortisone, see RM292.4.C67
666.C76 Coumarine
666.C84 Cromolyn sodium
666.C94 Curare
666.C95 Curare-like agents
666.C975 Cyclacillin
666.C976 Cyclic nucleotides
666.C978 Cyclosporine
666.C985 Cytidine diphosphate choline

Drugs and their actions
Individual drugs and other agents, A-Z -- Continued

666.C987 Cytokines
666.D26 Dandelions
666.D3 Datura stramonium
Declomycin, see RM666.D375
666.D37 Deferoxamine
Dehydroepiandrosterone, see RM296.5.D45
666.D375 Demeclocycline
666.D38 Desipramine
666.D45 Dextrose
666.D458 Diazoxide
666.D46 Dibenamine
666.D47 Dicumarol
666.D48 Diflunisal
666.D5 Digitalis
666.D557 Dimethyl sulfone
666.D56 Dimethyl sulphoxide
Diphenylhydantoin, see RM666.P58
666.D574 Dipyridamole
666.D575 Dipyrone
(666.D58) Disodium cromoglycate
see RM666.C84
666.D583 Disulfiram
666.D59 Dithiocarbamates
666.D63 Dobutamine
666.D65 Domperidone
666.D66 Dopamine
666.D68 Doxorubicin
666.D7 Doxycycline
Dried green barley juice, see RM666.B34
666.E34 Eggs
666.E38 Eicosanoids
666.E43 Eleutherococcus
666.E54 Emodin
666.E548 Enzyme inhibitors
666.E55 Enzymes
666.E58 Ephedrine
666.E78 Ergoloid mesylates
666.E8 Ergot
Essences and essential oils, see RM666.A68
666.E834 Erythropoietin
666.E84 Ethamsylate
666.E845 Ethylenediaminetetracetic acid
666.E847 Eucommia ulmoides
666.E86 Evening primrose oil
666.E87 Excitatory amino acids
Female sex hormones, see RM295
666.F4 Fenazepan
666.F42 Fenclofenac
666.F44 Feverfew
666.F47 Figs
666.F49 Filgrastim

Drugs and their actions
Individual drugs and other agents, A-Z -- Continued

666.F495 FK-506
666.F5 Flumazenil
666.F52 Flunitrazepam
666.F57 Folic acid. Vitamin M
666.F58 Folic acid antagonists. Vitamin M antagonists
666.F62 Forskolin
666.F64 Fosfomycin
666.F8 Furagin
666.F82 Furazolidone
666.F84 Furosemide
666.F85 Fusidic acid
666.G125 Galanthamine
666.G127 Gamma-hydroxybutyrate
Gamma globulin, see RM282.G3
666.G13 Gangleron
666.G15 Garlic
Gemstones, see RM666.P825
666.G44 Gentamicin
German chamomile, see RM666.C3797
666.G46 Germanium
666.G48 Ghee
666.G488 Ginger
666.G489 Ginkgo
666.G49 Ginseng
Glucocorticoids, see RM292.3+
666.G5 Glucosides
Glycosides, Cardiac, see RM349
666.G7 Gold
Gonadotropin, see RM291.2.G6
666.G75 Grapes
Green barley, see RM666.B34
666.G95 Gynostemma pentaphyllum
666.H24 Haloperidol
666.H245 Hawthorns
Including individual species
666.H25 Hematopoietic growth factors
666.H26 Henna
666.H28 Heparin
666.H3 Heptamycin
666.H33 Herbs. Herbal teas
Cf. RS164+, Pharmacy
666.H35 Heroin
666.H39 Hexoprenalin
666.H5 Histamine
666.H55 Honey
666.H57 Hot peppers. Capsaicin
666.H68 Hydazepam
666.H7 Hydralazine
666.H77 Hydrochloric acid
Hydrocortisone, see RM292.4.H9
666.H83 Hydrogen peroxide

Drugs and their actions
Individual drugs and other agents, A-Z -- Continued

| | |
|---|---|
| 666.H87 | Hydroxyethyl starch |
| 666.H88 | Hydroxytryptophan |
| | Hyperbaric oxygen, see RM666.O83 |
| 666.H9 | Hypophosphites |
| 666.I13 | INHA-17 |
| 666.I2 | Ichthyol |
| 666.I35 | Imidazoline |
| 666.I37 | Imiphos |
| 666.I4 | Imipramine |
| | Insulin, see RM293 |
| 666.I58 | Interferon |
| 666.I6 | Iodine |
| 666.I64 | Iodinol |
| 666.I7 | Ipecac |
| 666.I8 | Iron |
| 666.I82 | Iron chelates |
| 666.I9 | Iturine |
| 666.K36 | Kasugamycin |
| 666.K38 | Kava plant |
| | Lactam antibiotics, Beta, see RM666.B46 |
| 666.L3 | Lead |
| 666.L39 | Lebbek tree |
| 666.L4 | Lecithin |
| 666.L42 | Leflunomide |
| 666.L43 | Lemon |
| 666.L44 | Lettuce |
| 666.L45 | Lidoflazine |
| 666.L46 | Lincomycin |
| 666.L54 | Lipoic acid |
| 666.L56 | Lisuride |
| 666.L57 | Lithium |
| 666.L59 | Lonidamine |
| 666.L6 | Lorazepam |
| 666.L64 | Lormetazepam |
| | LSD, see RM666.L88 |
| | Lynestrenol, see RG137.6.L86 |
| 666.L88 | Lysergic acid diethylamide. LSD |
| 666.L9 | Lysozyme |
| 666.M25 | Macrolide antibiotics |
| 666.M26 | Macromolecules |
| 666.M3 | Magnesium |
| 666.M314 | Magnesium carbonate |
| 666.M317 | Maitaka |
| | Male sex hormones, see RM296 |
| 666.M324 | Mango |
| 666.M325 | Mannite |
| 666.M326 | Margosa |
| | Marijuana, see RM666.C266 |
| 666.M35 | MDMA |
| 666.M357 | Melaleuca alternifolia oil |
| 666.M4 | Menthol |

Drugs and their actions
Individual drugs and other agents, A-Z -- Continued

666.M43 Meprobamate
666.M5 Mercury
666.M512 Metalloproteinase inhibitors
666.M513 Metals
666.M514 Methisazone
666.M515 Methohexital
(666.M53) Methyl sulphoxide
see RM666.D56
666.M54 Methyldopa
Methylmethionine sulphonium, see RM666.V59
666.M546 Metoclopramide
666.M547 Metronidazole
Mineralocorticoids, see RM292.5+
666.M65 Minocycline
666.M68 Mistletoe
666.M75 Molasses
666.M8 Morphine
666.M83 Moxifloxacin
666.M85 Mulberries
666.M87 Mushrooms
666.N32 Nadolol
666.N34 Neem
666.N35 Neomycin
666.N44 Nettles
666.N48 Nicotine
666.N5 Nicotinic acid
666.N53 Nifedipine
666.N55 Nimodipine
666.N725 Nitroglycerine
666.N727 Nitroimidazoles
Nomifensine, see RC483.5.N66
Norepinephrine, see RM292.8.N6
Norethindrone, see RG137.6.N67
(666.N84) Novocaine
see RM666.P837
666.N85 Novoimanin
666.N87 Nucleic acids
Nucleotides, Cyclic, see RM666.C976
666.N92 Nutgrass
666.O25 Ocimum sanctum
666.O27 Octreotide acetate
666.O45 Omega-3 fatty acids
666.O47 Omeprazole
666.O5 Onions
666.O6 Opium
Opsonins, see RM282.O6
666.O7 Oranges
666.O73 Organic compounds
666.O78 Oxyfedrine
666.O8 Oxygen
666.O83 Oxygen, Hyperbaric

Drugs and their actions
Individual drugs and other agents, A-Z -- Continued
Oxytocin, see RM291.7.O9
666.O9 Ozone
666.P28 Pangamic acid. Vitamin B15
Parathyroid hormones, see RM290
666.P29 Pau d'arco
PCP, see RM666.P49
666.P35 Penicillin
666.P37 Pentazocine
666.P375 Pentoxifylline
666.P38 Pepper (Spice)
666.P385 Peppermint
Peptide hormones, see RM297.P4
666.P415 Peptides
666.P43 Peruvoside
666.P45 Petroleum
666.P48 Peyote
666.P49 Phencyclidine. PCP
666.P5 Phenol. Carbolic acid
666.P52 Phenothiazine
666.P53 Phenpentadiol
666.P54 Phenylbutazone
666.P56 Phenylindandione
666.P57 Phenylpropanolamine
666.P58 Phenytoin
666.P67 Phosphatidylserines
666.P73 Photosensitizing compounds
666.P757 Pimaricin
666.P764 Piper betle
666.P765 Piperacillin
666.P767 Pipothiazine
666.P77 Pipradrol
666.P774 Pirenzepine
666.P777 Piroxicam
Pituitary hormones, see RM291+
666.P78 Plasminokinase
666.P782 Platelet activating factor
666.P785 Plums
666.P795 Pollen
Pollen, Bee, see RM666.B375
666.P796 Polyene antibiotics
666.P797 Polymers
666.P798 Pomegranate
Posterior pituitary hormones, see RM291.5+
666.P8 Potassium
666.P822 Povidone
666.P824 Prazosin
666.P825 Precious stones
Prednisone, see RM292.4.P7
666.P826 Prenylamine
666.P828 Primaquine
666.P83 Pristinamycin

Drugs and their actions
Individual drugs and other agents, A-Z -- Continued

666.P837 Procaine
666.P84 Prochlorperazine
666.P847 Propolis
666.P85 Propranolol
666.P855 Prostacyclin
666.P857 Prostaglandins
666.P858 Prostanoids
666.P86 Prostigmine
666.P87 Proteins
666.P88 Psoralens
666.P89 Pulmonary surfactant
666.P92 Pumpkin
Quinine, see RM666.C53
666.Q55 Quinolone antibacterial agents
666.R24 Radish
666.R26 Ranitidine
666.R3 Ratany
666.R34 Rauwolfia
666.R37 Recombinant molecules
666.R38 Red yeast rice
666.R4 Reserpine
666.R5 Rhubarb
666.R54 Ribavirin
666.R55 Riboflavin. Vitamin B2
666.R554 Ribonucleic acid. RNA
666.R57 Rifamycins
666.R574 Rimazolium
666.R575 Risperidone
RNA, see RM666.R554
Roman chamomile, see RM666.C3797
666.R58 Rosemary
666.R59 Roses
666.R6 Royal jelly
666.R88 Rutin
666.S13 SP54
666.S15 Sage
666.S157 Saitarin
666.S165 Salicylates
666.S183 Salts
Salvarsan, see RM666.A77
666.S186 Salvinorin A
666.S193 Santonin
666.S195 Saponins
666.S2 Sarsaparilla
666.S28 Saw palmetto
666.S4 Scilla
666.S44 Seashells
666.S443 Seawater
Cf. RM819, Therapeutic use of seawater baths
666.S46 Serotonin
666.S465 Shiitake

Drugs and their actions
Individual drugs and other agents, A-Z -- Continued
Sex hormones, see RM294
666.S47 Sigmamycin
666.S5 Silver nitrate
666.S515 Sisomicin
666.S52 Snake venom proteins
666.S53 Sodium nitroferricyanide
666.S54 Sodium oxybate
Somatropin, see RM291.2.S6
666.S56 Sorbitol
666.S58 Sotalol
666.S59 Soybean. Soyfoods
666.S64 Spices
666.S66 Spironolactone
666.S662 Spirostan
666.S663 Spirulina
666.S67 Splenin
666.S68 Squalene
666.S72 Streptogramins
666.S73 Streptomycin
666.S75 Strophanthin
666.S8 Strychnine
666.S82 Subtilin
666.S822 Sucralfate (Therapeutics)
666.S823 Sugar
666.S825 Sulfalene
666.S827 Sulfinpyrazone
666.S836 Sulphamethoxazole
666.S85 Sulphanilamide
666.S87 Sulphapyridine
666.S88 Sulphonamides
666.S9 Sulphur. Sulphur drugs
666.S94 Sulpiride
666.T25 Tea fungus
666.T3 Terramycin
666.T33 Tetracyclines
666.T39 Theophylline
666.T4 Thialion
666.T42 Thiazines
666.T43 Thioctic acid
666.T44 Thiols
666.T5 Thymol
Thyroid hormones, see RM289
Thyrotropin, see RM291.2.T4
666.T53 Ticarcilin
666.T55 Ticlopidine
666.T6 Tobacco
666.T65 Tocopherol. Vitamin E
666.T73 Trace elements
666.T738 Transforming growth factors-beta
666.T74 Transition metal complexes
666.T75 Trasylol

Drugs and their actions
Individual drugs and other agents, A-Z -- Continued

666.T76 Trazodone
666.T78 Triamterene
666.T784 Triazolam
666.T79 Trichosanthin
666.T8 Trifluoperazine
666.T82 Trimethoprim
666.T83 Triparanol
666.T85 Tromethamine
666.T87 Tunicamycin
666.T88 Tumeric
666.U24 Ubiquinones. Coenzyme Q
666.U75 Uridine diphosphate sugars
666.U78 Ursodeoxycholic acid
666.V33 Valproic acid
Vasopressin, see RM291.7.V3
666.V49 Verapamil
666.V53 Vinblastine
666.V55 Vinegar
Including cider vinegar
Vitamin B2, see RM666.R55
666.V57 Vitamin B6
Vitamin B15, see RM666.P28
Vitamin BT, see RM666.C367
Vitamin C, see RM666.A79
Vitamin E, see RM666.T65
666.V58 Vitamin K
Vitamin M, see RM666.F57
Vitamin M antagonists, see RM666.F58
Vitamin P, see RM666.B48
666.V59 Vitamin U
666.W37 Watermelons
666.W45 Wheat
666.X9 Xylitol
666.Y63 Yogurt
666.Z55 Zinc
666.Z95 Zymosan

Nonprescription drugs. Patent medicines
Cf. RA401.A+, State regulation
Cf. RS250+, Materia medica

671.A1 General works
671.A2-Z Special, A-Z
Arrange by name of preparation if well known, otherwise by name of manufacturer
671.5.A-Z By region or country, A-Z

Mineral waters
For natural mineral water by region, country, or resort, see RA803, RA805, etc.

674 General works
676 Artificial mineral waters

Physical medicine. Physical therapy
Cf. RD52.P59, Postoperative physical therapy
Cf. RD736.P47, Orthopedics
Cf. RD792+, Orthopedic rehabilitation
For physical therapy for individual diseases, see the disease
For serum therapy for individual diseases, see the disease in RC or RM

695 Periodicals. Societies. Serials
696 Congresses
696.5 Dictionaries and encyclopedias
Directories
697.A2 General
697.A3-Z By region or country, A-Z
Instruments, apparatus, and appliances
698 General works
698.5.A-Z Special, A-Z
History
699 General works
699.3.A-Z By region or country, A-Z
Biography
699.5 Collective
699.7.A-Z Individual, A-Z
700 General works
701 General special
701.6 Problems, exercises, examinations
702 Popular works
Nurses' manuals, see RM700
705 Physical therapy as a profession
Study and teaching
706 General works
707.A-Z By region or country, A-Z
708 Research
708.2 Computer applications. Data processing
713 Practice of physical medicine and therapy. Physical medicine and therapy economics
Including business methods and employment surveys
Bloodletting, see RM182
Cupping, see RM184
Artificial hyperemia, see RM184
Mechanotherapy. Massage, exercise, etc.
719 General works
Massage
Including vibration
Cf. RA780.5, Personal health
721 General works
722 Massage therapy as a profession
723.A-Z Special methods, A-Z
723.A27 Acupressure
723.C5 Chinese massage
723.R43 Reflexology
723.S4 Segmental massage
Shiatsu, see RM723.A27

Physical medicine. Physical therapy
Mechanotherapy. Massage, exercise, etc.
Massage
Special methods, A-Z -- Continued
723.S8 Swedish massage
724 Manipulation
Exercise
Cf. RC350.E85, Neurology
Cf. RC684.E9, Cardiology
Cf. RD736.E88, Orthopedics
Cf. RJ53.E95, Pediatrics
Cf. RK528.E93, Orthodontics
725 General works
727.A-Z Special systems, A-Z
Aquatic exercises, see RM727.H8
727.C54 Ch'i kung
Hatha yoga, see RM727.Y64
727.H8 Hydrogymnastics. Aquatic exercises
727.I76 Isokinetic exercise
727.J64 Jogging
727.T34 T'ai chi ch'üan
727.W34 Walking
727.Y64 Yoga, Hatha
Cf. BL1238.56.H38, Hinduism
Cf. RA781.7, Exercise
Chiropractic, see RZ201+
733 Respiration as a remedy
Cf. RA782, Personal hygiene
Cf. RM824+, Aerotherapy
Occupational therapy. Rehabilitation
Cf. RA790+, Mental health
Cf. RC487, Psychiatry
Cf. RD795+, Orthopedics
735.A1 Periodicals. Societies. Serials
735.A3 Congresses
Biography, see RM699.5
History, see RM699+
735.A6-Z General works
735.3 Handbooks, manuals, etc.
735.32 Problems, exercises, examinations
735.33 Outlines, syllabi, etc.
735.36 Addresses, essays, lectures
735.4 Occupational therapy as a profession
Study and teaching
735.42 General works
735.44.A-Z By region or country, A-Z
735.447 Computer applications. Data processing
735.45 Clinical cases
735.6 Practice of occupational therapy. Occupational therapy economics
Including business methods and employment surveys
735.63 Instruments, apparatus and appliances
735.65 Examination. Diagnosis

Physical medicine. Physical therapy
Occupational therapy. Rehabilitation
Examination. Diagnosis -- Continued
735.67 Interviewing
735.7.A-Z Special occupational therapies, A-Z
735.7.G37 Gardening
735.7.H35 Handicraft
735.7.K54 Knitting
736 Rest as a remedy
736.5 Sleep therapy
Cf. RC489.S5, Psychotherapy
736.7 Recreational therapy
Cf. RA999.R42, Nursing homes
Hydrotherapy and balneotherapy
801 Periodicals. Societies. Serials
805 History
General works
810 Through 1800
811 1801-
813 General special
817.A-Z Systems and establishments. By name of system or place of establishment, A-Z
Bath, Eng. Hot Springs, see RA850.B3
817.H5 Hindo-yogi system
817.J47 Jesenik, Czechoslovakia. Wasserheilanstalt
817.K8 Kneipp system
817.M3 Malvern, Eng. Water Cure Establishment
Priessnitz method, see RM817.J47
Baths
819 Seawater
Cf. RA794, Seashore resorts, sea air, and sea bathing
Cf. RM666.S443, Therapeutic use of seawater
820 Russian and Finnish
821 Turkish
Cf. RM865+, Thermotherapy
822.A-Z Other, A-Z
Brine baths, see RM822.M9
822.C6 Cold baths
822.D7 Douche baths
822.H68 Hot baths
Medicated baths, see RM822.V2
822.M9 Mud, peat, sand, or brine baths
822.N3 Nauheim bath (Artificial)
Peat baths, see RM822.M9
Sand baths, see RM822.M9
Shower baths, see RM822.D7
822.V2 Vapor baths. Medicated baths
Cf. RM820, Russian baths
822.W2 Warm baths
Aerotherapy. Air as a remedy
Cf. RM161, Inhalatory medication
Cf. RM666.O8, Oxygen

Physical medicine. Physical therapy
Aerotherapy. Air as a remedy -- Continued
824 General works
825 General special
827 Compressed or rarefied air
Cf. RM666.O83, Hyperbaric oxygenation
Climatotherapy, see RA791+
Phototherapy. Radiotherapy. Actinotherapy
831 Periodicals. Societies. Serials
831.5 Congresses
Collected works (nonserial)
832 Several authors
832.2 Individual authors
833 General works
833.3 General special
Phototherapy
835 Periodicals. Societies. Serials
835.5 Congresses
Collected works (nonserial)
836 Several authors
836.2 Individual authors
837 General works
838 General special
Finsen's phototherapy
839.A1 Periodicals. Societies. Serials
839.A2-Z General works
840 Colored light
Cf. RZ414.6, Color therapy
841 Infrared rays
Cf. RM865+, Thermotherapy
841.5 Laser therapy
841.7 Photochemotherapy
Cf. RM666.P73, Photosensitizing compounds
842 Ultraviolet rays
843 Sun baths. Heliotherapy
844 Trade publications
Radiotherapy
Including x-ray, radium rays, and other radioactive elements
Cf. RC78.A6+, Diagnosis
845 Periodicals. Societies. Serials
845.5 Congresses
Collected works (nonserial)
846 Several authors
846.2 Individual authors
847 General works
849 General special
849.3 Problems, exercises, examinations
852 Radiopharmaceuticals
854 Safety measures
855 Positioning
857 Infrared rays
858 Radioisotopes

Physical medicine. Physical therapy
Phototherapy. Radiotherapy. Actinotherapy
Radiotherapy -- Continued
859 Radium
862.A-Z Other forms of radiotherapy, A-Z
862.A3 Actinium
862.E4 Electron beams
862.F37 Fast neutrons
862.M4 Mesons
862.N2 N-rays
862.R34 Radon. Radon baths
862.5 Instruments, apparatus, and appliances
862.7 Ultrasonic therapy
863 Cryotherapy. Therapeutic use of cold
Thermotherapy. Therapeutic use of heat
Including hot air treatments
Cf. RM821, Turkish baths
865 General works
867 Special
Including advertising
Fever therapy. Pyretotherapy
868 General works
868.5 Malaria fever therapy
Electrotherapy
Cf. RC77+, Electrodiagnosis
Cf. RD33.5, Electrosurgery
For applications to special diseases, see RC-RL, e.g. RC350.E5, Nervous diseases; RF54.E5, Diseases of the ear, nose and throat; RL115, Diseases of the skin
869 Periodicals. Societies. Serials
General works
870 Through 1900
871 1901-
872 General special
873 Handbooks, manuals, etc.
874 Diathermy
875 Addresses, essays, lectures
Special methods
880 Transcutaneous electrical nerve stimulation
884 Iontophoresis
885 Electric baths
886 Electrolysis
Cf. RL115+, Dermatology
889 Instruments, apparatus, and appliances
890 Advertising
Electrohomeopathy, see RZ420
893 Magnetotherapy
Cf. RZ422, Magnetic healing
894 Reflexotherapy
Animal magnetism and vital magnetism, see RZ430
Metallic tractors and metallotherapy, see RZ425
Hypotism, hypnosis, and suggestion therapeutics, see RC490+

Rehabilitation therapy
Cf. HD7255.A2+, Rehabilitation of disabled workers
Cf. HV1551+, Protection, assistance, and relief of the handicapped
Cf. RC439.5, Rehabilitation of mental patients
Cf. RD795+, Rehabilitation of the physically handicapped
Cf. RT120.R4, Rehabilitation nursing
Cf. UB360+, Rehabilitation of disabled veterans

930.A1 Periodicals. Societies. Serials
930.A5-Z General works
930.5.A-Z By region or country, A-Z
930.7 Life care planning. Life care plans
930.8 Functional assessment
931.A-Z Special therapies, A-Z
931.A65 Animals. Pet therapy (General)
Cf. RC489.P47, Psychotherapy
931.A77 The arts
931.D35 Dance therapy
931.D63 Dogs
Cf. HV1780+, Guide dogs
Cf. HV2509, Hearing ear dogs
931.H6 Horseback riding
Pet therapy, see RM931.A65
950 Rehabilitation technology
For individual artificial organs, instruments, or apparatus, see RD, RF, RK, etc.

Pharmacy and materia medica
1 Periodicals. Societies. Serials
3 Congresses
Boards of pharmacy registration
North America
United States
4.A1-A5 Periodicals. Societies. Serials
4.A6-Z General works
5.A-Z By region or state, A-Z
6.A-Z Canada. British America, A-Z
*Under each country:*
*.x General works*
*.x2 Local. By province, department, etc., A-Z*
7.A-Z Other North American regions or countries, A-Z
Apply table at RS6.A-Z
7.C7 Costa Rica
Apply table at RS6.A-Z
7.C9 Cuba
Apply table at RS6.A-Z
7.M6 Mexico
Apply table at RS6.A-Z
8.A-Z South America, A-Z
Apply table at RS6.A-Z
Europe
Great Britain
11.A1-A5 Periodicals. Societies. Serials
11.A6-Z General works
11.5.A-Z By region or country, A-Z
Apply table at RS6.A-Z
12.A-Z Other European regions or countries, A-Z
Apply table at RS6.A-Z
14.A-Z Asia, A-Z
Apply table at RS6.A-Z
15.A-Z Africa, A-Z
Apply table at RS6.A-Z
Australia
16 General works
16.5.A-Z By state or territory, A-Z
16.7 New Zealand
17.A-Z Pacific islands, A-Z
Apply table at RS6.A-Z
21 Yearbooks
Collected works (nonserial)
41 Several authors
43 Individual authors
51 Dictionaries and encyclopedias
Including dictionaries of drugs, e.g. Merck index
53 Classification of drugs
55 Nomenclature. Terminology. Abbreviations
55.2 Generic drugs. Generic drug substitution
Cf. RM301.45, Therapeutic equivalency
56 Communication in pharmacy

RS

Communication in pharmacy -- Continued
56.2 Information centers
56.4.A-Z By region or country, A-Z
56.7 Pharmaceutical telecommunication
Including pharmacy on radio
57 Pharmaceutical arithmetic. Statistical methods.
Handbooks, manuals, calculations, etc.
Cf. QC81+, Weights and measures
Labels in pharmacy
Including imprints on pills, capsules, etc.
58 General works
59.A-Z By region or country, A-Z
History
61 General works
62 General special
63 Ancient
64 Medieval
65 Modern
67.A-Z By region or country, A-Z
*Under each country:*
*.x General works*
*.x2 Local, A-Z*
(68) Pharmaceutical companies
see HD9665+
Biography
71 Collective
73.A-Z Individual, A-Z
Directories
For directories of supplies, see RS355+
74 General
By region or country
75 United States
76.A-Z Other regions or countries, A-Z
General works
Through 1900
78 Pharmacies. Apothecaries
Drugs
Cf. RS169.A3+, Early works on American materia medica
Cf. RS178+, Early works on Oriental materia medica
79 General works
80 Pamphlets
Organic drugs
Cf. RS161+, Pharmaceutical substances
81 Vegetable
83 Animal
85 Inorganic drugs
Cf. RS166+, Pharmaceutical substances
Secrets. Panaceas. Arcana, etc.
87 Collections
88.A-Z Individual, A-Z
88.B2 Balsamo virgen

General works
Through 1900
Secrets. Panaceas. Arcana, etc.
Individual, A-Z -- Continued
88.P8 Pulvus sympaticus
91 1901-
92 General special
93 Laboratory manuals of pharmacy
Cf. RS189+, Biological assay manuals
Cf. RS407, Pharmaceutical chemistry manuals
Tests and analyses of substances, see RS189+, RS400+
97 Problems, exercises, examinations
98 Outlines, syllabi, etc.
99 Addresses, essays, lectures
99.5 Anecdotes, facetiae, etc.
Practice of pharmacy. Pharmaceutical economics
Including business methods and employment surveys
100 General works
By region or country
United States
100.3 General works
100.35.A-Z By region or state, A-Z
100.4.A-Z Other regions or countries, A-Z
100.5 Pharmaceutical ethics
Study and teaching
Including schools
101 General works
103 Directories
105 Entrance examination aids
By region or country
United States
110 General works
111.A-Z By region or state, A-Z
Canada
113 General works
114.A-Z By province, A-Z
115.A-Z Other American regions or countries, A-Z
Apply table at RS67.A-Z
Europe
117.A1 General works
118.A2-Z By region or country, A-Z
Apply table at RS67.A-Z
Asia
119.A1 General works
119.A2-Z By region or country, A-Z
Apply table at RS67.A-Z
Africa
120.A1 General works
120.A2-Z By region or country, A-Z
Apply table at RS67.A-Z
Australia, New Zealand
121.A1 General works

Study and teaching
By region or country
Australia, New Zealand -- Continued
121.A2-Z By region or country, A-Z
Apply table at RS67.A-Z
122 Research. Experimentation
122.2 Computer applications. Data processing
Pharmacy as a profession
122.5 General works
122.9 Women in pharmacy
122.95 Pharmacy technicians
Museums. Exhibitions
123.A2 General works
123.A3-Z By region or country, A-Z
*Under each country:*
.x *General works*
.x2 *Special. By city, A-Z*
Formularies. Collected prescriptions
125 General works
127 Popular works
By region or country
North America
131.2 United States (General)
131.23 Canada
131.24 Mexico
131.25.A-Z Central America. By region or country, A-Z
131.27.A-Z South America. By region or country, A-Z
Europe
131.28 General works
131.3 Great Britain
131.32 Austria
131.34 Belgium
131.36 Denmark
131.38 France
131.4 Germany
Including West Germany
131.415 East Germany
131.42 Greece
131.44 Netherlands
131.46 Italy
131.48 Norway
131.5 Portugal
131.52 Soviet Union
131.54 Spain
131.56 Sweden
131.58 Switzerland
131.62.A-Z Other European regions or countries, A-Z
Asia
131.63 Near East
131.64 China
131.67 Pakistan
131.68 India
131.683 Sri Lanka

Formularies. Collected prescriptions
By region or country
Asia -- Continued
131.685 Burma
131.7 Japan
131.75.A-Z Other Asian regions or countries, A-Z
131.75.T87 Turkey
131.8 Australia
131.82 New Zealand
131.85.A-Z Pacific islands, A-Z
131.9.A-Z Africa. By region or country, A-Z
Pharmacopoeias
139 Universal
By region or country
North America
141.2 United States (General)
141.23 Canada
141.24 Mexico
141.25.A-Z Central America. By region or country, A-Z
141.27.A-Z South America. By region or country, A-Z
Europe
141.28 General works
141.3 Great Britain
141.32 Austria
141.34 Belgium
141.36 Denmark
141.38 France
141.4 Germany
Including West Germany
141.415 East Germany
141.42 Greece
141.44 Netherlands
141.46 Italy
141.48 Norway
141.5 Portugal
141.52 Soviet Union
141.54 Spain
141.56 Sweden
141.58 Switzerland
141.62.A-Z Other European regions or countries, A-Z
Asia
141.63 Near East
141.64 China
141.67 Pakistan
141.68 India
141.683 Sri Lanka
141.685 Burma
141.7 Japan
141.75.A-Z Other Asian regions or countries, A-Z
e.g.
141.75.T87 Turkey
141.8 Australia
141.82 New Zealand

Pharmacopoeias
By region or country -- Continued
141.85.A-Z Pacific islands, A-Z
141.9.A-Z Africa. By region or country, A-Z
Dispensatories
By region or country
North America
151.2 United States
151.23 Canada
151.24 Mexico
151.25.A-Z Central America. By region or country, A-Z
151.27.A-Z South America. By region or country, A-Z
Europe
151.3 Great Britain
151.32 Austria
151.34 Belgium
151.36 Denmark
151.38 France
151.4 Germany
Including West Germany
151.41 East Germany
151.42 Greece
151.44 Netherlands
151.46 Italy
151.48 Norway
151.5 Portugal
151.52 Soviet Union
151.54 Spain
151.56 Sweden
151.58 Switzerland
151.62.A-Z Other European regions or countries, A-Z
Asia
151.64 China
151.67 Pakistan
151.68 India
151.683 Sri Lanka
151.685 Burma
151.7 Japan
151.75 Turkey
151.8 Australia
151.82 New Zealand
151.85.A-Z Pacific islands, A-Z
151.9.A-Z Africa. By region or country, A-Z
152 Hospital pharmacy
Cf. RA975.5.P5, Pharmacy departments
Materia medica
Cf. RC953.7, Geriatric materia medica
Cf. RJ560+, Pediatric materia medica
Cf. RM1+, Therapeutics and pharmacology
Cf. RS79+, Early works on drugs
Cf. RS91, Pharmacy and materia medica
Dictionaries and encyclopedias, see RS51
153 General works

Materia medica -- Continued
154 Organic materia medica (General)
Cf. RS160+, Pharmacognosy
155 Additions to materia medica. New remedies
156 Handbooks, manuals, etc.
156.2 Problems, exercises, examinations
156.3 Outlines, syllabi, etc.
158 Popular works
Cf. RS127, Formularies and collected prescriptions
158.5 Addresses, essays, lectures
159 Collection and preservation of drugs
159.5 Packaging of drugs
Cf. RS58+, Labels in pharmacy
Pharmacognosy. Pharmaceutical substances (Plant, animal, and inorganic)
Cf. RM283+, Endocrines
Cf. RM666.A+, Pharmacology and therapeutics of individual drugs
160 General works
160.7 Marine substances
For marine algae, see RS165.A45
Organic substances
Cf. RS81+, Early works
161 General works
Animal substances
162 General works
163.A-Z Individual substances, A-Z
163.P3 Pantocrine
163.S8 Steroids
Vegetable substances. Medicinal herbs. Plant drugs
Cf. RM666.A+, Pharmacological use of herbs
Cf. RS190.P55, Assay methods
Cf. RS431.M37, Pharmaceutical chemistry
Cf. RV1+, Botanic and Thomsonian medicine
Cf. RX615.V43, Homeopathy
164 General works
By region or country, see RS169+
165.A-Z Individual plants and substances, A-Z
165.A24 Acanthopanax senticosus
165.A3 Aconite
165.A33 Adonis vernalis
165.A45 Algae
165.A48 Aloe
165.A5 Angelica
165.A6 Angostura
165.A7 Aphanizomenon
165.A84 Astragalus
165.B24 Bamboo
165.B28 Belladonna
165.B3 Belleric myrobalan
165.B4 Berberine

Materia medica
Pharmacognosy. Pharmaceutical substances (Plant, animal, and inorganic)
Organic substances
Vegetable substances. Medicinal herbs. Plant drugs
Individual plants and substances, A-Z -- Continued

| | |
|---|---|
| 165.C17 | Calendula |
| | Camomile, see RS165.C24 |
| 165.C2 | Cannabis |
| 165.C225 | Celandine |
| 165.C24 | Chamomile (Camomile) |
| 165.C247 | Chelidonium |
| 165.C255 | Chicory |
| 165.C26 | Chlorophyll |
| 165.C265 | Chondrodendron tomentosum |
| 165.C3 | Cinchona |
| 165.C5 | Coca |
| 165.D5 | Digitalis |
| 165.E4 | Echinacea |
| 165.E47 | Elders |
| 165.E5 | Eleutherococcus |
| 165.E7 | Ergot |
| 165.F72 | Fungi |
| 165.G45 | Ginseng |
| 165.G6 | Glycosides |
| | Hashish, see RS165.C2 |
| | Herbs, see RS164+ |
| 165.H45 | Helichrysum arenarium |
| 165.H67 | Hops |
| 165.H95 | Hypericum perforatum |
| 165.L94 | Lycium chinense |
| 165.M32 | Malva |
| | Marijuana, see RS165.C2 |
| | Marine algae, see RS165.A45 |
| 165.M38 | Mints |
| 165.O3 | Ocimum |
| 165.O45 | Oldenlandia affinis |
| 165.O6 | Opium |
| 165.P38 | Penicillin |
| 165.P44 | Peyote |
| 165.R25 | Rauwolfia |
| 165.R44 | Rhaponticum carthamoidae |
| 165.R48 | Rhubarb |
| 165.S35 | Sea buckthorn |
| 165.S4 | Senna |
| 165.S9 | Sugar |
| 165.T37 | Terminalia chebula |
| 165.T8 | Turmeric |
| 165.V34 | Valeriana officinalis |
| 165.W58 | Withania somnifera |
| 165.Y35 | Yams |

Materia medica
Pharmacognosy. Pharmaceutical substances (Plant, animal, and inorganic) -- Continued
Inorganic substances
Cf. RS85, Early works
166 General works
167.A-Z Individual substances, A-Z
167.S5 Silver
167.T5 Titanium
Antibiotics, see RM265+
Geographical distribution. Natural sources
For drugs from the sea, see RS160.7
169.A2 General works
By region or country
America
General works
169.A3-Z Through 1800
170 1801-
North America
United States
171 General works, 1801-
172.A-Z By region or state, A-Z
173.A-Z Other North American regions or countries, A-Z
South America
174 General works
175.A-Z By region or country, A-Z
Europe
176 General works
177.A-Z By region or country, A-Z
Asia
General works
178 Through 1800
179 1801-
180.A-Z By region or country, A-Z
Africa
181 General works
182.A-Z By region or country, A-Z
182.5.A-Z Indian Ocean islands, A-Z
Australia
183 General works
184.A-Z By region or country, A-Z
184.5 New Zealand
185.A-Z Pacific islands, A-Z
Assay methods. Standardization. Analysis
Including bioassay, microscopy, isolation, and separation technologies
189 General works
189.5.A-Z Special methods, A-Z
189.5.C34 Capillary electrophoresis
189.5.C48 Chromotography
189.5.F56 Flow injection analysis
189.5.H54 High performance liquid chromatography

RS

| | |
|---|---|
| | Materia medica |
| | Assay methods. Standardization. Analysis |
| | Special methods, A-Z -- Continued |
| 189.5.S65 | Spectrum analysis |
| 189.5.T45 | Thermal analysis |
| 190.A-Z | Assay of special substances, A-Z |
| 190.A48 | Allergens |
| 190.A5 | Antibiotics |
| 190.A53 | Anticonvulsants |
| 190.B55 | Biological products |
| 190.D77 | Drugs of abuse |
| 190.E5 | Enzymes |
| 190.H6 | Hormones |
| | Infusions, see RS190.I5 |
| 190.I5 | Injections. Infusions |
| 190.O63 | Opium |
| 190.P37 | Particles |
| 190.P4 | Penicillin |
| 190.P55 | Plant drugs |
| 190.P78 | Psychotropic drugs |
| 190.R34 | Radiopharmaceuticals |
| 190.S83 | Steroids |
| 190.T5 | Thyrotropin |
| 190.V5 | Vitamins |
| 192 | Pharmaceutical technology |
| 199.A-Z | Individual pharmaceutical processes, A-Z |
| 199.C63 | Coating |
| 199.D78 | Drying |
| 199.F5 | Filtration |
| 199.F67 | Formulation |
| 199.F74 | Freeze-drying |
| 199.G73 | Granulation |
| 199.M53 | Microbial quality control |
| 199.P36 | Pelletizing |
| 199.P4 | Percolation |
| 199.S73 | Sterilization |
| 199.W37 | Water purification |
| 199.5 | Drug delivery systems |
| 200 | Pharmaceutical dosage forms |
| 201.A-Z | Special dosage forms, vehicles, etc., A-Z |
| 201.A5 | Ampuls |
| 201.A56 | Antibody-drug conjugates |
| 201.B54 | Bioadhesive drug delivery systems |
| 201.B56 | Biopolymers |
| 201.C3 | Capsules. Microcapsules |
| | Carriers, Drug, see RS201.V43 |
| 201.C6 | Collodions |
| 201.C64 | Controlled release drugs |
| 201.D3 | Decoctions. Infusions |
| | Delayed action preparations, see RS201.C64 |
| | Drug carriers, see RS201.V43 |
| | Drug vehicles, see RS201.V43 |
| 201.E4 | Elixirs |

Materia medica
Pharmaceutical technology
Drug delivery systems
Pharmaceutical dosage forms
Special dosage forms, vehicles, etc., A-Z -- Continued

201.E5 Emulsions
201.E7 Essences and essential oils
201.E87 Excipients
201.E9 Extracts
201.G44 Gels
201.G5 Glycerites. Honeys. Mucilages
Honeys, see RS201.G5
Infusions, see RS201.D3
201.L53G5 Lipoprotein drug carriers
201.L55 Liposomes
Microcapsules, see RS201.C3
201.M53 Microspheres
201.M6 Mixtures
Mucilages, see RS201.G5
201.N35 Nanoparticles
Officinal waters, see RS201.W3
Oils, Essential, see RS201.E7
201.O3 Ointments
201.O5 Oleates
201.O6 Oleoresins
201.P37 Parenteral solutions
201.P5 Pills
201.P6 Plasters
201.P65 Polymeric drugs
201.P8 Powders
201.R4 Resins
201.S57 Solids
201.S6 Solutions
Solutions, Parenteral, see RS201.P37
201.S85 Suppositories
201.S95 Syrups
201.T2 Tablets
201.T7 Tinctures
201.V43 Vehicles, Drug. Drug carriers
201.W3 Waters, Officinal
210 Drug delivery devices
Cf. RM170.5, Infusion pumps

Commercial preparations. Patent medicines
Cf. RM671+, Therapeutics
250 General works
252.A-Z Special, A-Z

Pharmaceutical supplies
355 General works
356 Commercial publications
Including catalogs
For dictionaries of drugs, see RS51

Pharmaceutical microbiology, see QR46.5

RS

| | |
|---|---|
| | Materia medica -- Continued |
| 380 | Pharmaceutical biotechnology |
| | Pharmaceutical chemistry |
| | Cf. QD71+, Analytical chemistry |
| | Cf. RB40, Clinical chemistry |
| | Cf. RS189+, Analysis and testing of drugs |
| 400 | Periodicals. Societies. Serials |
| 401 | Congresses |
| 402 | Collected works (nonserial) |
| 402.5 | Dictionaries and encyclopedias |
| | History |
| 402.8 | General works |
| 402.9.A-Z | By region or country, A-Z |
| 403 | General works |
| 404.5 | Handbooks, manuals, etc. |
| 405 | Problems, exercises, examinations |
| 405.2 | Outlines, syllabi, etc. |
| 407 | Laboratory manuals |
| 410 | Addresses, essays, lectures |
| 418 | Computer applications. Data processing |
| 419 | Combinatorial chemistry |
| 420 | Drug design |
| 422 | Drug lipophilicity |
| 424 | Drug stability |
| | Drug radiolabeling |
| 425 | General works |
| 425.5.A-Z | Special methods, A-Z |
| 425.5.I63 | Radioiodination |
| 429 | Drug stereochemistry. Chiral drugs |
| 431.A-Z | Individual substances, A-Z |
| 431.A53 | Alkaloids |
| 431.A57 | Amines |
| 431.A58 | Aminodeoxy sugar antibiotics |
| 431.A584 | Amphetamines |
| 431.A586 | Anthracyclines |
| 431.A59 | Antibacterial agents |
| 431.A6 | Antibiotics |
| 431.A62 | Antifungal agents |
| 431.A64 | Antineoplastic agents |
| 431.A66 | Antiviral agents |
| 431.A95 | Auranofin |
| 431.A98 | Autonomic drugs |
| 431.B48 | Beta lactam antibiotics |
| 431.B49 | Bicyclic diazepines |
| 431.B55 | Bleomycin |
| 431.C23 | Carbohydrates |
| 431.C25 | Cardiovascular agents |
| 431.C5 | Clay minerals |
| 431.C6 | Corticosteroids |
| 431.D58 | Diuretics |
| 431.E73 | Ergot alkaloids |
| 431.F55 | Fluorides |
| 431.H34 | Hallucinogenic drugs |

Materia medica
Pharmaceutical chemistry
Individual substances, A-Z -- Continued

431.H95 Hyoscyamus
431.I53 Indandione
431.I56 Insulin
431.M37 Medicinal plants
431.M45 Metals
431.M47 Methamphetamine
431.N37 Narcotics
431.O73 Organofluorine compounds
431.P35 Penicillin
431.P37 Peptide antibiotics
431.P38 Peptides
431.P45 Petroleum products
431.P456 Phenothiazine
431.P46 Phorbol esters
431.P55 Plant antiviral agents
431.P68 Progesterone derivatives
431.P7 Prostaglandins
431.P75 Proteins
431.P9 Pyrazolines
431.R34 Radiopharmaceuticals
431.R4 Resins
431.S78 Steroids
431.S94 Sunscreens
431.T4 Tetracyclines
431.T44 Tetrahydrocannabinol
431.T75 Triterpenoid saponins
441 Microscopical examination of drugs

Nursing
1 Periodicals. Societies. Serials
3 Congresses
By region or country
Including licensure, registration, history, etc.
North America
United States
4 General works
5.A-Z By region or state, A-Z
Canada
6.A1 General works
6.A2-Z By province, etc., A-Z
7.A-Z Other North and Central American regions or countries, A-Z
*Under each country:*
*.x General works*
*.x2 Local, A-Z*
7.C4 Central America
7.C7 Costa Rica
Apply table at RT7.A-Z
7.C9 Cuba
Apply table at RT7.A-Z
7.M6 Mexico
Apply table at RT7.A-Z
South America
8.A1 General works
8.A2-Z By region or country, A-Z
Apply table at RT7.A-Z
Europe
10 General works
11 Great Britain
12.A-Z Other European regions or countries, A-Z
Apply table at RT7.A-Z
Asia
13.A1 General works
13.A2-Z By region or country, A-Z
Apply table at RT7.A-Z
Africa
14.A1 General works
14.A2-Z By region or country, A-Z
Apply table at RT7.A-Z
15 Australia
16 New Zealand
Pacific islands
17.A1 General works
17.A2-Z By island or group of islands, A-Z
21 Dictionaries and encyclopedias
22 Nomenclature. Terminology. Abbreviations
Communication in nursing
23 General works
24 Nursing writing
Directories
25.A2 General

Directories -- Continued
25.A3-Z By region or country, A-Z
27 Placement agencies
Statistics and surveys
29 General works
By region or country, see RT4+
History
31 General works
By region or country, see RT4+
Biography
For army nurses, see UH341+
For missionary nurses, see R722.3+
For navy nurses, see VG226+
34 Collective
37.A-Z Individual, A-Z
General works
40 Through 1900
41 1901-
42 General special
44 Instruments, apparatus, and appliances
48 Nursing assessment
Including observation and examination of the patient
48.5 Diagnostic techniques. Laboratory tests, etc.
48.55 Patient monitoring
48.6 Nursing diagnosis
49 Nursing care plans. Planning
50 Nursing records
50.5 Computer applications
Including electronic data processing
51 Handbooks, manuals, etc.
52 Outlines, syllabi, etc.
55 Problems, exercises, examinations
61 Popular works
Including home nursing
61.5 Juvenile works
62 Practical nursing
63 Addresses, essays, lectures
65 Medicine and surgery for nurses
67 Hygiene for nurses
68 Mathematics for nurses. Statistical methods
English language for nurses, see PE1116.N8
Microbiology for nurses, see QR46
Physical therapy for nurses, see RM700
Therapeutics and materia medica for nurses, see RM125
69 Textbooks combining several basic subjects
e.g. Physiology, anatomy, etc.
Study and teaching
Cf. RT90+, Teaching as a specialty in nursing
71 General works
73 General special
73.5 Audiovisual aids
73.7 Educational evaluation and measurement. Ability testing

| | |
|---|---|
| | Study and teaching -- Continued |
| 74 | Practical nursing education |
| 74.5 | Associate degree nursing |
| | Cf. RT82.5, Associate degree nurses |
| 74.7 | Preceptorships in nursing education |
| 75 | Graduate nursing education |
| 76 | Continuing nursing education |
| | Including in-service training |
| | By region or country |
| | United States |
| 79 | General works |
| 80.A-Z | By region or state, A-Z |
| | *Under each state:* |
| | *.x* *General works* |
| | *.x2* *Local, A-Z* |
| 81.A-Z | Other regions or countries, A-Z |
| | Apply table at RT7.A-Z |
| 81.5 | Research. Experimentation |
| 81.6 | Clinical cases |
| 82 | Nursing as a profession |
| 82.3 | Certification in nursing |
| 82.5 | Associate degree nurses |
| 82.8 | Nurse practitioners |
| | Cf. R729.5.N87, Nurse-physician joint practice |
| 82.9 | Gay nurses. Lesbian nurses |
| 83 | Male nurses and attendants |
| | Minorities in nursing |
| 83.3 | General works |
| 83.5 | Black nurses |
| 84 | Nurses' aides |
| 84.5 | Philosophy of nursing. Nursing models |
| 85 | Nursing ethics |
| 85.2 | Religious aspects |
| | Cf. RT120.P37, Parish nursing |
| 85.5 | Standards for nursing care. Nursing audit. Evaluation and quality control of nursing care |
| 85.6 | Nursing errors |
| 86 | Psychology of nursing |
| 86.3 | Nurse and patient |
| 86.4 | Nurse and physician or other health professionals |
| | Cf. R729.5.N87, Nurse-physician joint practice |
| 86.45 | Clinical supervision of nurses. Mentorship |
| 86.5 | Social aspects |
| 86.54 | Transcultural nursing |
| | Practice of nursing. Nursing economics |
| | Including business methods and employment surveys |
| 86.7 | General works |
| | By region or country |
| | United States |
| 86.73 | General works |
| 86.74.A-Z | By region or state, A-Z |
| 86.75.A-Z | Other regions or countries, A-Z |
| 87.A-Z | Special topics in basic nursing care, A-Z |

Special topics in basic nursing care, A-Z -- Continued
Amusements for invalids, see GV1231
Cookery for the sick, see RM219+
Feeding patients, see RT87.N87
Moving patients, see RT87.T72
87.N87 Nutritional care. Feeding patients
87.P35 Pain
87.P67 Positioning patients
87.S24 Safety measures
87.S49 Sex. Sexuality
Cf. RC556+, Sexual problems
87.T45 Terminal care
87.T72 Transferring and moving patients
Specialities in nursing
Administration
89 General works
89.3 Personnel management
Teaching
Including nursing education and patient education
90 General works
90.3 Health promotion. Health education
90.5 Team nursing
90.7 Primary nursing
Pediatric nursing, see RJ245+
Geriatric nursing, see RC954
Cancer nursing, see RC266
Cardiovascular disease nursing, see RC674
Dental nursing, see RK60.5
Eye, ear, nose, and throat nursing, see RE88, RF52.5
Respiratory disease nursing, see RC735.5
Dermatologic nursing, see RL125
Gynecological nursing, see RG105
Maternity nursing, see RG951
Neurological nursing, see RC350.5
Obstetrical nursing, see RG951
Psychiatric nursing, see RC440
School nursing, see RJ247
Surgical nursing, see RD99+
Orthopedic nursing, see RD753
Communicable disease nursing
95 General works
Poliomyelitis nursing, see RC180.8
Tuberculosis nursing, see RC311.8
97 Home nursing, see RT61, RT120.H65
Public health nursing
Cf. HV691.A2+, Medical charities
Cf. RJ247, School nursing
98 Community health nursing
Including nursing in voluntary health agencies, visiting nurse associations
Cf. RT120.H65, Home nursing
Industrial nursing, see RC966
Aviation nursing, see RC1097
102 Institutional nursing

Specialities in nursing -- Continued
104 Private-duty nursing
108 Red Cross nursing
Including peacetime and disaster nursing
Government nursing services
Army nurses and nursing, see UH341+, UH490+
Navy nurses, see VG226+, VG350+
Public health nursing, see RT97
By region or country
United States
116 General works
118.A-Z Special services, A-Z
Army nursing service, see UH493+
118.I5 Indian nursing service
118.N38 National Institutes of Health nursing service
Navy nursing service, see VG353+
118.V4 Veterans' Administration nursing service
Other regions or countries, see RT6.A+
120.A-Z Other special types of nursing, A-Z
120.C3 Camps
120.C45 Chronic diseases
120.C5 Civil defense
120.E4 Emergency nursing
120.F34 Family nursing
Forensic nursing, see RA1155
120.H65 Home nursing
Cf. RT61, Popular works
120.I5 Intensive care nursing
120.L64 Long-term care facilities
Including nursing homes
Nursing homes, see RT120.L64
120.O9 Outpatient facilities
120.P37 Parish nursing
120.R4 Rehabilitation
120.R87 Rural nursing
120.S83 Subacute care
120.W3 War

Botanic, Thomsonian, and eclectic medicine
1 Periodicals. Societies. Serials
General works
3 Through 1850
5 1851-
Biography
7 Collective
8.A-Z Individual, A-Z
9 Addresses, essays, lectures
Eclectic medicine
11 Periodicals. Societies. Serials
15 Yearbooks
21 Congresses
Collected works (nonserial)
31 Several authors
33 Individual authors
41 General works
45 Examination. Diagnosis
50 Handbooks, manuals, etc.
51 Problems, exercises, examinations
52 Outlines, syllabi, etc.
53 Popular works
61 History
Biography
71 Collective
76.A-Z Individual, A-Z
81 Addresses, essays, lectures
Study and teaching
By region or country
America
United States
100 General works
101.A-Z Individual schools. By place, A-Z
151.A-Z Other American regions or countries, A-Z
Europe
170 General works
171 Great Britain
181.A-Z Other European regions or countries, A-Z
Diseases, treatment, etc.
211 Fevers
Diseases due to specific infection
221 General works
225.A-Z Individual diseases, A-Z
Diseases due to diathesis
231 General works
235.A-Z Individual diseases, A-Z
Diseases of the nervous system
241 General works
246.A-Z Individual diseases, A-Z
Diseases of the circulatory system
251 General works
256.A-Z Individual diseases, A-Z
Diseases of the respiratory system

Eclectic medicine
Diseases, treatment, etc.
Diseases of the respiratory system -- Continued
261 General works
266.A-Z Individual diseases, A-Z
Diseases of the digestive system
271 General works
276.A-Z Individual diseases, A-Z
Diseases of the genitourinary system
281 General works
286.A-Z Individual diseases, A-Z
291 Diseases of the head and neck
293 Diseases of the chest and abdomen
297 Diseases of the pelvis
Surgery
301 General works
305 Conditions requiring surgery
311 Neoplasms. Tumors
Diseases of the eye
321 General works
331.A-Z Individual diseases, A-Z
Diseases of the ear, nose, and throat
Including works on the nose and throat combined
341 General works
343 Diseases of the ear
345 Diseases of the nose
347 Diseases of the throat
Gynecology and obstetrics
361 General works
363.A-Z Individual classes, A-Z
365 Obstetrics
Diseases of children
375 General works
377.A-Z Individual diseases, A-Z
Diseases of the skin
381 General works
391.A-Z Individual diseases, A-Z
Materia medica and therapeutics
401 General works
411.A-Z Remedies, A-Z
Pharmacy
415 General works
421 Pharmacopoeias
431 Dispensatories

Homeopathy
Cf. RZ412, Biochemic system
1 Periodicals. Societies. Serials
Hospitals, clinics, etc.
6 General works
6.5.A-Z By region or country
11 Yearbooks
21 Congresses
Collected works (nonserial)
31 Several authors
33 Individual authors
41 Dictionaries and encyclopedias
46 Directories
51 History
Biography
61 Collective
66.A-Z Individual, A-Z
68 Hahnemann's works
71 General works
72 General special
73 Handbooks, manuals, etc.
73.3 Problems, exercises, examinations
73.4 Outlines, syllabi, etc.
74 Examination. Diagnosis
75 Clinical cases
76 Popular works
78 Addresses, essays, lectures
Theory. Principles
81 General works
85 Antihomeopathic literature
Study and teaching
91 General works
101.A-Z By region or country, A-Z
*Under each country:*
*.x General*
*.x2A-Z Local, A-Z*
Diseases, injuries, treatment, etc.
211 Fevers
Diseases due to specific infections
221 General works
226.A-Z Individual diseases, A-Z
Acquired immune deficiency syndrome, see RX226.A35
226.A35 AIDS
226.C5 Cholera
226.D6 Diphtheria
226.Y4 Yellow fever
Diseases due to diathesis
Including constitutional diseases, hereditary diseases, etc.
241 General works
261.A-Z Individual diseases, A-Z
Arthritis, see RX261.R4

Diseases, injuries, treatment, etc.
Diseases due to diathesis
Individual diseases, A-Z -- Continued
261.C3 Cancer
Class here works on medical treatment only
For works on surgery, see RX376
261.R4 Rheumatism. Arthritis
261.S9 Sycosis
Diseases of the nervous system
281 General works
301.A-Z Individual diseases, A-Z
301.B8 Brain diseases
301.C7 Convulsions
301.H5 Headache
301.I57 Insomnia
301.M45 Mental disorders
301.N5 Neuralgia
Diseases of the blood, lymphatics, and endocrine glands
305 General works
309.A-Z Individual diseases, A-Z
309.P9 Purpura
Diseases of the circulatory system
311 General works
316.A-Z Individual diseases, A-Z
Diseases of the respiratory system
321 General works
326.A-Z Individual diseases, A-Z
326.C2 Catarrh
326.C7 Colds, Common
Common colds, see RX326.C7
326.H3 Hay fever
Diseases of the digestive system
331 General works
332 Diseases of the stomach
333 Diseases of the liver
336.A-Z Individual diseases, A-Z
336.C7 Constipation
336.D9 Dyspepsia
Diseases of the rectum
341 General works
343 Hemorrhoids
346.A-Z Other diseases, A-Z
Diseases of the genitourinary system
Cf. RX460+, Gynecology and obstetrics
351 General works
356.A-Z Individual diseases, A-Z
356.B8 Bright's disease
360 Diseases of the chest
Surgery adapted to homeopathy
366 General works
367 General special
Conditions requiring surgery

Diseases, injuries, treatment, etc.
Surgery adapted to homeopathy
Conditions requiring surgery -- Continued
368 General works
376 Neoplasms. Tumors
For medical treatment of cancer, see RX261.C3
Wounds and injuries
390 General works
395.A-Z By type or causative agent, A-Z
395.S66 Sports injuries
Diseases of the eye
401 General works
431.A-Z Individual diseases, A-Z
431.C37 Cataract
Diseases of the ear, nose, and throat
441 General works
446 Diseases of the ear
451 Diseases of the nose
456 Diseases of the throat
Gynecology and obstetrics
460 Periodicals. Societies. Serials
461 General works
463 General special
465 Popular works
467 Menstruation
469 Menopause. Change of life
471 Leucorrhea
473.A-Z Other diseases, A-Z
476 Obstetrics
Diseases of children
501 General works
503 Popular works
510 Underdeveloped children
531.A-Z Individual diseases, A-Z
531.A77 Attention-deficit hyperactivity disorder
540 Diseases of the teeth
Diseases of the skin
561 General works
581.A-Z Individual diseases, A-Z
581.A25 Acne
581.R5 Ringworm
590.A-Z Other diseases, A-Z
590.S75 Stress
Materia medica and therapeutics
601 General works
603 Noncomprehensive. Additions, new remedies, etc.
606 Handbooks, manuals, etc.
606.2 Problems, exercises, examinations
606.3 Outlines, syllabi, etc.
615.A-Z Remedies, A-Z
615.A74 Arnica
615.B42 Bee venom
615.C2 Carbolic acid

| | |
|---|---|
| | Materia medica and therapeutics |
| | Remedies, A-Z -- Continued |
| 615.F55 | Flower remedies |
| | Herbal remedies, see RX615.V43 |
| 615.M55 | Mineral remedies |
| 615.P67 | Potassium chloride |
| 615.S9 | Sulphur |
| 615.V43 | Vegetable remedies |
| 621 | Therapeutics |
| | Repertories of symptoms |
| 631 | General works |
| 635 | Tongue symptoms |
| 637 | Head symptoms |
| | Materia medica and pharmacy |
| 671 | General works |
| 675 | Pharmacopoeias |
| 681 | Trade publications |

Other systems of medicine
Chiropractic
201 Periodicals. Societies. Serials
205.A-Z Boards of chiropractic registration. By region or country, A-Z
For certification lists, see RZ233
*Under each country:*
.*x* *General works*
.*x2A-Z* *Local, A-Z*
211 Yearbooks
213 Congresses
Collected works (nonserial)
215 Several authors
216 Individual authors
History
221 General works
225.A-Z By region or country, A-Z
Biography
231 Collective
232.A-Z Individual, A-Z
Practice of chiropractic. Chiropractic economics
Including business methods and employment surveys
232.2 General works
By region or country
United States
232.3 General works
232.32.A-Z By region or state, A-Z
232.4.A-Z Other regions or countries, A-Z
233 Directories
235 Atlases. Pictorial works
236 Chiropractic as a profession
236.3 Chiropractic assistants
236.5 Chiropractic ethics
Study and teaching
237 General works
238.A-Z By region or country, A-Z
241 General works
242 General special
242.9 Handbooks, manuals, etc.
243 Problems, exercises, examinations
243.2 Outlines, syllabi, etc.
244 Popular works
244.5 Juvenile works
245 Addresses, essays, lectures
Diagnosis
250 General works
251.A-Z Special diagnostic methods, A-Z
251.A65 Applied kinesiology
251.R33 Radiography
255 Therapeutics
Diseases, injuries, treatment, etc.
260 Diseases of the eye, ear, nose, and throat
Diseases of children

| | |
|---|---|
| | Chiropractic |
| | Diseases, injuries, treatment, etc. |
| | Diseases of children -- Continued |
| 263 | General works |
| 264.A-Z | Individual diseases, A-Z |
| 265.A-Z | Diseases of other organs or systems, A-Z |
| | Ankle, see RZ265.F66 |
| 265.C7 | Cranium |
| 265.F66 | Foot. Ankle |
| 265.H4 | Headache |
| 265.J64 | Joints |
| 265.K53 | Knee |
| 265.M45 | Mental disorders |
| 265.M8 | Muscles |
| 265.N4 | Neck. Torticollis |
| 265.N45 | Nervous system |
| | Scoliosis, see RZ265.S64 |
| 265.S64 | Spine. Scoliosis |
| | Torticollis, see RZ265.N4 |
| | Wounds and injuries |
| 270 | General works |
| 275.A-Z | By type or causative agent, A-Z |
| 275.S65 | Sports injuries |
| 275.W48 | Whiplash injuries |
| | By organ or system, see RZ265.A+ |
| | Osteopathy |
| 301 | Periodicals. Societies. Serials |
| | Hospitals, clinics, etc. |
| 302 | General works |
| | By region or country |
| | United States |
| 302.5 | General works |
| 303.A-Z | By region or state, A-Z |
| 304.A-Z | Other regions or countries, A-Z |
| | Boards of registration. By region or country |
| 305 | United States |
| 307.A-Z | Other regions or countries, A-Z |
| 311 | Yearbooks |
| 313 | Congresses |
| | Collected works (nonserial) |
| 315 | Several authors |
| 316 | Individual authors |
| | History |
| 321 | General works |
| 325.A-Z | By region or country, A-Z |
| | Biography |
| 331 | Collective |
| 332.A-Z | Individual, A-Z |
| 333 | Directories |
| 336 | Osteopathy as a profession |
| | Study and teaching |
| 337 | General works |
| 338.A-Z | By region or country, A-Z |

Osteopathy -- Continued
341 General works
342 General special
342.9 Handbooks, manuals, etc.
343 Problems, exercises, examinations
343.2 Outlines, syllabi, etc.
344 Popular works
345 Addresses, essays, lectures
345.7 Practice of osteopathy. Osteopathic business
Including business methods and employment surveys
Diseases, treatment, etc.
347 Fevers
Diseases due to specific infection
350 General works
351.A-Z Individual diseases, A-Z
Diseases due to diathesis
353 General works
354.A-Z Individual diseases, A-Z
Diseases of the nervous system
356 General works
357.A-Z Individual diseases, A-Z
Diseases of the endocrine glands
358 General works
358.5.A-Z Individual diseases, A-Z
358.5.T59 Thyroid gland diseases
Diseases of the circulatory system
359 General works
360.A-Z Individual diseases, A-Z
Diseases of the respiratory system
362 General works
363.A-Z Individual diseases, A-Z
Diseases of the digestive system
365 General works
366.A-Z Individual diseases, A-Z
Diseases of the rectum
368 General works
369.A-Z Individual diseases, A-Z
Diseases of the genitourinary system
371 General works
372.A-Z Individual diseases, A-Z
Surgery adapted to osteopathy
374 General works
376 Conditions requiring surgery
378 Neoplasms. Tumors
Diseases of the eye
380 General works
381.A-Z Individual diseases, A-Z
381.C37 Cataract
Diseases of the ear, nose, and throat
Including works limited to the nose and throat
382 General works
383 Diseases of the ear
384 Diseases of the nose

Osteopathy
Diseases, treatment, etc.
Diseases of the ear, nose, and throat -- Continued
385 Diseases of the throat
386 Gynecology and obstetrics
Diseases of children
390 General works
391.A-Z Individual diseases, A-Z
Diseases of the skin
393 General works
394.A-Z Individual diseases, A-Z
Orthopedia
397 General works
397.5 Temporomandibular joint
399.A-Z Osteo-magnetics, neuropathy, etc., A-Z
Cf. RM721+, Massage
Cf. RZ201+, Chiropractic
399.C73 Craniosacral therapy
399.N5 Neuropathy
399.O8 Osteo-magnetics
399.S7 Spondylotherapy
Mental healing
Cf. BT732.5+, Spiritual healing
Cf. BT732.55+, Spiritual healing
Cf. BV4337, Pastoral medicine
Cf. RC49+, Psychosomatic medicine
Cf. RC435+, Psychiatry
Cf. RC475+, Psychotherapy
400.A1 Periodicals. Societies. Serials
400.A4 Dictionaries and encyclopedias
400.A6-Z General works
401 General special
403.A-Z Systems of mental healing, A-Z
Christian Science healing, see BX6950
403.P75 Psychic surgery
403.R45 Reiki
403.S56 Silva Mind Control
Cf. BF1156.S55, Mental suggestion
403.Z37 Zarrow miracle psychic healing
403.Z6 Zodic force control
Clinical cases
405 Collective
406.A-Z Individual, A-Z
Biography of mental healers
407 Collective
408.A-Z Individual, A-Z
Miscellaneous systems and treatments
409.7 Anthroposophical therapy
410 Baunscheidtism. (Exanthematic method)
412 Biochemic system
413 Broussaisism. Writings and doctrines of Francois J.V.Broussais

Miscellaneous systems and treatments -- Continued
413.5 Brunonianism. Brownism. Writings and doctrines of John Brown
414 Chronothermal system
414.6 Color therapy
415 Crystal healing
Dianetics, see BP605.S2
416 Dosimetric system. Alkaloidal system
420 Electrohomeopathy
Graphology, see BF905.M43
422 Magnetic healing
424 Medicine wheels
425 Metallic tractors. Metallotherapy
430 Mesmerism, animal magnetism, etc.
Cf. BF1111+, Parapsychology
Cf. RC490+, Hypnotism and hypnosis (Psychiatry)
Naturopathy
433 Dictionaries and encyclopedias
Biography
439.5 Collective
439.7.A-Z Individual, A-Z
440 General works
Study and teaching
444 General works
445.A-Z By region or country, A-Z
460 Orgonomic medicine
501 Phrenology
Class here medical aspects of phrenology
For psychological aspects, see BF866+
520 Polarity therapy
600 Radiesthesia
Cf. BF1628.3, Occult sciences
Cf. RC271.R24, Cancer therapy
605 Radionics
999 Other systems and treatments not otherwise provided for

RZ

.A1-.A5 Official publications
.A6A-Z Nonofficial works. By author
.A7-.Z Individual institutions. By name, A-Z
*Under each:*
*.xA1-.xA7 Official publications*
*.xA1-.xA4 Serial*
*.xA5-.xA7 Nonserial*
*.xA8-.xZ Other works. By author, A-Z*

| | |
|---|---|
| 1 | General works |
| 2.A-Z | Local, A-Z |
| 3 | Collective biography |
| | For individual biography see R154 |

| | |
|---|---|
| 1 | General works |
| 2 | General special |
| 3.A-Z | Local, A-Z |
| | Biography |
| 4.A1 | Collective |
| 4.A2-Z | Individual, A-Z |

TABLE

| | |
|---|---|
| 1 | General works |
| 2.A-Z | Local, A-Z |

| | |
|---|---|
| 1 | General works |
| 2.A-Z | Local, A-Z |

| | |
|---|---|
| .A1 | Official publications |
| .A2A-Z | Local, A-Z |
| .A3-.Z | Individual institutions. By name, A-Z |

## A

## B

## D

## E

G

## I

## L

## M

## O

P

## Q

## R

## V

## W

## X



## Y

Z